Prentice Hall LITERATURE

PENGUIN EDITION

Unit Six
Resources

The American Experience

PEARSON

Upper Saddle River, New Jersey
Boston, Massachusetts
Chandler, Arizona
Glenview, Illinois
Shoreview, Minnesota

13-digit ISBN: 978-0-13-366467-6
10-digit ISBN: 0-13-366467-8

1 2 3 4 5 6 7 8 9 10   12 11 10 09 08

PEARSON

CONTENTS

For information about the Unit Resources, a Pronunciation Guide, and a Form for Analyzing Primary Source Documents, see the opening pages of your Unit One Resources.

"Everything Stuck to Him" by Raymond Carver

"Traveling Through the Dark" by William Stafford

"The Secret" by Denise Levertov

"The Gift" by Li-Young Lee

"Who Burns for the Perfection of Paper" by Martin Espada

"Camouflaging the Chimera" by Yusef Komunyakaa

"Streets" by Naomi Shihab Nye

Urban Renewal by Sean Ramsey

Playing for the Fighting 69th by Wiliam Harvey

"One Day, Broken in Two" by Anna Quindlen

"Mother Tongue" by Amy Tan

"For the Love of Books" by Rita Dove

from **The Woman Warrior** by Maxine Hong Kingston

from **The Names** by N. Scott Momaday

Concept Map Unit 6
The Contemporary World: (1970–Present)

Three Essential Questions serve as lenses through which to view the literature—

How does literature shape or reflect society?

What is the relationship between place and literature?

What makes American literature American?

Reflected in these selections:

Reflected in these selections:

Reflected in these selections:

Forms and Movements

which are demonstrated in these selections:

- Short Story
- Lyric Poetry/Voice/Identity
- Essay/Memoir/Postmodernism

Characteristics of the Period and Its Literature

In the 1970s, cultural diversity is reflected in literature and new voices are heard.

National and personal security become focal points for many Americans.

Technological advances change the way Americans communicate and see the world.

Writers explore individual voice in a self-conscious way.

Writers experiment with uses of language to create complex characters.

Writers address ideas of freedom and oppression and react to political events.

Elements and Techniques

which are demonstrated in these selections:

- Foreshadowing/Epiphany
- Characterization
- Parody/Satire

UNIT 6 STUDENT LOG

VOCABULARY

WRITING & EXTEND YOUR LEARNING

WORKSHOPS

Name _____ Date _____

Unit 6 Introduction
Names and Terms to Know

A. DIRECTIONS: *Write a brief sentence explaining each of the following names and terms. You will find all of the information you need in the Unit Introduction in your textbook.*

1. Ronald Reagan: _____
_____

2. 9/11: _____
_____

3. Watergate: _____
_____

4. Sally Ride: _____

5. Al Gore: _____

6. Bicentennial. _____
_____

B. DIRECTIONS: *Use the hints below to help you answer each question.*

1. How has the Internet changed the way people communicate? [*Hints: What is the Internet? What are the various ways people communicate on the Internet? How are these different from communication by letter, telephone, or mass media?*]
_____
_____
_____

2. What challenges did the new millennium present to Americans? [*Hints: What new dangers did Americans face after 2000? What new problems did the U.S. face overseas?*]
_____
_____
_____

3. What problems or controversies marked American politics during this time? [*Hints: What was Watergate? What happened to President Nixon? What happened during the 2000 election?*]
_____
_____
_____

Name _____ Date _____

Essential Question 1: How does literature shape or reflect society?

A. DIRECTIONS: *Answer the questions about the first Essential Question in the Introduction, about whether literature shapes or reflects society. All the information you need is in the Unit 6 Introduction in your textbook.*

A. *Political and Social Events with the Greatest Impact*

    1. Give examples of the ways in which computers became part of daily life. _____
    _____

    2. How have historians changed their views about the cultural contributions of minority populations?_____
    _____

    3. How did the terrorist attacks on September 11, 2001, affect Americans in general?
    _____

B. *American Values and Attitudes*

    1. How do computers enhance both self-expression and anonymity? _____
    _____

    2. What has become the American toward maintaining individual cultural identities? _____
    _____

C. *Expression of Values and Attitudes in American Literature*

    1. List the various types of diversity reflected in American literature of this period.
    _____

    2. How does the new technology affect the way literature now reaches Americans?
    _____

    3. List some of the themes explored by American writers during this time.
    _____

B. DIRECTIONS: *Answer the questions that include the Essential Question Vocabulary words.*

    1. Would *diversity* on a menu suggest many or few choices? Explain. _____
    2. What would a *commercial* view of a product be likely to involve? _____
    3. From which of the mass *media* do you get most of your news? _____

Unit 6 Introduction

Essential Question 2: What is the relationship between place and literature?

A. **DIRECTIONS:** *On the lines provided, answer the questions about the second Essential Question in the Introduction, about the relationship between place and literature. All the information you need is in the Unit 6 Introduction in your textbook.*

A. *Places Americans Write About*

    1. What are "ordinary places" and what contemporary American writers write about these ordinary places? _____
_____

    2. Give examples of ways in which Americans are writing about "ordinary places transformed." _____
_____

B. *Global Awareness*

    1. What environmental problems are explored in contemporary American writings? _____
_____

    2. Give examples of contemporary writers whose nonfiction, fiction, and poetry develops environmental themes. _____
_____

C. *Impact of Electronic Technology*

    1. How has electronic technology changed the way characters, authors, and readers communicate with each other? _____
_____

    2. Contemporary literature includes many references to such areas of popular culture as
_____

    3. What is cyberliterature? _____
_____

B. **DIRECTIONS:** *Answer the following questions based on Essential Question Vocabulary words.*

  1. Would a story set in *cyberspace* be old-fashioned or futuristic? Explain. _____
_____

  2. Would local property taxes be a *global concern*? _____
_____

  3. If you were to *transform* your house, what would be the first thing you'd do? _____
_____

Unit 6 Introduction

Essential Question 3: What makes American literature American?

A. DIRECTIONS: *On the lines provided, answer the questions about the third Essential Question in the Introduction, about what makes American literature American. All the information you need is in the Unit 6 Introduction in your textbook.*

A. *Qualities in Contemporary American Literature*

    1. Why would you expect American literature to display cultural diversity? _____
    _____

    2. How has the definition of "literature" expanded in recent decades?
    _____

B. *Postmodern American Literature*

    1. What does it mean to say a literary work is "self-conscious"?
    _____

    2. Why is contemporary literature "released" from the need to mean something?
    _____

    3. What attitude toward the past does much contemporary literature display?
    _____

C. *Growth of Suburbia and American Literature*

    1. Give examples of American prose writers whose works look toward the future.
    _____

    2. List some twenty-first century American poets.
    _____

B. DIRECTIONS: *Answer the questions based on the Essential Question Vocabulary words.*

    1. What might a poet who wants to experiment with a different *genre* write? _____
    2. Name one *innovation* in contemporary automobiles. _____
    3. Is someone who is *self-conscious* likely to be relaxed or nervous? Explain. _____
    _____

Unit 6 Introduction

Following-Through Activities

A. CHECK YOUR COMPREHENSION: *Use this chart to complete the Check Your Comprehension activity in the Unit 6 Introduction. In the middle box, fill in a key concept in contemporary American literature. In the right box, fill in a key author. The concept-author pairing for American Literature has been done for you.*

Common Theme	New / Changed Form	Element of Style
Place and Imagination		
American Literature	Cultural Identity	Amy Tan
Literature and Society		

B. EXTEND YOUR LEARNING: *Use this graphic organizer to help you compare directions to a real-world location and a location on the Internet.*

Real-World Location:	**Internet Location**

Travel Directions:	**Travel Directions:**

From the Author's Desk
Julie Alvarez Introduces "Antojos"

DIRECTIONS: *Use the lines provided to answer these questions based on Alvarez's introduction to the story "Antojos."*

1. According to Alvarez's first paragraph, what did "Antojos" eventually become?

_____

_____

2. What explanation does Alvarez give for writing a short story first, not a novel?

_____

_____

3. How did studying Emily Dickinson apparently affect Alvarez's writing?

_____

_____

4. How did reading about Thomas Wolfe help inspire Alvarez to write "Antojos"?

_____

_____

5. On what real-life person is the main character of "Antojos" based, and on what experience of that person?

_____

_____

6. What main point about going home does Alvarez suggest "Antojos" expresses?

_____

_____

7. According to Alvarez, how does "Antojos" differ from an essay?

_____

_____

8. Why did Alvarez include the Palmolive poster in "Antojos"? As what does the poster come to be seen?

_____

_____

Julia Alvarez
Listening and Viewing

Segment 1: Meet Julia Alvarez

- Where did Alvarez spend her childhood, and what was her family there like?
- After coming to America, what good and bad treatment did she encounter in school?

_____

_____

_____

_____

Segment 2: Julia Alvarez on the Short Story

- According to Alvarez, where should the action in a short story start?
- Citing Chekhov, where does Alvarez think a short story should end?

_____

_____

_____

_____

Segment 3: Julia Alvarez on the Writing Process

- What does Alvarez mean by "the habit of writing"?
- What does she say about trying to write a story or novel from beginning to end?

_____

_____

_____

_____

Segment 4: Julia Alvarez on the Rewards of Writing

- For Alvarez, what role do rewards from the larger world play in writing?
- According to Alvarez, how does writing help her in life?

_____

_____

_____

_____

Vocabulary Warm-up Word Lists

Study these words from the selection. Then, complete the activities.

Word List A

anniversary [an uh VER suh ree] *n.* annual date of a past event
Americans celebrate the <u>anniversary</u> of their independence on July 4th.

complexion [kuhm PLEK shuhn] *n.* color and general appearance of a person's face
His sunburned <u>complexion</u> was a sign of lots of outdoor activity.

conversing [kahn VERS ing] *v.* talking; sharing thoughts and ideas
After <u>conversing</u> with our partners for quite a while, we made a decision.

craved [KRAYVD] *v.* wanted intensely
After a month without sweets, Owen desperately <u>craved</u> a dessert.

descent [dee SENT] *n.* downward passage
The jet aircraft began its <u>descent</u> some fifty miles away from the airport.

gratifying [GRAT uh fy ing] *adj.* pleasing; satisfying
After every feeding, the baby gave its mother a <u>gratifying</u> smile.

obscuring [uhb SKYOOR ing] *v.* concealing; hiding
Unfortunately, the tall building is <u>obscuring</u> our view of the water.

relishing [REL ish ing] *v.* enjoying; taking keen pleasure in
<u>Relishing</u> the movie, Cassandra stared with delight at the screen.

Word List B

appease [uh PEEZ] *v.* to satisfy
In an effort to <u>appease</u> the child, the babysitter gave him more milk.

congregated [KAHN gruh gayt uhd] *v.* came together in a group
Waiting for the grand opening, shoppers <u>congregated</u> in front of the store.

dissuade [di SWAYD] *v.* to convince someone not to do something
Mark tried to <u>dissuade</u> his son from diving off the high platform.

docile [DAHS uhl] *adj.* easy to direct or manage; obedient
The puppy is so <u>docile</u> that it has been easy to train him.

listlessly [LIST lis lee] *adv.* without energy; in a lethargic manner
Without seeming to care, Philip <u>listlessly</u> shook his neighbor's hand.

loath [LOHTH] *adj.* unwilling; reluctant
Wendy needs to walk around a lot, and she is <u>loath</u> to go on a long car ride.

momentous [moh MEN tuhs] *adj.* of great significance or importance
Today's graduation is a <u>momentous</u> event for all the students in the class.

wayward [WAY wuhrd] *adj.* difficult to control; unruly
Every so often, you can see <u>wayward</u> flowers growing among the weeds.

Unit 6 Resources: New Voices, New Frontiers
9

Name _____ Date _____

"Antojos" by Julia Alvarez
Vocabulary Warm-up Exercises

Exercise A *Fill in the blanks, using each word from Word List A only once.*

On their fifth wedding [1] _____, Ken and Jen wanted to visit Everglades National Park in south Florida. As the plane made its [2] _____ to the Miami airport, Jen could see that Ken was looking forward to the experience. He had been eagerly [3] _____ with their seatmate Bill, who turned out to be a retired park ranger. Bill was enthusiastic, obviously [4] _____ telling some of his best alligator stories. From the ranger's healthy [5] _____, Ken and Jen could see that he'd led an active, outdoor life. They themselves worked every day in a large office building and [6] _____ a holiday in the out-of-doors. Just now, a few clouds were [7] _____ the view of downtown Miami. Looking down from the plane, though, Ken and Jen were sure that this would be a(n) [8] _____ vacation.

Exercise B *Decide whether each statement below is true or false. Circle* T *or* F, *and explain your answer.*

1. If you successfully <u>appease</u> someone, that person feels dissatisfied.
   T / F _____

2. People who have <u>congregated</u> have spread out in all directions.
   T / F _____

3. You <u>dissuade</u> someone from behaving in a certain way if you feel the behavior is improper.
   T / F _____

4. A wild tiger can normally be expected to be <u>docile</u>.
   T / F _____

5. Someone acting <u>listlessly</u> feels full of energy.
   T / F _____

6. If you are <u>loath</u> to do something, you are reluctant.
   T / F _____

7. History textbooks typically ignore <u>momentous</u> events.
   T / F _____

8. If a child's behavior is <u>wayward</u>, parents usually have nothing to worry about.
   T / F _____

Name _____ Date _____

"Antojos" by Julia Alvarez
Reading Warm-up A

Read the following passage. Pay special attention to the underlined words. Then, read it again, and complete the activities. Use a separate sheet of paper for your written answers.

On the second <u>anniversary</u> of the day she began her journal, Inez decided to become a writer. For two years, as she recorded observations and experiences, she had considered a writing career. Now, as she stared in the mirror, she tried to recognize the <u>complexion</u> of a famous writer. As her eyes widened, she was pleased to see a <u>gratifying</u> look of surprise on her face. The ability to be surprised by people and things was a quality a good writer needed; writers were always taking pleasure in the unexpected and <u>relishing</u> with delight the quirky aspects of human nature.

As she thought about her journal, Inez realized she was a compulsive eavesdropper. If two people were <u>conversing</u> on the bus, for example, she would strain her ears to catch bits of dialogue. By now, she knew that most people have a distinctive way of speaking, and Inez would practice expanding the snippets she overheard. She believed that readers <u>craved</u> realism in books; they yearned for fictional characters to sound and act like real people.

Inez also knew she loved storytelling. At the art museum, for example, one of her favorite paintings showed a young woman reading a letter. It had been painted several hundred years ago, somewhere in Europe. Instead of <u>obscuring</u> its meaning for Inez, however, these origins posed mysteries demanding to be solved. Who was the young woman? Who had written the letter, and why? What would the woman think or do as a result? For Inez, the painting had all the makings of a story.

Her reverie was interrupted by her mother's call that dinner was ready. Still thinking about her future career, Inez slowly made her <u>descent</u> downstairs to the kitchen, imagining the joy she would feel on the day her first novel was published.

1. Underline the words in this sentence and the next sentence that give a clue to the meaning of <u>anniversary</u>. Use the word *anniversary* in an original sentence.

2. Circle the words in this sentence and the next sentence that give a clue to the meaning of <u>complexion</u>. Write a definition for *complexion* in your own words.

3. Underline the words that give a clue to the meaning of <u>gratifying</u>. What is a synonym for *gratifying*?

4. Circle the words that offer a clue to the meaning of <u>relishing</u>. What are two antonyms for *relishing*?

5. Circle the words in this sentence that offer clues to the meaning of <u>conversing</u>. What is a synonym for *conversing*?

6. Underline the word in this sentence that gives a clue to the meaning of <u>craved</u>. What is a synonym for *craved*?

7. Circle the words in this sentence that give a clue to the meaning of <u>obscuring</u>. What is the opposite of *obscuring*?

8. Circle the word that helps explain the meaning of <u>descent</u>. What is an antonym for *descent*?

11

"Antojos" by Julia Alvarez
Reading Warm-up B

Read the following passage. Pay special attention to the underlined words. Then, read it again, and complete the activities. Use a separate sheet of paper for your written answers.

During Julia Alvarez's lifetime, some <u>momentous</u> changes have made a deep impact on life in her homeland, the Dominican Republic. For foreigners, perhaps the most obvious of these changes has been the growth of the Dominican tourist industry. Hundreds of new tourist resorts have sprung up. Whether visitors enjoy the active lifestyle or want to laze <u>listlessly</u> on a beach towel, the Dominican Republic is a pleasant and charming vacation getaway.

Besides the sunny, warm weather, an important factor favoring tourism is the country's increased political stability. After a somewhat <u>wayward</u> history of twists and turns, the Dominican Republic is now regarded by visitors as a safe and welcoming destination.

Another great change affecting Dominican life has been rapidly increasing urbanization. Rural Dominicans have been <u>loath</u> to remain in the countryside, where economic opportunity seems limited. Instead, they have <u>congregated</u> in the cities, gathered together in places such as the capital Santo Domingo, as well as Santiago and La Romana. For hundreds of years, the *campesinos*, or poor farmers, were fundamentally <u>docile</u> and content with their lot. For many, however, this is no longer the case. To <u>appease</u> their appetite for a better standard of living, people have migrated to the city in droves.

Dominicans are also participating in another relocation: emigration. Here again the causes are mostly economic. It is hard for the Dominican government to <u>dissuade</u> citizens from emigrating to other countries. It is hard to convince people to stay when they see so much opportunity available elsewhere, especially in the United States. In the last 40 years, more than 10% of the country's total population has moved away to settle abroad. It will be interesting to see whether this trend continues.

1. Underline the words that give a clue to the meaning of <u>momentous</u>. Write a sentence using **momentous**.

2. Circle the words in this sentence that give a clue to the meaning of <u>listlessly</u>. What is an antonym for **listlessly**?

3. Circle the words in this sentence that hint at the meaning of <u>wayward</u>. What is the opposite of **wayward**?

4. Underline the words in this sentence that give clues to the meaning of <u>loath</u>. What are two synonyms for **loath**?

5. Circle the words in this sentence that help explain the meaning of <u>congregated</u>. Write a definition of **congregated**.

6. Underline the words in this sentence that give a clue to the meaning of <u>docile</u>. What is a synonym for **docile**?

7. Underline the words in the sentence that give a clue to the meaning of <u>appease</u>. Use the word **appease** in an original sentence.

8. Circle the words in the next sentence that hint at the meaning of the word <u>dissuade</u>. What is an antonym for **dissuade**?

"Antojos" by Julia Alvarez
Literary Analysis: Plot Structure

Plot structure is the sequence of events in a literary work. A plot usually begins by introducing the setting, the characters, and the basic situation. However, authors sometimes begin in medias res, in the middle of an action. For example:

For the first time since Yolanda had reached the hills, there was a shoulder on the left side of the narrow road.

Writers use in medias res to grab readers' attention by cutting to the climax or to an interesting part of the story. They then go back to the beginning to fill in the details. To accomplish this, writers make use of flashbacks, which highlight a scene or event from an earlier time, thus providing valuable information about the characters' backgrounds, personalities, and motives. Writers also add interest through foreshadowing, the use of clues to suggest events that have yet to occur.

Use the chart below to provide examples from "Antojos" of each of these techniques: in medias res, flashback, and foreshadowing. In each case, explain the use of the technique and what it adds to the development of the plot.

Example of Technique	Explanation of Technique	What It Adds to the Story
In medias res:		
Flashback:		
Foreshadowing:		

"**Antojos**" by Julia Alvarez
Reading: Make Predictions

As you read a selection, you often wonder how a story will end. One strategy for understanding the way a story unfolds is to pause and make predictions about what will happen. Often a story contains hints that foreshadow things to come.

DIRECTIONS: *On the lines following each excerpt from "Antojos," record what predictions you might make about the rest of the story.*

1. She [Yolanda] would have to wait until she got to the coast to hear news of the hunger march in the capital.

   _____

   _____

2. It crossed her mind that her family had finally agreed to loan her a car because they knew she'd be far safer on the north coast than in the capital city where revolutions always broke out.

   _____

   _____

3. She hadn't seen her favorite *antojo*, guavas, since her last trip seven years ago.

   _____

   _____

4. —She was going up north? By herself? A woman alone on the road! "This is not the states." Her old aunts had tried to dissuade her. "Anything can happen."

   _____

   _____

5. "You must excuse him, Dona," she apologized. "He's not used to being among people." But Yolanda knew the old woman meant, not the people in the village, but the people with money who drove through Altamira to the beaches on the coast.

   _____

   _____

6. Branches scraped the sides and pebbles pelted the underside of the car. Yolanda wanted to turn back, but there was no room to maneuver the car around.

   _____

   _____

Name _____ Date _____

"Antojos" by Julia Alvarez
Vocabulary Builder

Words From Spanish

A *machete* is a large, heavy knife used to cut down vegetation. The word is taken directly from Spanish, in which it has the same meaning. Many other words in English come from Spanish.

A. DIRECTIONS: *The following words are derived from Spanish. Consult a dictionary, and then write down their different meanings. Tell which words are taken directly from Spanish, like* machete, *and which have been changed slightly.*

1. hammock _____

2. plaza _____

3. patio _____

4. cocoa _____

Using the Word List

    appease   collusion   dissuade   docile   enunciated   machetes

B. DIRECTIONS: *For each Word List word, choose the word or phrase that is* most similar *in meaning. Circle the letter of your choice.*

1. dissuade
   A. persuade   B. destroy   C. discourage   D. encourage

2. appease
   A. apply   B. control   C. provoke   D. satisfy

3. machetes
   A. artillery   B. shovels   C. knives   D. machines

4. collusion
   A. argument   B. conspiracy   C. disruption   D. interpretation

5. docile
   A. harmful   B. angry   C. obedient   D. foolish

"Antojos" by Julia Alvarez
Support for Writing

As you work on a new version of the story "Antojos," choose one of the men who help Yolanda when her tire goes flat. Tell the story through his eyes from a first-person point of view. Reread the story and enter information into the chart below.

"A Flat Tire," by _____

What we were doing that day	
What we thought when we first saw Yolanda	
Yolanda's behavior toward us/how we felt	
How we felt when Yolanda offered to pay us	

On a separate page, draft your new version of the event. Use your new information from the chart, along with information from the story. Provide dialogue and background for your character and other characters who may be in your new version. When you revise, check to be sure you have kept the viewpoint of the new character.

"Antojos" by Julia Alvarez
Enrichment: World Languages

When Yolanda was a young immigrant trying to learn English, her teacher told her "Language is power." In today's world, the need to know a language other than one's native tongue is increasingly important, not only for immigrants adjusting to new countries, but also in business and politics. The world we live in today is often known as the "global village." This term refers to the fact that mass media, computers, and rapid transportation have made the world seem quite small—as if it were one village. It is becoming easier than ever to communicate, conduct business, and share knowledge with people around the world.

DIRECTIONS: *Explore the need to know a variety of languages by answering the following questions:*

1. In what specific ways do you think the world has become smaller due to technology and transportation? Do you think the world should become smaller? Why, or why not?

   _____

   _____

   _____

2. What products do we import from and export to foreign countries? Why might some business people need to know more than one language in today's economy?

   _____

   _____

   _____

3. Why might knowing more than one language be helpful to people involved in space exploration programs throughout the world? How can the ability to share knowledge easily in this area be beneficial to the world?

   _____

   _____

   _____

4. If people throughout the world were conversant in a variety of languages, might countries enjoy better relationships? Why, or why not? How can being able to communicate effectively with people from other countries dispel prejudices and increase tolerance?

   _____

   _____

   _____

5. Respond to the statement of Yolanda's teacher—"Language is power." Do you agree? Why, or why not?

   _____

   _____

   _____

"Antojos" by Julia Alvarez
Open-Book Test

Short Answer *Write your responses to the questions in this section on the lines provided.*

1. In what respect does "Antojos" begin "in medias res," or in the middle of things? Briefly define this element of plot structure, and specify the element of the story that it exemplifies.

   _____

   _____

   _____

   _____

2. As Yolanda drives through the mountains in "Antojos," what event does the roar of an engine behind her car foreshadow?

   _____

   _____

   _____

3. What key piece of background knowledge about the Dominican Republic is most useful in understanding the following passage from "Antojos"?

   > Her family had been worried that trouble would break out, for the march had been scheduled on the anniversary of the failed revolution nineteen years ago today.

   _____

   _____

   _____

   _____

4. In the following passage from "Antojos," which phrase signals the beginning of a flashback?

   > There seemed to be plenty here to eat—except for guavas.

   > In the capital, her aunts had plied her with what she most craved after so many years away. "Any little *antojo*, you must tell us!" They wanted to spoil her. . . .

   _____

   _____

   _____

   _____

5. Yolanda's craving for guavas is a key element of "Antojos." Use the Idea Web below to organize Yolanda's thoughts, feelings, experiences, and associations in relation to guavas. Then, on the lines below, briefly summarize what guavas mean to her.

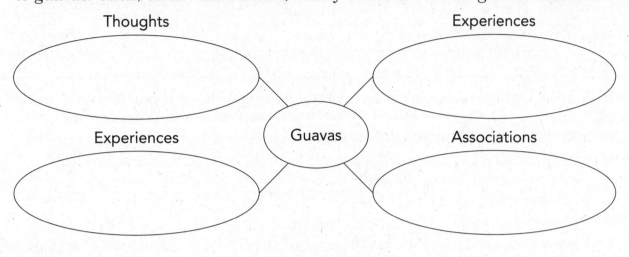

_____

_____

6. In "Antojos," when Yolanda's aunts ask her about her *antojos*, Yolanda does not know what *antojos* means. Why not? How does her lack of understanding of this word relate to a larger theme of the story?

_____

_____

_____

7. After Yolanda invites the boys to pile into the car to look for guavas, she notices that the road to the grove is very bumpy and the surroundings very desolate. We learn, "Yolanda wanted to turn back, but there was no room to maneuver the car around." What plot development is foreshadowed in this passage?

_____

_____

8. Based on what you know about the situation in the Dominican Republic at the time of the story, what can you predict about how Yolanda will react when she sees two men approaching her with machetes? Why?

_____

_____

_____

9. Based on your background knowledge of life in the Dominican Republic, what social reality of life in that country is shown by Jose's inability to get the rich people down the road to help Yolanda with her flat tire in "Antojos"?

_____

_____

_____

10. If your friend is usually very *docile,* would you likely have a problem in convincing your friend to do what you want? Why or why not? Base your answer on the meaning of *docile* as it used in "Antojos."

_____

_____

Essay

Write an extended response to the question of your choice or to the question or questions your teacher assigns you.

11. The background information provided about the Dominican Republic in your textbook and in the story "Antojos" helps the reader understand some of the social and economic realities portrayed in the story. Based in part on that background knowledge, write an essay on how the lives of Yolanda and her aunts are different from the lives of those she meets on her journey to find guavas.

12. In "Antojos," when Yolanda meets the two men with the machetes, she immediately assumes that these two poor men are potentially dangerous and might seek to take advantage of her. After her encounter with these men and after her experiences with Jose and his friends, how do her feelings change? Develop your thoughts in an essay supported by details from the story.

13. Write an essay in which you explain the significance of the title "Antojos." In your essay, discuss what antojos means, why guavas are Yolanda's *antojos,* and how *antojos* lead her to the experiences she has in the story.

14. **Thinking About the Essential Question: What is the relationship between place and literature?** In "Antojos," Yolanda seems torn between two very different kinds of places—the Dominican Republic of her childhood and the United States of her adulthood. Do you think people are shaped more decisively by the places of their youth or the places of their adulthood? Develop your thoughts in a brief essay.

Oral Response

15. Go back to question 2, 5, or 8 or to the question your teacher assigns you. Take a few minutes to expand your answer and prepare an oral response. Find additional details in "Antojos" that support your points. If necessary, make notes to guide your oral response.

"Antojos" by Julia Alvarez
Selection Test A

Critical Reading *Identify the letter of the choice that best answers the question.*

____ 1. The title of this story is "Antojos," which means "cravings." What is most likely Yolanda's most important craving?
A. the desire to take a new journey
B. the desire to drive a new car
C. the desire to connect to her homeland
D. the desire to meet new people

____ 2. The plot in "Antojos" begins in the middle of what action?
A. Yolanda walking down the road
B. Yolanda driving her car
C. Yolanda greeting her family
D. Yolanda joining a protest march

____ 3. In "Antojos," why doesn't Yolanda know what *antojos* means?
A. She has lost her ability to understand Spanish.
B. It is a Spanish word that is no longer in use.
C. Yolanda has never known how to speak Spanish.
D. Her aunts have not told her what the word means.

____ 4. In "Antojos," what prediction can you make about Yolanda's car trip based on her family's worries for her safety?
A. Nothing will happen.
B. She will have problems with her car.
C. She will cancel her trip.
D. She will ride a bicycle.

____ 5. What setting is introduced at the beginning of the plot of "Antojos"?
A. a city street in the capital of the Dominican Republic
B. a country road in the Dominican Republic
C. a shack on the side of the road
D. the estate of Yolanda's family

___ 6. Background about which country will help you make predictions in "Antojos"?

   A. Haiti

   B. Dominican Republic

   C. United States

   D. Cuba

___ 7. Why does Yolanda pretend to be an American to the men who change her tire in "Antojos"?

   A. She enjoys playing a part.

   B. She feels safer being seen as an outsider.

   C. She is ashamed of being Dominican.

   D. She is ashamed of her poor Spanish.

___ 8. Why does Yolanda offer the men money for changing her tire in "Antojos"?

   A. She believes they have earned it.

   B. She fears they are asking for pay.

   C. She knows it is a custom to pay for help.

   D. She feels bad that she distrusted them.

___ 9. In "Antojos," what prediction can you make based on the clue in the text that the road to the guava grove got "bumpier and bumpier"?

   A. Yolanda will drive smoothly on the road.

   B. Yolanda's car will run out of gas.

   C. Yolanda will pass a bus of loud men.

   D. The rough road will cause a flat tire on Yolanda's car.

___ 10. As Yolanda waits for help in "Antojos," what does her flashback reveal about feelings toward living in the United States?

   A. She is uncomfortable living there.

   B. She loves living there.

   C. She would never choose to leave the United States.

   D. She wants to move home and live with her family.

___ 11. What trick does Yolanda play on the men who stop to help her in "Antojos"?

   A. She lets them think she is an American and does not speak Spanish.

   B. She convinces them that she is from a royal family.

   C. She fools them into pushing her car.

   D. She makes them think she is injured.

_____ 12. Why is Jose walking slowly when Yolanda sees him on the road back from the Miranda's in "Antojos"?

A. He has hurt his foot.

B. He does not want to see her, because he could not bring help.

C. He is angry with her.

D. He is tired from picking guavas.

Vocabulary and Grammar

_____ 13. Which sentence best conveys the meaning of *dissuade* in this sentence: "Yolanda's aunts tried *dissuade* her from traveling alone"?

A. They invited her to travel with them.

B. They tried to talk her out of traveling alone.

C. They talked to her about staying at home.

D. They wanted her to travel alone.

_____ 14. Which of these sentences contains an absolute phrase that is set off from the noun it modifies?

A. "There seemed to be plenty here to eat."

B. "Yolanda came upon a small village."

C. "They quickly packed the guavas in the trunk."

D. "The hills turned into a plateau, the road widening."

Essay

15. At the beginning of "Antojos," Yolanda believes that strangers are usually dangerous and that if people know she has money, they will take advantage of her. What are her feelings at the end of the story? Write a brief essay to discuss your opinion.

16. In "Antojos," how are the lives of Yolanda and her aunts different from the lives of those she meets on her journey to find guavas? Write a brief essay to address the differences in their economic class.

17. **Thinking About the Essential Question: What is the relationship between place and literature?** In "Antojos," Yolanda thinks about two very different places—the Dominican Republic of her childhood and the United States of her adulthood. Write an essay in which you compare and contrast Yolanda's childhood experiences and her adult experiences in these different places.

"Antojos" by Julia Alvarez
Selection Test B

Critical Reading *Identify the letter of the choice that best completes the statement or answers the question.*

_____ 1. What are *antojos*?
   A. friends
   B. cravings
   C. fruits
   D. good deeds

_____ 2. What warning do family members give Yolanda?
   A. Do not travel north alone.
   B. Do not eat fruit at this time of year.
   C. Be prepared for bad weather.
   D. Be careful with your money.

_____ 3. What event or activity is interrupted **in medias res** as the story "Antojos" begins?
   A. Yolanda is talking to Jose.
   B. Yolanda is driving in the country.
   C. Yolanda is changing a tire.
   D. Yolanda is eating a guava.

_____ 4. What information is conveyed is this flashback in "Antojos":
   Her aunts were proven right: After so many years away, their niece was losing her Spanish.

   A. Yolanda lives at home with her aunts.
   B. Yolanda has not lived with her family in her native country in a long time.
   C. Yolanda's aunts are happy that Yolanda speaks English and Spanish.
   D. Yolanda is concerned that she forgets Spanish words.

_____ 5. In what way are Yolanda's aunts' warnings an example of foreshadowing in "Antojos"?
   A. They suggest that Yolanda will return to the Dominican Republic.
   B. They indicate that she will meet someone famous.
   C. They suggest that something will happen to Yolanda.
   D. They forecast an excursion with no problems.

_____ 6. Which of the following details about the country roads in "Antojos" can be used to make a prediction about Yolanda's trip?
   A. The roads are paved.
   B. The roads have no signs.
   C. The roads lead to the ocean.
   D. The roads are narrow and bumpy.

_____ 7. Why does Yolanda allow the men to believe she is American and cannot speak Spanish?
   A. Because of the fighting within her country, she feels she is safer being thought of as an outsider.
   B. She enjoys lying about her identity.
   C. She is ashamed of her heritage and plans to return to America anyway.
   D. She believes the men are American.

24

____ 8. How is Yolanda's behavior different from the behavior of the men who change her tire?
   A. Yolanda is rude to the men when they try to help her.
   B. The men treat Yolanda with caution while she tries to make conversation.
   C. Although Yolanda is suspicious of the men, they are not suspicious of her.
   D. Yolanda is friendlier than they are.

____ 9. Background information about Julia Alvarez, author of "Antojos," might help you make a prediction about what happens to which character in the story?
   A. Jose
   B. Yolanda
   C. Yolanda's aunt
   D. the man with the machete

____ 10. What happens when Jose tries to get help?
   A. He gets lost, gives up, and goes home.
   B. Because of the troubles in the country, people are suspicious and unwilling to help him.
   C. Many people respond sympathetically and try to follow him back to the broken-down car.
   D. People refuse to help him because they do not like Yolanda.

____ 11. How might you best describe the way Jose and Yolanda are feeling at the end of the story, after their experiences?
   A. excited
   B. somber
   C. tired
   D. annoyed

____ 12. What is the main reason the story is called "Antojos"?
   A. The name reflects Yolanda's craving for guavas.
   B. The name reflects Yolanda's craving to experience her homeland authentically.
   C. The name reflects suspicion, which is a theme in the story.
   D. The name reflects Yolanda's relationship with her family.

____ 13. What is the significance of the Palmolive poster in the story?
   A. The poster is a sign of the country's decline.
   B. The woman in the poster resembles Yolanda.
   C. To Yolanda, the woman in the poster represents people in her country calling out to her.
   D. The poster is a symbol of happiness and contentment.

____ 14. What is the main reason that Jose is upset when he returns from the Miranda's in "Antojos"?
   A. The guards thought he was lying.
   B. He hurt his foot walking.
   C. He wanted to see the men with the machetes.
   D. He does not want to go home.

Vocabulary and Grammar

_____ 15. What is the best meaning of the word *appease* as it is used in this sentence?

Enough guavas to appease even the greediest island spirit for life!

A. satisfy

B. include

C. support

D. disappoint

16. In which sentence is *docile* used correctly

A. The docile men in the bus were protesting loudly against the government.

B. Jose was docile and did what he mother asked.

C. The boys were docile, so they were eager to argue with Yolanda.

D. Yolanda was docile as a girl and never followed her aunt's advice.

_____ 17. Identify the complete absolute phrase in the following sentence:

She left them behind, her small car driving easily up the highway.

A. She left them behind, her small car driving easily

B. easily up the highway

C. She left them behind

D. her small car driving easily up the highway

Essay

18. In an essay, explain the function of the flashback scene in "Antojos." What happens in the scene? Why is it important to the story? What key information do readers get from this scene?

19. In an essay, explain the title "Antojos." What double meaning does it have in this story? When is the word used? What theme does it emphasize?

20. Explain how the background information about the country's political unrest contributes to Yolanda's initial reaction to the men with the machetes in "Antojos." Why does she respond the way she does? What does she think might happen? What is your prediction based on her reaction, and is your prediction correct? Is Yolanda's prediction about her own situation correct? Write a brief essay to discuss your ideas.

21. **Thinking About the Essential Question: What is the relationship between place and literature?** In "Antojos," Yolanda seems torn between two very different kinds of places—the Dominican Republic of her childhood and the United States of her adulthood. Do you think people are shaped more decisively by the places of their youth or the places of their adulthood? Develop your thoughts in a brief essay.

Vocabulary Warm-up Word Lists

Study these words from the selection. Then, complete the activities.

Word List A

centerpiece [SEN tuhr pees] *n.* decorative object or arrangement placed at the center of a table
    For the party, Eliza made a <u>centerpiece</u> out of pinecones and evergreens.

collards [KAHL uhrdz] *n.* the leaves of the vegetable kale
    Patricia makes <u>collards</u> from greens that she grows in her garden.

deliberately [di LIB uhr uht lee] *adv.* intentionally
    Otis <u>deliberately</u> designed his schedule so that he could take on extra work.

embrace [em BRAYS] *v.* to clasp or hold close
    Before saying good-bye, I wanted to <u>embrace</u> my old friend.

lavender [LAV uhn duhr] *adj.* of a pale, purple color
    Gina's <u>lavender</u> silk scarf is the color of black-raspberry ice cream.

orchid [OR kid] *n.* an unusually shaped flower, often purple or white
    For Mother's Day, we gave Mom an <u>orchid</u> to pin on her dress.

scalding [SKAWL ding] *adj.* burning hot; harshly critical, as if burning
    From Henry's <u>scalding</u> laugh, Jane could tell that he disliked her story.

temptation [temp TAY shuhn] *n.* desire to have or do something that should be avoided
    Candace fought the <u>temptation</u> to eat a cookie.

Word List B

dingy [DIN jee] *adj.* shabby; dirty
    Carl, who likes to look good, never wears <u>dingy</u> clothes to school.

doctrines [DAHK trinz] *n.* religious beliefs or principles
    A religious school may be expected to follow the <u>doctrines</u> of its church.

flannel [FLAN uhl] *adj.* made of a soft cloth, usually of wool and cotton
    In the winter, I make my bed with warm <u>flannel</u> sheets.

furtive [FER tiv] *adj.* sneaky
    In the twilight, we glimpsed a <u>furtive</u> person peeking over the fence.

ignorant [IG nuhr unt] *adj.* uneducated; unaware; uninformed
    Taking the advice of an <u>ignorant</u> person can land you in trouble.

mercilessly [MER suh less lee] *adv.* cruelly
    Ian <u>mercilessly</u> squashed the spider with his foot.

oppress [uh PRES] *v.* to keep down by unjust use of power or authority
    Dictatorships <u>oppress</u> their citizens and often deny them human rights.

witty [WIT ee] *adj.* clever and humorous
    People enjoy Jean's <u>witty</u> personality, especially when she jokes around.

Name _____ Date _____

"Everyday Use" by Alice Walker
Vocabulary Warm-up Exercises

Exercise A *Fill in the blanks, using each word from Word List A only once.*

Louise worked hard on the picnic preparations. Early in the morning, she chopped the

[1] _____ and put them in a huge pot of hot, [2] _____

water. Then she carefully and [3] _____ chose decorations for the long

picnic table. A [4] _____-colored tablecloth would give the table a fresh,

spring-like look, she decided. For a(n) [5] _____, she arranged dozens

of daffodils in a large vase, clustered around a single, large [6] _____.

Finally, Louise began to make her famous fried chicken, a(n) [7] _____

that few of her relatives could ever resist. Her brother Glen and his wife Darla were the

first guests to arrive, and when they rang the bell at noon, Louise rushed to the door to

greet and [8] _____ them.

Exercise B *Decide whether each statement below is true or false. Circle* T *or* F, *and explain
your answer.*

1. A costume that looks *dingy* would immediately attract purchasers.
   T / F _____

2. *Doctrines* are ideas or concepts in which few people believe.
   T / F _____

3. The best thing on a very hot day would be to cover yourself in *flannel*.
   T / F _____

4. A *furtive* person is generally to be trusted.
   T / F _____

5. Someone *ignorant* of a situation has little or no knowledge about it.
   T / F _____

6. Rulers acting *mercilessly* typically have compassion for their subjects.
   T / F _____

7. Employers who *oppress* their employees have the workers' best interests at heart.
   T / F _____

8. *Witty* remarks will often provoke smiles or laughter from those who hear them.
   T / F _____

Name _____ Date _____

"**Everyday Use**" by Alice Walker
Reading Warm-up A

Read the following passage. Pay special attention to the underlined words. Then, read it again, and complete the activities. Use a separate sheet of paper for your written answers.

In African American tradition, quilts and quilting have served a number of functions. Quilts were made for warmth, of course. However, in a culture of oral tradition, they also helped to preserve memories and events. On the Underground Railroad before the Civil War, quilts even functioned as "message boards" to guide slaves on their way north to freedom.

The African American artist and painter Faith Ringgold decided to <u>embrace</u> this tradition in her work and make it her own. In the 1970s, Ringgold became inspired by Asian paintings from Tibet. She began sewing fabric borders around her paintings. Consciously and <u>deliberately</u>, Ringgold developed works of art she called story quilts. The quilt thus became like a <u>centerpiece</u> to display narrative images telling original stories in the context of African American life and history. In her story quilts, Ringgold celebrates ordinary life with joy and inspiration. She uses bold, simple shapes and striking, bright colors, among them <u>lavender</u> hues. Beautiful flowers, such as sunflowers and <u>orchids</u>, are also prominent elements.

Folk artists sometimes yield to the <u>temptation</u> to sentimentalize their subject matter, but Ringgold consistently avoids such a trap. Much of her work challenges the stereotypes of black women, for example. Her first story quilt was entitled *Who's Afraid of Aunt Jemima?* Ringgold did not depict the central figure as an elderly cook, chopping <u>collards</u> in the kitchen and then tossing them into a pot of <u>scalding</u> water to boil. Instead, Aunt Jemima has been transformed into Jemima Blakey, a dynamic and successful businesswoman and restaurant owner. Jemima's story unfolds in a striking combination of acrylics and dyed, painted, and pieced fabric.

1. Underline the words in this sentence that give a clue to the meaning of <u>embrace</u>. Use the word *embrace* in a sentence.

2. Circle the word that gives a clue to the meaning of <u>deliberately</u>. Use a word meaning the opposite of *deliberately* in a sentence.

3. Underline the words in this and the two previous sentences that give a clue to the meaning of <u>centerpiece</u>. Where would you likely find a *centerpiece*?

4. Circle the clue to the meaning of <u>lavender</u> here. What feelings do *lavender* things evoke in you?

5. Circle the words that tell to the meaning of <u>orchids</u>. What is special about an *orchid*?

6. Underline the words in this sentence that give a clue to the meaning of <u>temptation</u>. Is it usually advisable or inadvisable to yield to *temptation*?

7. Circle the words in this sentence that give a clue to the meaning of <u>collards</u>. Use the word *collards* in a sentence.

8. Circle the clues to the meaning of <u>scalding</u>. Tell what scalding means.

"Everyday Use" by Alice Walker
Reading Warm-up B

Read the following passage. Pay special attention to the underlined words. Then, read it again, and complete the activities. Use a separate sheet of paper for your written answers.

All their lives, Lisa's older sister Kathy had been the smart one, whose underline{witty} comments had always amused and impressed teachers and parents. While Kathy projected confidence, Lisa was quiet and underline{furtive}, not wanting anyone to notice her.

How strange it was, then, when Kathy came home from her first semester at college such a different person. She had always dressed neatly, but now she wore underline{dingy} jeans she had bought at a second-hand store, and instead of her usual cashmere sweater, she wore an old, button-down shirt made of soft cotton underline{flannel}, like a carpenter or a woodsman.

"You look disgraceful," said their mother, who could hardly recognize her own daughter.

Kathy shrugged and said that clothes didn't matter. What mattered was the person inside.

"Go upstairs and change," said their mother, annoyed by Kathy's tone.

When Kathy refused, the first of a long series of fights resulted. Lisa tried to stay out of everybody's way, as Kathy underline{mercilessly} did things to bother their mother, dressing in old clothes, acting irresponsibly, and criticizing the small town where they lived. According to Kathy, the people who lived in their town were narrow-minded and completely underline{ignorant} of the world outside; at college, on the other hand, people questioned the ideas and underline{doctrines} they had been brought up to believe in. The fights went on and on, but Lisa noticed that they seemed to make Kathy only more and more unhappy.

Finally, the constant bickering began to underline{oppress} even Kathy, whom Lisa found one night crying in her bedroom. When Lisa asked why, Kathy said she would understand in a few years, when she went away to college herself.

1. Underline the words that give a clue to the meaning of underline{witty}. Write a sentence of your own using the word **witty**.

2. Circle the words in this sentence that give a clue to the meaning of underline{furtive}. What are two antonyms for **furtive**?

3. Underline the words in this sentence that offer clues to the meaning of underline{dingy}. Use a word meaning the opposite of **dingy** in a sentence of your own.

4. Underline the words in this sentence that give a clue to the meaning of underline{flannel}. Would you likely wear a **flannel** garment in hot weather or in cold weather?

5. Circle the words in this sentence that give a clue to the meaning of underline{mercilessly}. Use a word meaning the opposite of **mercilessly** in a sentence of your own.

6. Underline the words in this sentence and the previous one that hint at the meaning of underline{ignorant}. What are two synonyms for **ignorant**?

7. Circle the words in this sentence hinting at the meaning of underline{doctrines}.

8. Circle the words in this sentence that hint at the meaning of the word underline{oppress}. What is a synonym for **oppress**?

Name _____ Date _____

Literary Analysis: Characterization

Characterization is the revelation of characters' personalities. In "Everyday Use," the author uses language to show different sides of characters' personalities. For example, the story's narrator uses Standard English to reveal her internal thoughts:

Maggie attempts to make a dash for the house, in her shuffling way, but I stay her with my hand.

The narrator uses dialect, however, in her outward expressions:

"I reckon she would," I said. "I promised to give them quilts to Maggie, for when she marries John Thomas."

This duality of language causes readers and Dee to have very different perceptions of the narrator. Use the chart below to provide two examples of each kind of expression used by the narrator—Standard English and dialect. For each example, explain what the use of language reveals about the narrator's character.

Standard English, Example 1:	What it reveals about narrator's character:
Standard English, Example 2:	What it reveals about narrator's character:
Dialect, Example 1:	What it reveals about narrator's character:
Dialect, Example 2:	What it reveals about narrator's character:

"Everyday Use" by Alice Walker
Reading Strategy: Contrast Characters

Good writers use specific details to depict characters. In depicting characters who are very different, writers use contrasting details. For example, recall the ways in which the three female characters in "Everyday Use" are dressed:

The narrator: I wear flannel nightgowns to bed and overalls during the day.

Maggie: her thin body enveloped in pink skirt and red blouse

Dee: A dress down to the ground, in this hot weather. A dress so loud it hurt my eyes. There are yellows and oranges enough to throw back the light of the sun. . . . Earrings gold, too, and hanging down to her shoulders.

Nowhere does Alice Walker come out and write, "The narrator was practical; Maggie was plain, simple, and solid; Dee, on the other hand, was flashy and bold." Instead of making such "telling" remarks, Walker shows us how the characters are different by using specific and concrete details and letting us draw our own conclusions.

Below are several specific details, some drawn from "Everyday Use." After each, describe a contrasting detail. (It, too, may be from "Everyday Use.") An example is given.

Example: The mother opened her arms and ran across the room to embrace her daughter.

Answer: Her arms folded across her chest, the mother stared at her daughter from across the room.

1. He smiles broadly; his teeth shiny white as pearls.

   _____

   _____

2. She cooked the freshly killed pork over an open fire.

   _____

   _____

3. She hung back in the kitchen, her scarred hands hidden in the folds of her tattered skirt.

   _____

   _____

4. She rifled through the trunk to find the precious quilts.

   _____

   _____

5. She talked a blue streak over the sweet potatoes and the rest of the meal.

   _____

   _____

"Everyday Use" by Alice Walker
Vocabulary Builder

Using the Roots *-doc-/-doct-*

The roots *-doc-* and *-doct-* mean "teach." The Word List word *doctrines*, which means "ideas, beliefs, or rules that are taught," is formed from the root *-doct-*.

A. DIRECTIONS: *Complete each of the following sentences by choosing the best word for each sentence. Use context clues and what you know about the meaning of -doc-/-doct- to make your selection.*

docent   doctorate   doctrinaire   documented

1. She received her _____ in veterinary science from the state university.
2. Wanting a record of their family reunion, the Hernandez family _____ the event on videotape.
3. The _____ who teaches our honors class is not a regular faculty member.
4. The tutor's inflexible and _____ methods did not inspire his students.

Using the Word List

furtive   cowering   oppress   doctrines

B. DIRECTIONS: *Choose the word or phrase that is most nearly* opposite *in meaning to each numbered Word List word. Circle the letter of your choice.*

1. furtive
   A. shifty
   B. hidden
   C. honest
   D. annoying
2. cowering
   A. retreating
   B. swaggering
   C. thriving
   D. despising
3. oppress
   A. enslave
   B. control
   C. punish
   D. free
4. doctrines
   A. beliefs
   B. doubts
   C. creeds
   D. theories

"Everyday Use" by Alice Walker

Grammar and Style: Transitional Expressions

Writers often use **transitional expressions**—transitions and transitional phrases to show the relationships between ideas. A transition is a single word, and a transitional phrase is a group of words. Transitions and transitional phrases show time relationships, comparisons, degrees of importance, and spatial relationships. Read the following examples from "Everyday Use":

Maggie will be nervous *until after* her sister goes. . . . (shows a time relationship)

This house is in pasture, too, *like* the other one. (shows a comparison)

A. PRACTICE: For each sentence, underline the transition or transitional phrase. Then tell whether it shows a time relationship, a comparison, or a spatial relationship.

1. One winter I knocked a bull calf straight in the brain between the eyes with a sledge hammer. . . .

   _____

2. But that was before we raised the money, the church and me, to send her to August to school.

   _____

3. The dress is loose and flows, and as she walks closer, I like it.

   _____

4. "You must belong to those beef-cattle people down the road," I said.

   _____

5. You didn't even have to look close to see where hands pushing the dasher up and down to make butter had left a kind of sink in the wood.

   _____

6. "Some of the pieces, like those lavender ones, come from old clothes her mother handed down to her," I said. . . .

   _____

B. WRITING APPLICATION: *Write a paragraph based on the characters and/or situations portrayed in "Everyday Use." Use transitions and transitional phrases to show the relationships between ideas.*

_____

_____

_____

_____

_____

_____

_____

_____

"Everyday Use" by Alice Walker
Support For Writing

To write a critical review of "Everyday Use," begin by rereading the story and noting your reactions. Enter your responses in the chart below.

Review of "Everyday Use"

Story Plot	My Opinion	Examples from Story
_____ _____	_____ _____	_____ _____
Story Characters _____ _____	**My Opinion** _____ _____	**Examples from Story** _____ _____
Story Message _____ _____	**My Opinion** _____ _____	**Examples from Story** _____ _____

Summary of My Opinion:
_____
_____
_____
_____

On a separate page, begin your draft by making a general statement about your opinion of the story. Then, write individual paragraphs to address each of the items in your chart. When you revise your work, replace weak modifiers with strong and precise adjectives.

"Everyday Use" by Alice Walker
Enrichment: Art

Quilting is the process of stitching together two layers of fabric. This simple definition, however, hardly describes the intricate and highly skilled handiwork found in countless examples of American quilts. Lone Star and Walk Around the Mountain, the patterns of Grandma Dee's quilts, are just two examples among the great number and variety of quilt patterns.

Quilting became very popular in America in the eighteenth and nineteenth centuries. The quilts were often made from, and the patterns created around, the scraps of fabric saved from petticoats, shirts, long underwear, old wedding dresses, and other articles of clothing. These scraps of fabric are a tactile history of our ancestors' lives. Grandma Dee's quilts, for example, contain scraps from her dresses, Grandpa Jarrell's shirts, and Great Grandpa Ezra's Civil War uniform. Some quilts "tell" a family's story through embroidered outlines of hands, trees, flowers, animals, and other symbols significant to individual family members. Sometimes, a poem is stitched or written on the quilt.

DIRECTIONS: *Answer each of the following questions. Then use your answers to help you imagine a quilt that tells about your family. Represent each member of your family in one of the quilt squares. Use colored pencils to draw your quilt idea in the area provided.*

1. List each family member to be presented in your quilt, including yourself.

   _____

2. What color(s) will you use for each family member? What color of thread will you use to unite the different squares?

   _____

   _____

3. What object or symbol will you use for each family member? What does the object or symbol tell about the person?

   _____

   _____

4. What else will you include in your quilt? Special fabrics? Why?

   _____

Name _____ Date _____

"Everyday Use" by Alice Walker
Open-Book Test

Short Answer *Write your responses to the questions in this section on the lines provided.*

1. From the language she uses to describe herself, what impression do you get of Dee's mother in "Everyday Use"? Give details from the text.

   _____

   _____

   _____

2. What contrast between Maggie and Dee is revealed in the following passage from "Everyday Use"?

   > Maggie will be nervous until after her sister goes: she will stand hopelessly in corners, homely and ashamed of her burn scars . . . eying her sister with a mixture of envy and awe. She thinks that her sister has held life always in the palm of one hand . . .

   _____

   _____

3. In "Everyday Use," Dee's mother fantasizes about meeting up with Dee on a television show that reunites parents and children who have not seen each other for a long time. Why do you think she has this fantasy? What does it show about her relationship with Dee?

   _____

   _____

   _____

4. Why has Dee come to visit her mother and sister? Cite a quotation from the story that explains why she has come to visit them.

   _____

   _____

   _____

5. According to Dee's mother, what motivates Dee to read to her mother and sister in "Everyday Use"?

   _____

   _____

   _____

6. Based on the language the narrator uses to describe her life with Maggie in the first and last paragraphs of "Everyday Use," briefly explain why Maggie and her mother are satisfied with their lives in a way that Dee is not with hers.

   _____

   _____

   _____

   _____

7. Use the graphic organizer to sort out and analyze the contrasting character traits and personalities of Maggie and Dee in "Everyday Use." Then, on the lines below, summarize their contrasting characters.

Maggie's Traits

_____

_____

_____

Dee's Traits

_____

_____

_____

Difference

_____

_____

_____

_____

_____

_____

_____

8. The narrator of "Everyday Use" wants Maggie, not Dee, to have the quilts that have been crafted by their family members. Based on clues provided in the story, briefly describe how you think Maggie would use the quilts as opposed to how Dee would use them. Then explain how this difference reveals a contrast in the characters of the two sisters.

_____

_____

_____

_____

9. What does the narrator's language in this passage from "Everyday Use" reveal about the character of Maggie?

It was Grandma Dee and Big Dee who taught her [Maggie] how to quilt herself. She stood there with her scarred hands hidden in the folds of her skirt. She looked at her sister with something like fear but she wasn't mad at her.

_____

_____

_____

10. If you cast a *furtive* glance at your friend during class, would other people be likely to notice it? Why or why not? Base your answer on the meaning of *furtive* as it is used in "Everyday Use."

_____

_____

Essay

Write an extended response to the question of your choice or to the question or questions your teacher assigns you.

11. What do you think is the significance of the title of the story, "Everyday Use"? In an essay, explain Walker's use of this title and what it reveals about the contrasting outlooks and personalities of the main characters. Support your answer with details from the story.

12. Throughout "Everyday Use," Dee expresses an interest in her family's cultural heritage through her admiration of objects such as the butter churn and the quilts. Maggie, in her own way, also shows an appreciation of the family's background. In an essay, explain how Dee's appreciation of her family's heritage differs from Maggie's. Support your answer with details from the story.

13. In commenting on her cultural heritage in "Everyday Use," Dee states that she has rejected the name her mother gave her because "I couldn't bear it any longer, being named after the people who oppress me." In an essay, explain whether Dee has also been kept down by her family. Include examples from the text to support your opinion.

14. **Thinking About the Essential Question: How does literature shape or reflect society?** In "Everyday Use," Walker portrays the impact of an older daughter's changing tastes and values on her more traditional mother and younger sister. Do you think that Walker is merely reflecting a state of society in this story, or is she commenting on how people should relate to their cultural heritage? Explain your answer in an essay supported by details from the story.

Oral Response

15. Go back to question 1, 2, or 5 or to the question your teacher assigns you. Take a few minutes to expand your answer and prepare an oral response. Find additional details in "Everyday Use" that support your points. If necessary, make notes to guide your oral response.

Name _____   Date _____

"**Everyday Use**" by Alice Walker
Selection Test A

Critical Reading *Identify the letter of the choice that best answers the question.*

____ 1. Who is telling the story "Everyday Use"?
   A. Maggie
   B. Dee
   C. Maggie and Dee's mother
   D. a character outside the story

____ 2. Based on Dee's personality in "Everyday Use," why would Dee be embarrassed to have her friend speak with her mother?
   A. because her mother laughs too much
   B. because of the way her mother talks
   C. because her mother his arrogant
   D. because her mother takes care of Maggie

____ 3. How does Maggie feel that she is different from Dee in "Everyday Use"?
   A. Dee is lucky, and she is not.
   B. Dee is kind, and she is not.
   C. She is educated, and Dee is not.
   D. She is friendly, and Dee is not.

____ 4. What language of Maggie's in "Everyday Use" shows that she is surprised and at a loss for words?
   A. "How do I look, Mama?"
   B. "Wa-su-zo-Tean-o!"
   C. "Uhnnnh."
   D. "She can have them, Mama."

____ 5. Why is the name Wangero important to Dee in "Everyday Use"?
   A. It is her grandfather's name.
   B. It is a non-slave name.
   C. It is her husband's name.
   D. It is her Aunt Dee's real name.

____ 6. How does the author of "Everyday Use" show that language is an important part of Dee's personality?
   A. She speaks with a fancy accent.
   B. She loves to read.
   C. She collects books.
   D. She teaches others to use Standard English.

_____ 7. Why is Maggie shy in public in "Everyday Use"?
   A. She does not read well.
   B. She does not like her name.
   C. She cannot make quilts.
   D. She has been scarred in a fire.

_____ 8. What major difference between Maggie and Dee is revealed at the end of "Everyday Use"?
   A. what their mother means to them
   B. what the quilts truly mean to them
   C. how they feel about Dee's husband
   D. how they feel about the house

_____ 9. What meaning does the title "Everyday Use" have in connection with the story's events?
   A. Quilts should be hung to look pretty.
   B. Things made to be used have a special beauty.
   C. Beauty and use do not go together.
   D. Using things every single day wears them out.

_____ 10. How does Mama grow as a character at the end of "Everyday Use"?
   A. She dips some snuff.
   B. She understands her heritage.
   C. She stands up to Dee.
   D. She becomes more religious.

_____ 11. Who gets to the keep the quilts at the end of "Everyday Use?"
   A. the narrator   C. Dee
   B. Hakim-a-barber   D. Maggie

Vocabulary and Grammar

_____ 12. Which word best replaces *doctrines* in this sentence: "The young man explained the *doctrines* he had been raised with"?
   A. emotions   C. people
   B. religious beliefs   D. history books

_____ 13. Which is the most appropriate word to describe the boys who used to sneak around Dee's house when she was younger?
   A. furtive
   B. oppressive
   C. comfortable
   D. visible

____ **14.** Which of the following sentences most accurately uses a transitional expression?

   A. In the mean time, Maggie is shy with strangers; she is comfortable at home with her mother.

   B. Maggie is shy with strangers; for example, she is comfortable at home with her mother.

   C. Maggie is shy with strangers; similarly, she is comfortable at home with her mother.

   D. Maggie is shy with strangers; however, she is comfortable at home with her mother.

____ **15.** Which of the following sentences most effectively uses a transitional expression to join these two independent clauses?

   Dee is dismissive of her family. Her comments about her sister are cruel.

   A. Dee is dismissive of her family; in the mean time, her comments about her sister are cruel.

   B. Dee is dismissive of her family; on the other hand, her comments about her sister are cruel.

   C. Dee is dismissive of her family; in fact, her comments about her sister are cruel.

   D. Dee is dismissive of her family; however, her comments about her sister are cruel.

Essay

16. In "Everyday Use," Dee says to her mother and Maggie, "You just don't understand . . . your heritage." Is she right? Who has the more realistic sense of heritage that goes with the quilts—Dee, or Mama and Maggie? In what ways? Write a brief essay to respond.

17. What standards of human beauty are expressed in "Everyday Use"? How does Mama express these standards? Why is it interesting that she is the person to speak about them? Write a brief essay to address these questions.

"Everyday Use" by Alice Walker
Selection Test B

Critical Reading *Identify the letter of the choice that best completes the statement or answers the question.*

____ 1. "Everyday Use" is the story of
   A. a young woman's return home.
   B. a house that burns down.
   C. a new marriage.
   D. a young man meeting his inlaws.

____ 2. Maggie looks forward to Dee's visit with
   A. anticipation and confidence.
   B. worry and fear.
   C. excitement and scorn.
   D. nervousness and awe.

____ 3. Why is Maggie timid and insecure?
   A. She knows that her mother loves Dee more.
   B. She grew up in poverty.
   C. Her mother gives away her possessions.
   D. She was scarred by a fire.

____ 4. When the author has Maggie repeat the phrase, "Uhnnnh," she characterizes Maggie as
   A. someone who likes to sing.
   B. inarticulate, almost like an animal.
   C. someone who is delighted with the sound of her own voice.
   D. eager and ready to join the conversation.

____ 5. Why doesn't Dee bring her friends home?
   A. She does not like her family.
   B. Her friends embarrass her.
   C. She is ashamed of her poverty.
   D. She has no friends.

____ 6. Which words best describe Wangero?
   A. generous and shy
   B. homely and shy
   C. stylish and shallow
   D. caring and respectful

____ 7. The narrator says Dee would prefer her to have "skin like an uncooked barley pancake," meaning
   A. moist and smooth.
   B. light in color.
   C. soft and sticky.
   D. fresh smelling.

Unit 6 Resources: New Voices, New Frontiers
43

____ 8. The narrator calls Dee "Miss" Wangero to show that Dee is
   A. more important than she is.
   B. an older woman.
   C. arrogant and distant from her.
   D. a stranger to her.

____ 9. Why did Dee embrace an African language when she chose a new name for herself—
Wangero Leewanika Kemanjo?
   A. It is the only language she knew.
   B. She wants to forget everything about her own family.
   C. She wants to be closer to her heritage.
   D. Her new name was her great-grandmother's name.

____ 10. What do the specific details in this passage reveal about Maggie?

> It was Grandma Dee and Big Dee who taught her [Maggie] how to quilt herself. She stood there with her scarred hands hidden in the folds of her skirt. She looked at her sister with something like fear but she wasn't mad at her.

   A. Maggie has no feeling for the quilts.
   B. Maggie is afraid of her sister.
   C. Maggie is a needy person who depends upon her mother and sister.
   D. Maggie accepts the hardships life has handed her.

____ 11. What do the specific details in this passage reveal about Dee (Wangero)?

> After dinner Dee (Wangero) went to the trunk at the foot of my bed and started rifling through it. . . . Out came Wangero with two quilts. . . . "Mama," Wangero said sweet as a bird. "Can I have these old quilts?"

   A. Dee is a considerate and loving daughter.
   B. Dee brashly goes after what she wants.
   C. Dee respects her mother's privacy.
   D. Dee has very fond memories of her grandmother's quilts.

____ 12. What do the specific details in this passage reveal about the narrator's relationship with each of her daughters?

> I did something I never had done before: hugged Maggie to me, then dragged her on into the room, snatched the quilts out of Miss Wangero's hands and dumped them into Maggie's lap.

   A. The narrator loves Maggie's faith and is brave enough herself to challenge Dee's bossy, spoiled behavior.
   B. The narrator pities Maggie, but respects Dee, who has left home to make something of herself.
   C. The narrator loves Dee more than Maggie.
   D. The narrator is afraid of "Miss Wangero," who bosses both Maggie and the narrator.

____ 13. How does the author of "Everyday Use" show that language is an important part of Dee's personality?
   A. She speaks with a fancy accent.
   B. She collects books.
   C. She loves to read.
   D. She teaches others to use Standard English

____ 14. Who gets to the keep the quilts at the end of "Everyday Use?"
    A. the narrator   C. Dee
    B. Hakim-a-barber   D. Maggieh

Vocabulary and Grammar

____ 15. The Word *doctrines* means _____.
    A. honorary degrees
    B. visiting teachers or professors
    C. meek personalities
    D. beliefs or rules that are taught

____ 16. What does the word *furtive* mean in the following sentence?
    The boys were furtive, hiding in the bushes, when they came around looking for Dee.
    A. sneaky   C. comfortable
    B. oppressive   D. visible

____ 17. Which of the following sentences most accurately uses a transitional expression?
    A. In the mean time, Maggie is shy with strangers; she is comfortable at home with her mother.
    B. Maggie is shy with strangers; for example, she is comfortable at home with her mother.
    C. Maggie is shy with strangers; similarly, she is comfortable at home with her mother.
    D. Maggie is shy with strangers; however, she is comfortable at home with her mother.

____ 18. Which of the following transitional expressions would best join these two independent clauses?
    Dee is dismissive of her family. Her comments about her sister are cruel.
    A. in the mean time   C. in fact
    B. on the other hand   D. however

Essay

19. Walker uses specific details to describe the narrator, Dee, and Maggie. These details also illustrate the differences among these three characters. In an essay, analyze the physical, emotional, and intellectual differences between the narrator and her two daughters. Support your answer with descriptive details from "Everyday Use."

20. In an essay, analyze what motivates Dee's interest in her heritage. Compare and contrast Dee's motivations with Maggie's knowledge of specific stories and details about their heritage. How does their appreciation of their heritage differ?

21. In "Everyday Use," Dee is energetic, talkative, and showy, while Maggie is quiet and still. Write an essay in which you explain Dee's and Maggie's personality using the story's last line

"And then the two of us sat there just enjoying, until it was time to go in the house and go to bed."

Would Dee be content sitting on the porch with her mother? Is Dee capable of "just enjoying"? What does it say about Maggie and her appreciation of her family that she can act in this way?

Study these words from the selections. Then, complete the activities.

Word List A

dozed [DOHZD] *v.* napped; slept lightly
　School started so early that Trinh often <u>dozed</u> during first period.

jiggled [JIG uhld] *v.* rocked or bounced lightly; gave little jerks to
　Andrew <u>jiggled</u> the key in the lock to make it work.

marveled [MAHR vuhld] *v.* admired and wondered; was amazed by
　Caroline's parents <u>marveled</u> at her extraordinary talent for singing.

overcast [OH ver kast] *adj.* dark or gray cloudy sky
　On an <u>overcast</u> day, we had no need for an umbrella to give us shade.

refills [ree FILZ] *v.* fills up again
　The waiter <u>refills</u> the water glasses as soon as they are empty.

striking [STRI king] *adj.* noticeable; extraordinary; stands out
　Malcolm bore a <u>striking</u> resemblance to his beloved dog, Bailey.

survivor [ser VY ver] *n.* a person with strength and resilience who can get through hard times successfully
　Jill faced hardship but she was a <u>survivor</u> so she overcame her problems.

waterfowl [WAWT er FOWL] *n.* birds that live in water, such as ducks
　We saw several types of <u>waterfowl</u> swimming in the lake.

Word List B

ambitions [am BISH uhnz] *n.* desires for success; big goals
　One of his <u>ambitions</u> is to become a movie star.

attractive [uh TRAK tiv] *adj.* pleasing appearance; appealing
　The boots in that store window are <u>attractive</u>.

correspondence [KAWR uh spahn duhns] *n.* letters received or written
　Jacob and Christine had a lengthy <u>correspondence</u> by mail.

involves [in VAHLVZ] *v.* includes; relates to
　The story <u>involves</u> a wolf, a little girl in a red cloak, and a grandma.

letterhead [LET er hed] *n.* stationery with name and address printed at the top
　Stefan uses the company <u>letterhead</u> for his business correspondence.

maintain [mayn TAYN] *v.* to keep in good condition by taking care of
　Molly learned to <u>maintain</u> trucks at her vocational school.

minor [MY ner] *adj.* of smaller or lesser importance
　Dr. Dan said the cut was a <u>minor</u> one and did not require stitches.

utilities [yoo TIL uh teez] *n.* public services supplied to homes like water, sewer, gas, electricity and phone services
　Some landlords include the cost of <u>utilities</u> in the rent for an apartment.

46

"Everything Stuck to Him" by Raymond Carver
Vocabulary Warm-up Exercises

Exercise A *Fill in the blanks, using each word from Word List A only once.*

Maria's aunt suggested she try to get a modeling job due to her beautiful,

[1] _____ appearance and tall height. Unfortunately, at her first inter-

view, the front door of the modeling agency office seemed to be stuck. When Maria

[2] _____ it, the door flew open, whacked her nose terribly, and she ended

up in the emergency room. The doctor [3] _____ at Maria's injury, saying

it was amazing. He gave Maria a prescription saying, "Be sure the pharmacy

[4] _____ the prescription, if you need more." Maria left the hospital with

a large bandage across her nose. The gray, [5] _____ sky seemed to mir-

ror her depressed spirits. She sat down on a bench next to a pond where some

[6] _____ were swimming. Maria soon [7] _____ off to

sleep. She awoke a few minutes later, re-energized. She realized that, deep down, she

was pretty tough, a [8] _____. She decided not to wait until her nose

healed to pursue a career. Maybe she'd investigate something else, perhaps a career as

a pharmacist.

Exercise B *Decide whether each statement below is true or false. Circle T or F, and explain your answer.*

1. If your house burns down, it is a <u>minor</u> calamity.
   T / F _____

2. A project that <u>involves</u> you is one that you participate in.
   T / F _____

3. <u>Letterhead</u> is a kind of animal you would find in a swamp.
   T / F _____

4. Washing machines and dryers are <u>utilities</u>.
   T / F _____

5. If you <u>maintain</u> a garden that means you ignore it.
   T / F _____

6. A person's <u>correspondence</u> might include letters and hand-written notes.
   T / F _____

7. A person without a desire to succeed has <u>ambitions</u>.
   T / F _____

8. If you find a person <u>attractive</u> that means you have some positive feelings for that
   person.
   T / F _____

"Everything Stuck to Him" by Raymond Carver
Reading Warm-up A

Read the following passage. Then, complete the activities.

After the long car ride with his family to Uncle Milton's house in the mountains, Jeremy is exhausted. The road was monotonous, and the sky was <u>overcast</u>, gray, and dreary for the entire trip. Upon arrival, Jeremy can't wait to sit down. Unfortunately, they have to wait until Uncle Milton, who is quite old and very formal, invites them to sit. Finally the old man gestures to them to take a seat in the living room.

His parents chat on and on with Uncle Milton. Jeremy's mother is exaggerating about Jeremy's career on the high school football team. She is insisting that everybody in the stadium has admired and <u>marveled</u> at his passes and interceptions. She is telling about the time Jeremy got tackled by half the opposing team, and how he is such a <u>survivor</u>, so he got through that hard moment just fine.

But Uncle Milton isn't paying much attention. While she is talking he walks to the kitchen. When he returns, he <u>refills</u> their glasses with lemonade until they are all full again, and starts a new conversation about something else entirely, <u>waterfowl</u>.

At the lake we will tour tomorrow, he is saying, the wood ducks are fascinating. Their appearance is extraordinary, really quite <u>striking</u>. He starts describing the head of the male wood duck, which has shiny green, blue, and purple feathers, red eyes, and black and white stripes. Jeremy hears nothing more about wood ducks because he has <u>dozed</u> off. He has just started dreaming about a giant purple and green bird when he feels his arm being <u>jiggled</u> by his mother. She jerks it just enough to wake him, while nodding her head at Uncle Milton, who now holding an ancient football and describing his own glory days on the field.

1. Underline the words that help to explain the meaning of <u>overcast</u>. Write a sentence describing an *overcast* sky.

2. Circle the word that has a meaning similar to <u>marveled</u>. Give another synonym for *marveled*.

3. Underline the phrase that is a clue to the meaning of <u>survivor</u>. Tell about a *survivor* you know.

4. Underline the phrase that tells what Uncle Milton <u>refills</u>. Use the word *refills* in a sentence.

5. Circle the words in a nearby sentence that give a clue to the meaning of <u>waterfowl</u>. Name another type of *waterfowl*.

6. Circle nearby words that are synonyms for <u>striking</u>. Give another synonym for the word *striking*.

7. Underline one of the phrases that gives you the clue to the meaning of <u>dozed</u>. Write your own definition for the word *dozed*.

8. Circle the words that explain the meaning of <u>jiggled</u>. Use the word *jiggled* in a sentence.

"Everything Stuck to Him" by Raymond Carver

Reading Warm-up B

Read the following passage. Then, complete the activities.

Many people have <u>ambitions</u> to achieve the American dream of home ownership. Owning a home is an admirable goal. However, renting a home is also a desirable choice for many Americans.

Renting a home can be an <u>attractive</u> choice for several reasons. One thing that makes renting pleasing is that it usually costs less than buying. When you rent, you do not have to spend as much money or time to <u>maintain</u> your home; keeping it in good condition is the responsibility of its owner. Certainly a renter needs to do <u>minor</u>, less important things like cleaning and taking care of the yard, if there is a garden. But renting <u>involves</u> less work than owning, because a renter's chores do not usually include fixing the roof, furnace, or a major appliance. Those tasks usually belong to the owner.

Renters may be required to pay extra money for <u>utilities</u> like electricity, gas, and water service. The landlord's <u>correspondence</u> will explain what is included in the rent fee. These letters and forms are likely to be printed on <u>letterhead</u>, with the landlord's name, address, and other contact information at the top of the pages.

The majority of people rent a home at some point in their lives. Most young, single people living independently for the first time are renters. Renters also include families relocating to new areas, low-income households, recent immigrants, and older citizens who may find renting a good choice as their children grow up and move away.

The goal of home ownership is an excellent one, yet for people who rent by choice or by circumstance, freedom from the additional costs and chores of home ownership can offer flexibility and time to pursue an art, a degree, a profession, or other unique goals and dreams.

1. Underline the words in a nearby sentence that have a meaning similar to <u>ambitions</u>. Write a sentence describing one of your *ambitions*.

2. Circle the word that is described by <u>attractive</u>. Give a synonym for the word *attractive*.

3. Underline the words that explain the meaning of <u>maintain</u>. Write a sentence telling about something you *maintain*.

4. Circle the words that have the same meaning as <u>minor</u>. Give an antonym for *minor*.

5. Underline the phrase that tells why renting <u>involves</u> less work. Write a sentence using the word *involves*.

6. Circle the words that explain the meaning of <u>utilities</u>. What *utilities* are used in the place where you live?

7. Underline the words in a nearby sentence that help to explain the meaning of <u>correspondence</u>. Describe the *correspondence* you have with people, whether it is on paper or through an electronic media.

8. Underline the phrase that describes the meaning of <u>letterhead</u>. Use the word *letterhead* in a sentence

49

Name _____ Date _____

"Everything Stuck to Him" by Raymond Carver
Literary Analysis: Author's Style

Every work of fiction reflects its **author's style**—the author's choice and arrangement of words and details and how these elements work together to establish mood and meaning. Some authors use detailed descriptions in their narratives, whereas others avoid elaborate descriptions in favor of simple dialogue or a spare recounting of events. Raymond Carver usually favors an economical, pared-down approach that features an economy of words and a minimum of description. Critics have often labeled Carver's style as a minimalist, a term used to describe work that has been reduced to its bare essentials.

DIRECTIONS: *The left-hand column one of the chart below lists several notable features of Carver's minimalist approach in "Everything Stuck to Him." In the right-hand column, briefly explain how that feature adds to the overall impact of the story.*

Minimalist Feature	How It Adds to Impact of the Story
No quotation marks in dialogue	
No names given to the father and daughter	
The husband and wife are called "boy and girl"	
No descriptions of physical features of characters	
Simple, direct language	

"Everything Stuck to Him" by Raymond Carver
Reading Strategy: Ask Questions

When you read news articles, poems, or short stories, you may sometimes need to **ask questions** about what is happening, why things happen, or why the writer expresses something in a particular way. Do you pay attention, or do you just read on? If you do pay attention to the questions in your mind, you may gain fuller understanding of what you are reading. For example, readers may find themselves asking questions about the time shifts in "Everything Stuck to Him"

DIRECTIONS: *As you read "Everything Stuck to Him," ask yourself these questions. It is possible that you might not be able to answer the questions right way. You might have to piece together information or clues to come cup with the answers after you finish the story.*

1. What is the relationship of the two characters who are speaking to each other as the story opens? How can you tell?

   _____

   _____

   _____

2. Who narrates the "outer" story that opens and closes "Everything Stuck to Him?" Who narrates the "inner story" that comes in between?

   _____

   _____

3. At one point "boy" expresses some romantic interest in "girl's" two sisters. What does this admission say about the possible future of the marriage between "boy" and "girl"?

   _____

   _____

4. What has happened to the marriage of "boy" and "girl" by the time the scene shifts back to the "outer" story toward the end of "Everything Stuck to Him"? How can you tell?

   _____

   _____

5. What do you think is the meaning of the title "Everything Stuck to Him"?

   _____

   _____

Name _____ Date _____

"Everything Stuck to Him" by Raymond Carver
Vocabulary Builder

Word List

ambitions   coincide   fitfully   striking

A. DIRECTIONS: *Think about the meaning of the underlined World List word in each sentence. Then, answer the question.*

1. His birthday often seemed to <u>coincide</u> with one of his final exams. Was the boy often free of exam pressures on his birthday? How do you know?

   _____

   _____

2. Juanita is known for her <u>ambitions</u>. Does Juanita lack goals that she wants to achieve? How do you know?

   _____

   _____

3. The hotel was known for the <u>striking</u> decor of its lobby? Would people be likely to notice the decor of the hotel lobby? How do you know?

   _____

   _____

4. If someone said that he had slept <u>fitfully</u>, would he have slept soundly through the night? How do you know?

   _____

   _____

B. DIRECTIONS: *On each line, write the letter of the word or phrase that is closest in meaning to the Word List word.*

___ 1. coincide
    A. delight
    B. predict
    C. declare
    D. overlap

___ 2. ambitions
    A. encounters
    B. aspirations
    C. triumphs
    D. schemes

___ 3. striking
    A. tiring
    B. pressuring
    C. noticeables
    D. fulfilling

___ 4. fitfully
    A. faithfully
    B. sporadically
    C. diligently
    D. carelessly

"Everything Stuck to Him" by Raymond Carver
Support for Writing

When you finished reading "Everything Stuck to Him," did you find the ending happy or unhappy or somewhere in between? Try to sketch arguments for all sides of this issue before settling on the viewpoint you will take in your essay on this subject. Answer the questions below to help you organize your thoughts before you write your essay. Think about plot elements, key bits of dialogue, and the main characters' reactions to events, memories, and each other.

1. What arguments can be made for viewing the ending as happy?

_____

_____

_____

_____

_____

2. What arguments can be made for viewing the ending as unhappy?

_____

_____

_____

_____

_____

3. What arguments can be made for viewing the ending as neither happy nor unhappy, but somewhere in between?

_____

_____

_____

_____

_____

After you decide which of these three views of the ending is the most convincing to you, write a rough draft of an essay in which you defend your opinion. Support your opinion with clear logic and details from the story.

"Everything Stuck to Him" by Raymond Carver
Enrichment: Hunting

The main conflict between the husband and wife in "Everything Stuck to Him" is provoked by the husband's desire to go goose hunting with his friend even though his infant daughter appears to be ill.

Originally, the hunting and killing of animals by humans was a means of survival. Today, the legal hunting of game animals still provides foods such as venison, and many hunters regard their activity as a useful method of controlling the population of certain species that tend to overbreed in certain rural areas, such as deer or geese. Others argue that there are more natural, less violent methods available to control animal populations and that by the ethics of the modern world, hunting and killing animals in the wild is a cruel, unethical practice that should be banned.

Work with a partner to present a debate about hunting. Gather information from the Internet and the library to enter into the graphic organizer below. Summarize the positions of each of the four groups. Then, choose a classmate who holds the view that is opposite from yours as a partner for the debate.

Hunting: Pro or Con?

Hunters	Animal Rights Supporters	Farmers	Environmentalist
Reason for position: _____ _____	Reason for position: _____ _____	Reason for position: _____ _____	Reason for position: _____ _____
Facts that support position: _____ _____ _____	Facts that support position: _____ _____ _____	Facts that support position: _____ _____ _____	Facts that support position: _____ _____ _____

As you debate, take notes of your opponent's arguments to be able to rebut effectively, and show respect for your opponent's viewpoints.

"Everything Stuck to Him" by Raymond Carver
Open-Book Test

Short Answer *Write your responses to the questions in this section on the lines provided.*

1. Raymond Carver's writing style has often been called "minimalist." Based on a reading of the first few paragraphs of "Everything Stuck to Him," why do you think this label applies to Carver's writing style? Cite an example or two to support your answer.

   _____

   _____

   _____

2. What is the relationship between the first two people who speak in the story? What detail helps the reader to clarify this relationship?

   _____

   _____

   _____

   _____

3. If you wanted to get a sense of the economic status of the husband and wife in the story, which detail would first give a major clue about this?

   _____

   _____

   _____

   _____

4. What is it about the way in which the narrator refers to the husband and wife that contributes to the "minimalist" style of "Everything Stuck to Him"? Give an example from the text.

   _____

   _____

   _____

   _____

5. Does the narrator ever describe the physical appearance of the boy, the girl, or their daughter? What does this aspect of the story say about the author's style and intentions? Explain.

   _____

   _____

   _____

   _____

6. After being repeatedly awakened by the crying baby, the narrator says that the boy "did a terrible thing. He swore." Why would swearing seem like a terrible thing in this context? Why do you think the boy's swearing upset his wife?

_____

_____

_____

_____

7. What causes the girl's attitude toward the boy to soften after she tells him that he must choose between Carl and "us"? Why does her attitude soften?

_____

_____

_____

8. The title "Everything Stuck to Him" refers in part to the incident where the breakfast plate falls into the boy's lap. Do you think that the title has any other meaning? If so, what do you think it is?

_____

_____

_____

9. Of the three characters in "Everything Stuck to Him"—the father, the mother, and the daughter—which one is noticeably not present by the end of the story? What is the significance of this absence?

_____

_____

10. If you slept *fitfully* during the night, would you likely feel rested in the morning? Why or why not? Base your answer on the meaning of *fitfully* as it is used in "Everything Stuck to Him."

_____

_____

Essay

Write an extended response to the question of your choice or to the question or questions your teacher assigns you.

11. In "Everything Stuck to Him," Raymond Carver provides almost no physical descriptions of the characters. In an essay, write a brief description of what you think each of the characters looks like—the girl and the boy and, later in the story, the father and the daughter. Do you think that adding your descriptions to the story would add to or subtract from its impact? Why? Support your opinion with clear reasoning and relevant examples.

12. In "Everything Stuck to Him," Carver does not tell the reader outright what happened to the boy and girl and their marriage after the events recounted in the story—he provides only hints. Based on those hints and your own inferences and imagination, write an essay in which you describe the subsequent course of the marriage of the boy and girl. Support your answer with clear reasoning and details from the story.

13. Near the end of "Everything Stuck to Him," the older version of the boy tells his now-grown daughter, "Things change . . . I don't know how they do. But they do without your realizing it or wanting them to." In an essay, explain how this story illustrates this idea of change happening no matter what. In your answer, specify what has changed, and give the reason for the change(s). Support your answer with details from the story.

14. **Thinking About the Essential Question: What makes American literature American?** Even though "Everything Stuck to Him" is set in Milan, the recollected story is set in America. What gives this story its distinctively American character? Develop your thoughts in a brief essay. Provide details to support your ideas.

Oral Response

15. Go back to question 1, 2, or 6 or to the question your teacher assigns you. Take a few minutes to expand your answer and prepare an oral response. Find additional details in "Everything Stuck to Him" that support your points. If necessary, make notes to guide your oral response.

"Everything Stuck to Him" by Raymond Carver
Selection Test A

MULTIPLE CHOICE

Critical Reading *Choose the answer that best answers the question or completes the statement.*

____ 1. What is the setting of "Everything Stuck to Him"?
A. Milan at Christmas
B. New York in the summer
C. Indiana in autumn
D. California for Easter

____ 2. The story within the story in "Everything Stuck to Him" is about
A. a winter night in Italy
B. a young couple and their baby
C. a father and his adult daughter
D. a Christmas celebration

____ 3. In "Everything Stuck to Him," the young woman wants to hear a story about
A. her father's job
B. her mother's cooking
C. her childhood
D. a hunting trip

____ 4. Which of the following best describes Raymond Carver's style in "Everything Stuck to Him?
A. tragic
B. elaborate
C. suspenseful
D. minimalist

____ 5. In "Everything Stuck to Him," what does the reader want to know about the narrator?
A. Where does the narrator live?
B. Is the narrator the father of the young woman?
C. Does the narrator travel often?
D. What is the narrator's name?

____ 6. As the narrator tells the story in "Everything Stuck to Him," the reader can understand the plot by asking
A. "Will I find out that the boy in the story is the narrator?"
B. "In what city does the young couple live?"
C. "Did the young couple have any more children?"
D. "Do I need to know when the narrator and young girl met?"

____ 7. When the narrator explains that the boy in "Everything Stuck to Him" was "a little in love" with his wife's sister, he reveals that the boy

   A. noticed other woman.

   B. was interested only in his wife.

   C. is still in love with the sister.

   D. the sister was in love with the boy.

____ 8. In "Everything Stuck to Him," what does the girl's anxiety for the crying baby tell you about her?

   A. She does not care about the baby.

   B. She wants to sleep.

   C. She knows what is wrong.

   D. She is an inexperienced mother.

____ 9. In "Everything Stuck to Him," why is the girl angry about the boy's choice to go hunting when the baby is crying?

   A. She wants to go hunting, too.

   B. She is scared and wants his support at home.

   C. She knows he will not come back.

   D. She wants him to cook breakfast.

____ 10. In "Everything Stuck to Him," why does the girl tell the boy he's "going to have to choose" between hunting and having a family?

   A. She wants a bigger house.

   B. She wants more children.

   C. She wants to force him to stay home.

   D. She wants him to go away.

____ 11. In "Everything Stuck to Him," does the boy go hunting?

   A. No, he stays home.

   B. He stays home in the morning and goes hunting in the afternoon.

   C. Yes, he goes hunting.

   D. Yes, he goes hunting but comes home early.

____ 12. The dialogue in "Everything Stuck to Him" is minialist because

   A. it is brief.

   B. it is filled with vivid adjectives.

   C. it occurs between two people.

   D. some of it occurred in the past.

___ **13.** At the end of "Everything Stuck to Him," the narrator reveals that
  A. he was the boy in the story.
  B. he does not care about the past.
  C. he does not remember the young woman.
  D. he did now know the boy in his story.

Vocabulary

___ **14.** In which sentence is the word *fitfully*, from "Everthing Stuck to Him,"used correctly?
  A. The baby slept fitfully, waking up over and over throughout the night.
  B. She napped fitfully and slept for three hours.
  C. The child played fitfully and with much energy.
  D. The argument continued fitfully because neither person would stop.

___ **15.** In the following sentence, what does he word *coincide*, from "Everything Stuck to Him," mean?

  My babysitting job and my sister's soccer game coincide.

  A. happen at different times
  B. happen at the same time
  C. cancel each other
  D. happen twice

Essay

16. In an essay, discuss the two frames in the story "Everything Stuck to Him." Identify the characters and the plots of each story. Tell how the two stories are related to each other.

17. In an essay, describe the relationship between the narrator in "Everything Stuck to Him" and the young woman who is visiting him. Do they have a close relationship? Is the young woman eager to talk with him? Is he eager to talk to her? How do they treat each other?

18. **Thinking About the Essential Question: What makes American literature American?** Even though "Everything Stuck to Him"is set in Milan, the story being told within the story is set in America. What characteristics make the story being told seem "American"? Develop your thoughts in a brief essay.

"Everything Stuck to Him" by Raymond Carver
Selection Test B

MULTIPLE CHOICE

Critical Reading *Choose the answer that best answers the question or completes the statement.*

_____ 1. Why is the young woman asking the narrator for stories about her childhood in "Everything Stuck to Him"?
   A. She wants to learn more about her parents.
   B. She likes to hear the narrator talk.
   C. She is writing a book about her youth.
   D. She in unsure about where she grew up.

_____ 2. When the narrator in "Everything Stuck to Him" describes the young woman as a "survivor from top to bottom," what does he mean?
   A. She is a tall woman.
   B. She handles adversity successfully.
   C. She has survived a car accident.
   D. She will live longer than the narrator.

_____ 3. The author of "Everything Stuck to Him" immediately draws the reader into the story when he
   A. describes the setting.
   B. discusses the characters' past.
   C. tells the identify of the characters.
   D. begins the story in the middle of the characters' conversation.

_____ 4. What is the best answer to the question, "Why doesn't the narrator want to tell a story to the young woman?"
   A. He is shy about speaking aloud.
   B. He wants to forget the past.
   C. He is afraid she will laugh at him.
   D. He is suspicious of her.

_____ 5. "Everything Stuck to Him" has which characteristic of a minimalist story?
   A. It has elaborate details.
   B. There is much dialogue.
   C. There are two characters.
   D. It has a basic plot.

_____ 6. In "Everything Stuck to Him," why are the boy and girl awake most of the night before the boy's hunting trip?
   A. The girl is ill.
   B. They have to work.
   C. Their baby is crying.
   D. Their neighbors are noisy.

_____ 7. Which line in this passage from "Everything Stuck to Him" refers to the outer story that includes the narrator and the young woman?

> Sally was the girl's sister. She was striking. I don't know if you've seen pictures of her. The boy was a little in love with Sally, just as he was a little in love with Betsy, who was another sister the girl had.

A. Sally was the girl's sister.

B. She was striking.

C. I don't know if you've seen pictures of her.

D. The boy was a little in love with Sally.

_____ 8. In "Everything Stuck to Him," what does the boy's interaction with his baby daughter reveal about his personality?

A. He cares about the baby.

B. He is nervous.

C. He dislikes helping with the baby.

D. He is distant from his wife.

_____ 9. Which question would the reader likely ask during the argument between the boy and the girl in "Everything Stuck to Him"?

A. Why is the young woman in Milan?

B. What are the characters' names?

C. Will the boy go hunting or stay home?

D. What time is it in the story?

_____ 10. In "Everything Stuck to Him," what happens when the boy begins to eat his breakfast?

A. He spills his plate of waffles into his lap.

B. The baby starts crying.

C. The girl knocks his plate on the floor.

D. The phone rings.

_____ 11. To what is the narrator probably referring when he speaks the following line in "Everything Stuck to Him"?

> "Things change, he says. I don't know how they do. But they do without realizing it or wanting them to."

A. His relationship with his wife

B. The weather outside

C. His job with the dentist

D. His age

_____ 12. What is the young woman's reaction to the narrator's story in "Everything Stuck to Him"?

A. She cries.

B. She was interested.

C. She was angry.

D. She ignores him.

_____ 13. Which statement best describes Raymond Carver's style in "Everything Stuck to Him"?

A. extended discussions of characters

B. long descriptions of the setting

C. rich and expressive dialogue

D. emotion and action in few words

_____ 14. What question is a reader most likely to ask at the end of "Everything Stuck to Him"?
   A. Will the young woman tell a story?
   B. Why does the young woman study her nails?
   C. What happened to the young woman's mother?
   D. Why is the narrator in Milan?

_____ 15. What do the narrator and the young woman do at the end of "Everything Stuck to Him"?
   A. They go walk around Milan.
   B. They stay home.
   C. They go to a movie.
   D. They return to the United States.

Vocabulary

_____ 16. The baby daughter in "Everything Stuck to Him" was born during cold weather that happened to coincide with hunting season. The best meaning of the word *coincide* is
   A. happen at the same time
   B. occurr afterwards
   C. disappear
   D. happen again

_____ 17. What is the best meaning of the word *striking* in the following passage from "Everything Stuck to Him"?

   Sally was the girl's sister. She was striking.

   A. agressive   **C.** awkward
   B. vividly impressive   **D.** quietly sad

_____ 18. In which sentence is *ambitions* used correctly?
   A. Their ambitions kept them from trying anything new.
   B. With no ambitions, they had goals and dreams to attain.
   C. Their ambitions were modest, so they planned great adventures.
   D. They had ambitions to travel the world and have exciting jobs.

Essay

19. In an essay, discuss the two frames in the story "Everything Stuck to Him." Identify the characters and the plots in each story. Tell how the two stories are related to each other.

20. In an essay, describe the relationship between the narrator and the young woman who is visiting him in "Everything Stuck to Him."Do they have a close relationship? Are they eager to talk to each other? How do they treat each other? Explain why each character acts the way he or she does.

21. Raymond Carver writes in a minimalist style in "Everything Stuck to Him." Identify two or three characteristics of his style. Then discuss the atmosphere created by those characteristics.

22. **Thinking About the Essential Question: What makes American literature American?** Even though "Everything Stuck to Him" is set in Milan, the recollected story is set in America. What gives this story its distinctively American character? Develop your thoughts in a brief essay.

Vocabulary Warm-up Word Lists

Study these words from the selections. Then, complete the activities.

Word List A

aimed [AYMD] *v.* directed; pointed
Although I <u>aimed</u> for the target, the arrow flew off into a field.

canyon [KAN yuhn] *n.* a deep valley with steep sides
If you shout into the <u>canyon</u>, you can hear an echo.

glare [GLAIR] *n.* a harsh, bright light
In the <u>glare</u> of the flashlight, the cat's eyes looked red.

heap [HEEP] *n.* a mound or pile
The laundry lay in an untidy <u>heap</u> on the floor.

recent [REE suhnt] *adj.* not long ago
Put the most <u>recent</u> issue of the magazine at the top of the pile.

sliver [SLIV er] *n.* a small, sharp piece of something
Jake got a <u>sliver</u> in his foot while walking on the wooden path.

stumbled [STUM buld] *v.* walked in an unsteady way
In the darkness, Mara <u>stumbled</u> around looking for the light.

swerve [SWERV] *v.* turn sharply to the side
We had to <u>swerve</u> to avoid hitting that box in the street.

Word List B

assassin [uh SAS uhn] *n.* killer, especially of a political leader
More than one U.S. president has been killed by an <u>assassin</u>.

assuming [uh SOOM ing] *v.* supposing
If he was <u>assuming</u> that I'd be ready at six, he'll be disappointed.

hesitated [HEZ i tay ted] *v.* paused before acting
Dwayne <u>hesitated</u> on the high dive before jumping into the pool.

lowered [LOH werd] *adj.* reduced; diminished
The soft music and <u>lowered</u> lights made the restaurant romantic.

recited [ri SY ted] *v.* narrated; told; repeated aloud
Lila <u>recited</u> a tale of her childhood that held us all spellbound.

shard [SHAHRD] *n.* fragment; broken piece
Weeks after the vase broke, we found a <u>shard</u> behind the chair.

stiffened [STIF uhnd] *v.* became rigid
The sponge <u>stiffened</u> as it dried out.

wilderness [WIL der nis] *n.* an area of land that is not cultivated or inhabited
Kyle loved the untamed beauty of the <u>wilderness</u>.

Name _____ Date _____

Vocabulary Warm-up Exercises

Exercise A *Fill in the blanks, using each word from Word List A only once.*

My weekend bike rides are usually uneventful, so when I tell you about my most

[1] _____ ride, you won't believe it. I set out on the bike trail that runs

alongside that deep [2] _____ in the state park. Even though there's a

wooden fence to keep anyone from falling over the side, I kept my eyes [3]

_____ straight ahead. Suddenly the driver of a car that was coming

towards me flashed his headlights to let me know he saw me. The [4] _____

of the lights made me blink, so I didn't see the rock in my path until the last minute. I

had to [5] _____ to avoid hitting it, but I fell anyway and landed in a [6]

_____ on the trail. As I [7] _____ around, feeling my bones

to make sure nothing was broken, I grabbed onto the fence to steady myself. Of course,

that's when I got the [8] _____ in my hand. That was a painful day!

Exercise B *Decide whether each statement below is true or false. Circle T or F, and explain
your answer.*

1. When you are <u>assuming</u> something, you are certain of it.
   T / F _____

2. When a person has <u>hesitated</u>, he has plunged ahead without stopping.
   T / F _____

3. <u>Lowered</u> thermostats conserve energy.
   T / F _____

4. A person who has <u>recited</u> her life story has told others about herself.
   T / F _____

5. In the <u>wilderness</u> you would expect to see restaurants and stores.
   T / F _____

6. An <u>assassin</u> has the greatest respect for human life.
   T / F _____

7. A towel hung outside to dry may have <u>stiffened</u> in the sun.
   T / F _____

8. A <u>shard</u> of pottery can tell scientists about an early civilization.
   T / F _____

Unit 6 Resources: New Voices, New Frontiers
65

Name _____ Date _____

"Traveling Through The Dark" by William Stafford,
"The Secret" by Denise Levertov, and **"The Gift"** by Li-Young Lee
Reading Warm-up A

Read the following passage. Then, complete the activities.

Memory is a funny thing. You may be absolutely positive that you recall every detail of a day, a moment, or an event. But if someone then says to you, "No, I was there, and we didn't <u>swerve</u> around a squirrel that day, it was an armadillo," you may think, "Well, I was certain it was a squirrel that we had to veer around, but I suppose it's possible that I'm mistaken."

These different perspectives on memory can be particularly pointed where families are concerned. Whether the event was <u>recent</u> or occurred sometime in the past, brothers, sisters, and parents will often remember the same story differently. I was made aware of this again when I visited my sister last week.

"Remember the time we camped near that <u>canyon</u> in Arizona?" she asked me. I remembered looking down over the edge to the valley below.

"Sure," I said. "I remember that you got a sharp <u>sliver</u> in your finger when you climbed that tree."

"Well, yes," she answered, "Except that the climber was you. You were crying so hard when Mom pulled that bit of wood out of your finger that you collapsed into a <u>heap</u> in the tent."

"No, that's not exactly accurate," I replied. "*You* were crying, and you <u>stumbled</u> and staggered all over the campsite until you were the one that looked like a pile of old clothes on the ground."

My sister <u>aimed</u> her most intense gaze at me, her eyes directed straight at my forehead. In the <u>glare</u> of the kitchen light, her features looked a lot like our mother when she was irritated, and I wished it were not quite so bright in there.

And then she said, "Maybe we're remembering two different trips!" At that, feeling ridiculous, we both laughed.

1. Underline the word that has the same meaning as <u>swerve</u>. Give a word or phrase that means the opposite of *swerve*.

2. Underline the words that mean the opposite of <u>recent</u>. Define *recent* in your own words.

3. Circle the words that give a clue to the meaning of <u>canyon</u>. Name a famous *canyon*.

4. Circle the phrase that gives a clue to the meaning of <u>sliver</u>. How is a *sliver* in the finger usually removed?

5. Underline the word in a nearby sentence that has a similar meaning to <u>heap</u>. Is a *heap* something that is messy or neat? Explain your answer.

6. Circle the word with the same meaning as <u>stumbled</u>. Write a new sentence using the word *stumbled*.

7. Underline the words that explain the meaning of <u>aimed</u>. What else might be *aimed*?

8. Underline the words in the paragraph that give a clue to the meaning of <u>glare</u>. Use *glare* in a new sentence.

Name _____ Date _____

Reading Warm-up B

Read the following passage. Then, complete the activities.

Nedra was an urban girl, for whom the <u>wilderness</u> was not to be found in an unspoiled landscape far removed from people, but in the vacant lot down the block. So, when she told Van she had a story to relate about her latest adventure in nature, he supposed it would have nothing to do with the great outdoors. At the beginning, as she <u>recited</u> her tale, he was still <u>assuming</u> that it would be about a random bee she had seen.

"Here's what happened," Nedra started to say, then she <u>hesitated</u> for a moment as she broke a piece of peanut brittle into fragments, and took a bite of one <u>shard</u>. After that short pause, she resumed her narration.

"I was walking to school very early this morning," she said, "and it was still pretty dark, since I had to be there early for band practice. Because it was after 6:30, the streetlamps had been turned down, and the <u>lowered</u> lights gave the street an eerie atmosphere. Suddenly, I heard the sound of animal footsteps, and then, as I squinted through the mist, I recognized immediately that this was no dog. I <u>stiffened</u> in fear, and my heart was pounding so rapidly I could hear it. I remained rigid, but the coyote—for I'm certain that's what it was—just went casually about its business."

"That's when I saw that what the coyote was after was a rabbit, hopping blithely along towards the park. Just as the coyote was about to lunge, I shouted, 'Stop, <u>assassin</u> – you killer, you murderer!'

"The two animals ran in different directions, and I felt gratified that I had saved a life. At least, that's what I explained to all those attentive police officers who arrived a few moments later!"

1. Underline the words that help explain the meaning of <u>wilderness</u>. Give an example of something that you might find in the **wilderness**.

2. Circle the words in a nearby sentence that explain the meaning of <u>recited</u>. Then give a synonym for **recited**.

3. Circle the word in a nearby sentence that means nearly the same as <u>assuming</u>. Then underline the phrase that tells what he was **assuming**.

4. Underline the phrase that gives a clue to the meaning of <u>hesitated</u>. Then write a new sentence using the word **hesitated**.

5. Underline the word that gives a clue to the meaning of <u>shard</u>. Explain what a **shard** is in your own words.

6. Underline the phrase that gives a clue to the meaning of <u>lowered</u>. Give an antonym for **lowered**.

7. Circle the word that explains the meaning of <u>stiffened</u>. Define **stiffened** in your own words.

8. Underline the words that mean the same as <u>assassin</u>. Write a new sentence using the word **assassin**.

67

"**Traveling Through the Dark**" by William Stafford
"**The Secret**" by Denise Levertov "**The Gift**" by Li-Young Lee

Literary Analysis: Epiphany

Characters in literature or speakers in poems sometimes have a sudden flash of insight, which is called an **epiphany**. At the moment of the epiphany, the character may realize something significant about himself or herself, about another character, or about life in general.

DIRECTIONS: *On the lines below each of the following quotations, explain why that moment in the specified poem does or does not represent a true epiphany for the speaker.*

"Traveling Through the Dark"

1. Traveling through the dark I found a deer / dead on the edge of the Wilson River road.

    _____

    _____

    _____

2. I thought hard for us all—my only swerving— / then pushed her over the edge into the river.

    _____

    _____

    _____

"The Secret"

3. Two girls discover / the secret of life / in a sudden line of / poetry.

    _____

    _____

    _____

4. "I love them . . . / for wanting to know it, / for / assuming there is / such a secret, yes, / for that / most of all.

    _____

    _____

    _____

"The Gift"

5. To pull the metal splinter from my palm / my father recited a story in a low voice.

    _____

    _____

    _____

6. And I did not life up my wound and cry, / Death visited here! / I did what a child does / when he's given something to keep. / I kissed my father.

    _____

    _____

    _____

"Traveling Through the Dark" by William Stafford
"The Secret" by Denise Levertov **"The Gift"** by Li-Young Lee

Reading Strategy: Interpret Poetry

To deepen your understanding of a poem, you must *interpret*, or search to find meaning in its words, images and other elements, You can interpret by looking closely at a particular element, such as the poem's title, the identify of its speaker, or a particular image and then deciding how the element relates to the poem's central message. You can also use your understanding of a poet's overall meaning or social context to interpret is individual elements.

DIRECTIONS: *Practice your interpretation skills by answering the following questions, which are based on the poems you have read.*

1. Who is the speaker in Denise Levertov's poem "The Secret"? Use your knowledge of the speaker to interpret the following lines from the poem:
   I love them / for finding what / I can't find, and for loving me / for the line I wrote, / and for forgetting it / so that / a thousand times, till death / finds them, they may / discover it again, in other / lines / in other / happenings.

   _____

   _____

   _____

2. How does the title of the poem "Traveling Through the Dark" relate to its central message? How does the title help you understand the poem as you begin reading?

   _____

   _____

   _____

3. In the poem "The Gift," significant images are presented in the following lines:
   Had you entered that afternoon / you would have thought you saw a man / planting something in a boy's palm, / a silver tear, a tiny flame.

   How do you interpret the images "silver tear" and "tiny flame," and how do they relate to the overall meaning of the poem?

   _____

   _____

   _____

   _____

"Traveling Through the Dark" by William Stafford
"The Secret" by Denise Levertov **"The Gift"** by Li-Young Lee
Building Vocabulary

Using Related Words: *exhaust*

A. DIRECTIONS: *Complete each sentence with one of the following words related to the word* exhaust: exhausted, exhaustively, exhaustible.

1. Our current use of fossil fuels is depleting _____ energy sources.
2. At the end of their twelve-hour shifts, the relief workers were _____.
3. The environmental group _____ researched all sides of the issue.

Using the Word List

exhaust   shard   swerve

B. DIRECTIONS: *For each pair of numbered words, choose the lettered pair of words that best expresses a similar relationship. Circle the letter of your choice.*

___ 1. SWERVE : OBSTACLE ::
    A. price : payment
    B. climb : mountain
    C. avoid : danger
    D. solution : problem

___ 2. VASE : SHARD ::
    A. part : whole
    B. object : fragment
    C. craft : skill
    D. beauty : utility

___ 3. EXHAUST : POLLUTION ::
    A. ocean : salty
    B. disaster : fatality
    C. airplane : propeller
    D. grass : vegetation

"Traveling Through the Dark" by William Stafford
"The Secret" by Denise Levertov **"The Gift"** by Li-Young Lee
Support for Writing

Prepare to write a comparison-and-contrast essay about the relationship between the title of two of these poems and the two poems' relationship to each other. As an aid in your preparation, use the chart below to make preliminary notes on the meaning of each poem's title and how that meaning compares or contrasts to the meaning of the other poems.

Poem Title	How Title Relates to Meaning of Poem	How Meaning of Poem Relates to Meaning of Other Poems
"Traveling Through the Dark"		
"The Secret"		
"The Gift"		

"Traveling Through the Dark" by William Stafford
"The Secret" by Denise Levertov **"The Gift"** by Li-Young Lee
Enrichment: Science

Sensory experiences can make us recall the past. For example, the smell of burning leaves might take you back to childhood autumns in Maine, a certain song may remind you or your sixth-grade dance, or the first bite of a juicy, fresh orange may remind you of a family trip to Florida.

In these poems, the authors describe life-changing moments or epiphanies triggered by a sensory experience—the warmth of a living fawn in carcass of a dead doe, the intellectual excitement caused by certain combinations of words on a page, and a father's gentle touch in removing a splinter revealing the meaning of love and compassion. You, too, can delve into your sensory memory bank to recall a significant moment in your life.

DIRECTIONS: *Explore connections between your sense and your memory by completing the following chart. List an object or idea related to each sense. Next, describe the memory it triggers. Then explain the significance of each memory.*

Sense	Detail	Memory Triggered	Significance
1. Sight			
2. Sound			
3. Smell			
4. Taste			
5. Touch			

"Traveling Through the Dark" by William Stafford, **"The Secret"** by Denise Levertov, and
"The Gift" by Li-Young Lee
Open-Book Test

Short Answer *Write your responses to the questions in this section on the lines provided.*

1. "Traveling Through the Dark," on one level, is about the encounter of a driver and a dead deer on a narrow mountain road. Can this encounter be interpreted on a more general level? If so, what is that interpretation?

   _____
   _____
   _____

2. After the narrator of "Traveling Through the Dark" discovers that the doe is carrying a fawn, he says, "Beside that mountain road I hesitated." The speaker hesitates before carrying out what customary action? Why does he hesitate?

   _____
   _____
   _____

3. In lines 17–18 of "Traveling Through the Dark," the speaker says, "I thought hard for us all—my only swerving— / then pushed her over the edge into the river." Who is "us all" and what insight does the speaker finally arrive at in these lines?" What does the poem's title reveal about the certainty of his insight?

   _____
   _____
   _____
   _____

4. What epiphany—or flash of insight or understanding—is discussed in the opening lines of "The Secret"?

   _____
   _____
   _____

5. In "The Secret," the narrator writes that she loves the finders of the secret "for forgetting it / so that / a thousand times, till death / finds them, they may / discover it again, . . ." What do these images of forgetting and rediscovering tell the reader about the process of finding the secret of life?

   _____
   _____
   _____

6. For what does the narrator love the two girls "most of all"? What difference in outlook does this statement reveal between the narrator and the two girls?

_____

_____

_____

7. In "The Gift," the narrator recalls how his father's tenderness and firmness helped him to understand something important when he was a child. What insight did the narrator gain?

_____

_____

_____

8. What is the gift that the narrator received from his father as a little boy in "The Gift"? How does that gift still bear fruit later in his life?

_____

_____

_____

_____

9. Each of the poems in this grouping—"Traveling Through the Dark," "The Secret," and "The Gift"—is a lyric poem. A lyric poem often contains a flash of insight or understanding that is tied to a key recurring image. Using the chart below, identify the key recurring image of the poem and the major insight or theme that is tied to the image.

Poem	Key Recurring Image	Major Insight or Theme
"Traveling Through the Dark"		
"The Secret"		
"The Gift"		

10. If you were examining the *shard* of a vase, what could you assume had happened to the vase? Base your answer on the meaning of *shard* as it is used in "The Gift."

_____

_____

_____

_____

Essay

Write an extended response to the question of your choice or to the question or questions your teacher assigns you.

11. In "Traveling Through the Dark," the narrator faces an agonizing decision—whether to try to save the unborn foal or to toss aside the carcass of the doe that is carrying it. Do you think the narrator makes the right decision in the poem? Why or why not? Develop your thoughts in an essay supported by details from the poem.

12. Each of the poems in this grouping—"Traveling Through the Dark," "The Secret," and "The Gift"—communicates an important theme or message about life. In an essay, briefly summarize the theme of each poem, and explain which theme spoke to you the most strongly or persuasively. Support your answer with details from the poems.

13. Both "The Secret" and "The Gift" are poems about love. In an essay, compare and contrast each poem's treatment of the subject of love, and the effect that love has on the narrator and the object(s) of the narrator's love. Support your answer with details from the poems.

14. **Thinking About the Essential Question: How does literature shape or reflect society?** Each of the poems in this grouping—"Traveling Through the Dark," "The Secret," and "The Gift"—is a lyric poem. In lyric poetry, the insight or theme is usually of an intensely personal nature. Yet society can shape the perceptions and feelings of the individual. In which of the three poems in this grouping is the influence of society most apparent in the perceptions and insights of the poet? Develop your views in an essay supported by details from the poem you have chosen.

Oral Response

15. Go back to question 1, 2, or 4 or to the question your teacher assigns you. Take a few minutes to expand your answer and prepare an oral response. Find additional details in "Traveling Through the Dark," "The Secret," and "The Gift" that support your points. If necessary, make notes to guide your oral response.

"Poems" by William Stafford, Denise Levertov, and Li-Young Lee
Selection Test A

MULTIPLE CHOICE

Critical Reading *Choose the answer that best answers the question or completes the statement.*

____ 1. In "Traveling Through the Dark," what has happened to the deer the speaker finds by the side of the road?
   A. It has broken its leg.
   B. It has fought with another deer.
   C. It has been hit by a car.
   D. It has been shot.

____ 2. In "Traveling Through the Dark," what doe the speaker mean when he says the deer was "large in the belly"?
   A. The deer had just eaten.
   B. The deer was a large male.
   C. The deer had much fur.
   D. The deer was pregnant.

____ 3. When the speaker hesitates in "Traveling Through the Dark," what decision is he weighing?
   A. Whether to save the unborn fawn
   B. Whether to take the deer with him
   C. Whether to call for help
   D. Whether to look for other fawns

____ 4. What is the central image in "Traveling Through the Dark"?
   A. a highway
   B. a canyon
   C. a dead deer
   D. a car

____ 5. In "The Secret," the speaker is most pleased to discover that the girls
   A. are successful in school.
   B. think secreet of life is knowable.
   C. like to read poetry.
   D. forgot about the mistakes in her poem.

___ 6. Which of the following identifies a key image in "The Secret"?

A. Poetry

B. Poets

C. Girls

D. Nature

___ 7. Who discovers the secret of life in "The Secret"?

A. The poet

B. Two girls

C. A person talking to the speaker

D. A poetry critic

___ 8. In "The Secret," two girls discover their love of

A. friendship.

B. poetry.

C. school.

D. telling secrets.

___ 9. Which of the following expresses a theme in "The Secret"?

A. A poem can have many different meanings to different people.

B. It is easy to forget lines of poetry.

C. A poet remembers every detail in every poem she writes.

D. People read poetry to to forget their problems.

___ 10. What is in the boy's hand in "The Gift"?

A. A thorn

B. A metal splinter

C. A sliver of wood

D. A spec of glass

___ 11. Why does the father recite a story while he removes the splinter frome his son's hand in "The Gift"?

A. To amuse himself.

B. To explain how iron is made.

C. To remind his son of his family history.

D. To distract his son.

___ 12. What is the central image in the poem "The Gift"?

A. A flame

B. A thumbnail

C. Hands

D. Feet

____ 13. What "gift" does the father give his son in "The Gift"?

    A. Education

    B. A kiss

    C. A flower

    D. Tenderness

Vocabulary

____ 14. An appropriate word to describe the fumes from the car in "Traveling Through the Dark" is

    A. exhaust   C. swerving

    B. light   D. river

____ 15. In which sentence is the word *swerve* used correctly?

    A. We had to swerve, so we drove in a straight line.

    B. I wanted to swerve, so I could drive around the deer.

    C. I needed to swerve, because I wanted to go backwards down the driveway.

    D. The other drivers stopped their cars to swerve.

Essay

16. The speaker in "Traveling Through the Dark" says, "I thought hard for us all." In an essay, identify "us": for whom is the speaker thinking? What is he thinking about? What decision does he make?

17. In an essay, compare and contrast the meanings of the titles "The Secret" and "The Gift." Identify the what each title refers to. Does it refer to an object, an idea, or a feeling? Could the title have more than one meaning? Then compare and contrast the titles with each other.

18. **Writing About the Essential Question essay question**

                              TK

"Poems" by William Stafford, Denise Levertov, and Li-Young Lee
Selection Test B

MULTIPLE CHOICE

Critical Reading *Choose the answer that best answers the question or completes the statement.*

____ 1. Why does the speaker in "Traveling Through the Dark" say it is best to roll dead deer into the canyon?
A. To keep people from feeling sad when they see the dead animal.
B. To keep other animals from investigating the deer's body.
C. To discourage other drivers from stopping to talk to the speaker.
D. To prevent other cars from swerving to miss hitting the deer, which could cause a car wreck.

____ 2. How does the deer, the central image in "Traveling Through the Dark," change from the beginning of the poem to the middle of the poem?
A. It goes from being just a dead deer to being a dead deer with a live fawn.
B. It goes from being alive to being dead.
C. First it is a deer, then the speaker thinks it is a cow.
D. The speaker thinks it is dead but it is alive.

____ 3. What causes the speaker to hesitate after he drags the body of the deer in "Traveling Through the Dark"?
A. He realizes the fawn is alive.
B. He is tired from dragging the deer.
C. He cannot see into the canyon.
D. He is blinded by oncoming headlights.

____ 4. In what way does the speaker experience a shift in perspective at the end of "Traveling Through the Dark"?
A. He realizes the roads are dangerous.
B. He realizes he cannot save the fawn.
C. He admits that he does not like deer.
D. He admits that he needs help making decisions.

____ 5. What does the speaker do with the deer at the end of "Traveling Through the Dark"?
A. He pushes it into the river.
B. He puts it on his car.
C. He tries to save it.
D. He leaves it by the side of the road.

____ 6. In "Traveling Through the Dark," as the speaker thinks about what to do with the deer, his thoughts are "swerving," which means
A. he is thinking about driving on curving roads.
B. he thinks straight through his problem without wavering.
C. his thoughts shift back and forth from one idea to another.
D. he barely gives the deer any thought at all.

____ 7. Who wrote the line of poetry that deeply affected the two girls in "The Secret"?
   A. their teacher who taught the poem
   B. the speaker's husband
   C. the girls' friend
   D. the speaker

____ 8. What is the central image in "The Secret"?
   A. poetry   **B.** girls   **C.** poets   **D.** books

____ 9. How does the central image in "The Secret" differ at the end of the poem from what it was at the beginning?
   A. At the beginning, it was two girls; at the end, it is only one girl.
   B. At the beginning, it is a book; at the end, it is a poem.
   C. At the beginning, it was one poem; at the end, it is all poetry.
   D. At the beginning, it is the poem; at the end, it is the poet.

____ 10. The girls in "The Secret" find the secret of life in a line of poetry but the poet who wrote the line does not know the secret, which suggests that
   A. the girls are smarter than the poet.
   B. poems mean different things to different people.
   C. the poet did not really write the poem.
   D. poetry has no real meaning.

____ 11. In "The Secret," the speaker's flash of understanding is that
   A. some people think there is a secret of life.
   B. some people love to read poetry.
   C. she actually loves her own poetry.
   D. she meets people who read her poems.

____ 12. In "The Secret," what is the girls' relationship to the poem that helped them discover the secret of life?
   A. The remember every word of the poem.
   B. They do not remember the secret or what line of poetry contained it.
   C. They remember a line from the poem but not the secret.
   D. They do not remember reading the poem.

____ 13. In "The Gift", what does the father do while he pulls the splinter from his son's hand?
   A. He remains silent.   **C.** He recites a story.
   B. He talks to the boy's mother.   **D.** He sings a song.

____ 14. In "The Gift," what about the experience of having a splinter removed so impresses the boy?
   A. His father's tenderness   **C.** His mother's concern
   B. The size of the splinter   **D.** The location of the splinter

____ 15. In "The Gift," in what way does the central image change throughout the poem?
   A. It is the boy's splnter and then the wife's splinter.
   B. It is different hands:the father's, the boy's, the wife's, and the speaker's.
   C. It is the father's face, the boy's hand, and the splinter.
   D. It is a child and then the adult person.

____ 16. When the boy says of his father, "he's given me something to keep" in "The Gift," what are two possible meanings of "something"?
  A. His splinter and his wife's splinter
  B. The splinter and a bandage
  C. The splinter and a tender memory
  D. The splinter and a new story

____ 17. What is one theme of "The Gift"?
  A. A meaningful lesson can be taught in a simple act.
  B. People rarely remember when experiences turn out happily.
  C. Splinters are small things that create big problems.
  D. Many lessons are passed from fathers to sons.

____ 18. In "The Gift," the speaker is similar to his father because
  A. he, too, can remove a splinter tenderly.
  B. he also tells stories.
  C. he worries about causing pain but never does.
  D. he is dismissive of minor injuries.

Vocabulary

____ 19. An appropriate word to describe the fumes from the car in "Traveling Through the Dark" is
  A. light
  B. swerving
  C. exhaust
  D. river

____ 20. In "The Gift," an appropriate word to describe a *shard* is
  A. knife   C. lid
  B. fragment   D. point

Essay

21. In an essay, compare and contrast the meanings of the titles "The Secret" and "The Gift." Identify what each title refers to. Does it refer to an object, an idea, or a feeling? Could the title have more than one meaning? Then compare and contrast the titles with each other.

22. In "Traveling Through the Dark," how does the title of the poem match what happens in the poem? Would the deer have been hit by someone traveling during the day? What else might the dark symbolize besides the dark of night? Discuss these questions in a brief essay.

23. Identify and compare the epiphanies the occur in "Traveling Through the Dark," "The Secret," and "The Gift." Do the epiphanies bring a sense of happiness? With what or whom is the speaker of each poem engaged as he or she builds the shift in perspective that leads to deeper insight? Respond to these questions in a brief essay.

24.   TK

Vocabulary Warm-up Word Lists

Study these words from the selections. Then, complete the activities.

Word List A

bamboo [bam BOO] *n.* tall, woody grass with jointed, often hollow stems, growing in temperate or tropical areas
  Bamboo grows so well that it is always spreading to places where no one wants it.

branches [BRAN chez] *n.* woody extensions protruding from a tree's trunk or main limbs
  The tree's branches were so low that they scraped our heads as we walked by.

grackles [GRAK uhls] *n.* large American blackbirds having iridescent plumage
  The grackles were making so much noise that we couldn't hear her horn.

hummingbird [HUM ing berd] *n.* tiny, brightly colored bird with wings that vibrate so fast that they sometimes make a humming sound
  The hummingbird was attracted to the feeder my grandmother hung from a tree.

oozing [OOZ ing] *v.* seeping slowly, especially moisture
  There were some tiny holes in the package, so the ice dream came oozing out.

sluggish [SLUG ish] *adj.* slow in movement
  The elephant at the zoo appeared sluggish after he was fed.

songbirds [SONG berdz] *n.* birds that utter musical tones
  I love to visit the woods near my friend's house, as they are full of songbirds.

terrain [tuh RAYN] *n.* a piece of land and its physical features
  It is always a good idea to learn about the terrain of an area where you plan to hike.

Word List B

completely [kuhm PLEET lee] *adv.* fully carried out; thoroughly
  She always read through the test questions completely before answering the first one.

manufactured [man yoo FAK cherd] *v.* made from raw materials by hand or machinery
  The new company that moved into town manufactured car parts.

punchclock [PUNCH klahk] *n.* a machine that records time on a card via stamp or hole pattern
  I hate working in a place where you have to use a punchclock when you come and go.

perfection [per FEK shuhn] *n.* freedom from fault or defect
  Sometimes she feels like her parents will accept nothing short of perfection.

refreshed [ri FRESHD] *v.* revived; restored in strength
  I always wake refreshed when I take a short nap in the afternoon.

revolved [ri VAWLVD] *v.* turned around or rotated
  The carousel revolved more and more slowly as the motor failed.

spines [SPYNZ] *n.* spinal columns; bones that support the back
  Some animals have such flexible spines that they can twist their bodies into loops.

upturned [UP ternd] *v.* turned up or over
  We stopped when we saw the turtle upturned by the side of the road and turned it over.

Selections by Espada, Komunyakaa, and Nye
Vocabulary Warm-up Exercises

Exercise A *Fill in the blanks, using each word from Word List A only once.*

Bird watching is an interesting hobby. The only equipment you need is binoculars, a guide to birds, and a notebook to keep a record of what you see. You can start in nearby [1] _____, your back yard or a local park. A botanical garden, while designed to showcase plants, may also harbor birds in its stands of [2] _____ or near its slow-running and [3] _____ streams. Look up into the tree [4] _____ and listen for [5] _____. If this doesn't yield results, look for someplace where bright flowers might attract a tiny [6] _____. Early evening is often the best time to spot large iridescent [7] _____, as they look for big trees in which to spend the night. Unless you live near water, it might be necessary to take a trip to an [8] _____ marsh or swamp to see certain species.

Exercise B *Decide whether each statement below is true or false. Circle* T *or* F, *and explain your answer.*

1. Animals with *spines*, like dogs and cats, are known as vertebrates.
   T / F _____

2. An *upturned* pot on the porch was full of water after it rained.
   T / F _____

3. She had learned the vocabulary words so *completely* that she failed the test.
   T / F _____

4. Although he worked in a factory, he never had to use a *punchclock*.
   T / F _____

5. Many toys are *manufactured* in China and imported into the U.S.
   T / F _____

6. A person who doesn't work hard at anything often achieves *perfection*.
   T / F _____

7. If a carnival ride *revolved* rapidly, some of the riders might have become motion sick.
   T / F _____

8. If someone is *refreshed* after a shower, they feel lousy.
   T / F _____

Selections by Espada, Komunyakaa, and Nye
Reading Warm-up A

Read the following passage. Then, complete the activities.

According to the Audubon Society, birding is the number one sport in America. They report 51.3 million birders in the U.S. The sport is popular with people of all ages throughout the country. Serious birders often travel to areas of the country with types of <u>terrain</u> different from the land where they live. Various species of birds live in widely varying environments. A forest of tall, slender <u>bamboo</u> harbors species that would never be found in open grassland. Ducks, loons, grebes, and pelicans are water birds that must, of course, live around water. Shore birds, or waders, like the sandpiper feed along the edges of marshes and oceans. There, the trickling and <u>oozing</u> sand and soil yields up their favorite foods.

Some birds are easy to spot, perched on <u>branches</u> of trees or hopping down from the boughs to walk on the ground in the open. Other birds, like large and noisy <u>grackles</u> or melodious <u>songbirds</u>, make their presence known through their voices. The tiny yet brilliant <u>hummingbird</u> can be seen easily because of its colors. The rapid beating of its wings also makes the characteristic humming sound that may alert people to its presence. Hummingbirds feed on the nectar of brightly colored flowers, so some people plants gardens designed to attract them.

Like most birds, male hummingbirds are more colorful than females. Other male birds may even vary their colors during the course of a year. They exhibit their brightest coloration during mating season. Females may be duller in color so that they will not be noticeable when sitting on a nest, incubating their eggs. In a world where predators are on the lookout for the slow and <u>sluggish</u>, each species has certain features that aid in its survival.

1. Underline the word that helps explain the meaning of <u>terrain</u>. Use the word **terrain** in a sentence.

2. Circle the words that describe what <u>bamboo</u> looks like. Name some things that are made of **bamboo**.

3. Underline the word that gives a clue to the meaning of <u>oozing</u>. Give a word or phrase that means the same as **oozing**.

4. Underline the word that has a similar meaning to <u>branches</u>. Use **branches** in a sentence, making sure it has the same meaning.

5. Circle the words that tell what <u>grackles</u> are like. Name a kind of bird that is similar to a **grackle**.

6. Underline the word that describes <u>songbirds</u>. Use **songbirds** in an original sentence.

7. Underline the words that describe the <u>hummingbird</u>. Have you ever seen a **hummingbird**? If so, where?

8. Underline the word in the sentence that helps explain what <u>sluggish</u> means. Give an antonym for **sluggish**

Selections by Espada, Komunyakaa, and Nye
Reading Warm-up B

Read the following passage. Then, complete the activities.

Up to the 19th Century, skilled individuals and artisans made everything that people didn't make for themselves. Initially, each individual artisan would have been <u>completely</u> in charge, running the whole operation, from start to finish. Each item produced was solely his or her responsibility and craftsmen were paid for items produced.

Eventually, fine artisans started to train others, who would work with them as apprentices for a number of years to learn the trade. Teaching the apprentices new skills helped the master artisans to rejuvenate their own skills. In this way, the skills of artisans were <u>refreshed</u>. Both master and apprentices practiced hard to achieve a level close to <u>perfection</u> could be reached. Artisans also joined together in workshops to attain excellence.

Eventually, goods began to be <u>manufactured</u> in larger and larger workshops and then factories. One of the advantages was that complex processes could be broken up into smaller parts. This meant that one person might perform the same job over and over again as items <u>revolved</u> and rotated past them on a conveyor belt. They might have to stoop to adjust an exposed or <u>upturned</u> piece of machinery, for example. This type of repetitive task often caused injuries of their shoulders or <u>spines</u> from having to bend and twist their backbones so much. More efficient use of labor led to lower prices for the consumer. But these gains were often offset by the physical and mental costs to workers.

The amount of time they worked was stamped on a card by a <u>punchclock</u>, a machine that recorded when they arrived and when they left. Eventually, Congress enacted laws that regulated the number of hours a person could work and also limited the minimum age of workers, as young children had often been hired in factories.

1. Underline the words that help explain the meaning of <u>completely</u>. Give another word that means the same as *completely*.

2. Circle the words that tell what was <u>refreshed</u>. Use the word *refreshed* in a sentence of your own.

3. Underline the words that give hints to the meaning of <u>perfection</u>. Use the word *perfection* in a sentence.

4. Underline the words that give a clue to the meaning of <u>manufactured</u>. Name some things that are *manufactured*.

5. Circle the word that gives a clue to the meaning of <u>revolved</u>. What other things have you seen that *revolved*?

6. Underline the word that gives a hint as to the meaning of <u>upturned</u>. Give a word or phrase that has the opposite meaning to *upturned*.

7. Underline that word that tells what might happen to workers' <u>spines</u>. Do you think injuries to *spines* would be painful?

8. Underline the words in the sentence that tell what a <u>punchclock</u> is for. Do you know anyone with a job that measures his or her hours by *punchclock*?

"Who Burns for the Perfection of Paper" by Martin Espada
"Camouflaging the Chimera" by Yusef Komunyakaa
"Streets" by Naomi Shihab Nye

Literary Analysis: Voice

A poem's unique **voice** comes from its style, its tone, and the individual personality of its speaker. Reading closely, you will find that every poem has a particular voice. Think about the different voices of the poems you have read. In what way does each poet express a unique style, tone, and personality?

DIRECTIONS: *As you read the three poems, make notes describing the style, tone, and personality of each speaker. Include details from the poems that emphasize or help create the speaker's voice.*

Poem	Voice
"Who Burns for the Perfection of Paper"	
"Camouflaging the Chimera"	
"Streets"	

"Who Burns for the Perfection of Paper" by Martin Espada
"Camouflaging the Chimera" by Yusef Komunyakaa
"Streets" by Naomi Shihab Nye

Reading Strategy: Analyze Author's Implicit Beliefs

Poems are almost always subjective—that is, they are based on the poet's own experiences, opinions, and beliefs. Sometimes, a poet will offer his or her beliefs in the hopes that the reader will adopt them and act on them, too. However, these beliefs may not be directly stated. Instead, they may be implied through poem details. Use a graphic organizer like this one to analyze each **author's implicit beliefs.**

Poem	Author's Implicit Beliefs	Details That Reveal Beliefs
"Who Burns for the Perfection of Paper"		
"Camouflaging the Chimera"		
"Streets"		

"Who Burns for the Perfection of Paper" by Martin Espada
"Camouflaging the Chimera" by Yusef Komunyakaa
"Streets" by Naomi Shihab Nye
Vocabulary Builder

Word List

terrain   refuge   crevices

A. DIRECTIONS: *Read the incomplete paragraph below. On each line, write one of the words from the Word List. You will use each word more than once. Think about the meaning of the word in the context of the paragraph.*

As the soldiers marched toward their next objective, a nearby village, they found themselves on unfamiliar (1) _____. They had to make their way through thick underbrush, but at least the ground seemed solid, so there was no danger of slipping into unseen (2) _____. If necessary, the soldiers could take (3) _____ in the thick surrounding vegetation if they found themselves under attack. Soon they found themselves approaching a farm, and the open (4) _____ promised to make for an easier advance. But there was no cover in those open fields that would provide ready or easy (5) _____ if they were spotted by the enemy, not even small (6) _____ in which they could hide temporarily.

B. DIRECTIONS: *Think about the meaning of the italicized Word List word in each item below. Then answer the question, and explain your answer.*

1. A geologist analyzes various types of <u>terrain</u>. Does he spend most of his working hours on land or in the air?

    _____

2. A villager being chased by a tiger found <u>refuge</u> in a small cabin. Was the villager safer than he was before?

    _____

3. The hiking guide alerted us to be on the lookout for <u>crevices</u>. Was the guide warning us of a potential danger?

    _____

C. DIRECTIONS: *On each line, write the letter of the word that is most nearly opposite in meaning to the Word List word.*

___ 1. terrain
    A. organism
    B. fatigue
    C. sky
    D. surroundings

___ 2. refuge
    A. exposure
    B. relief
    C. denial
    D. pretense

___ 3. crevices
    A. fires
    B. particles
    C. bumps
    D. appearances

Name _____ Date _____

"Who Burns for the Perfection of Paper" by Martin Espada
"Camouflaging the Chimera" by Yusef Komunyakaa
"Streets" by Naomi Shihab Nye
Support for Writing

Each of these poems expresses a belief about some fundamental aspect of life. Prepare to write an analytical essay on how each poem's theme, or central meaning, comments on the life of all humans. As part of your preparation, use the following chart as an aid in organizing your thoughts.

Key Question	"Who Burns for the Perfection of Paper"	"Camouflaging the Chimera"	"Streets"
What would you say each poem is "about"?			
What personal insight or experience is described in each poem?			
How does this experience relate to all people?			
What wish for humanity does each poem express?			

After reflecting on your answers to these questions, write a rough draft of your essay on a separate sheet of paper. Your draft should include a clear statement of your thesis, supporting details from the poems, and a conclusion.

"Who Burns for the Perfection of Paper" by Martin Espada
"Camouflaging the Chimera" by Yusef Komunyakaa
"Streets" by Naomi Shihab Nye

Enrichment: Vietnam Veterans

Yusef Komunyakaa based his poem "Camouflaging the Chimera" on his experiences serving in the army in Vietnam, where he reported from the frontlines and earned a Bronze Star for bravery. Part of his process of coming to terms with his war experience was writing about it in his poetry. Thousands of others veterans of the Vietnam War carry with them memories of that prolonged and bitter conflict.

If you can find a Vietnam veteran in your community, ask whether you may conduct an interview about his or her experiences in the war. Ask questions requiring in-depth, not "yes" or "no," responses.

You might with to use some or all of the questions below in conducting your interview. Do not feel bound to a specific set of prepared questions, however. If follow-up questions occur to you in the course of the interview, pursue those points, returning to your prepared questions later if you wish.

Suggested Questions:

1. During which years did you serve in Vietnam?

   _____

2. In which branch of the armed forces did you serve?

   _____

3. Were you drafted or did you enlist? If you enlisted, why did you do so?

   _____

   _____

   _____

4. Did you see combat while in Vietnam? If so, how often and under what conditions?

   _____

   _____

5. Were you wounded, or did any of your fellow soldiers suffer casualties in combat? How did those casualties occur, and what was their result?

   _____

   _____

6. What was different or unusual about having to fight a guerilla-type war?

   _____

   _____

7. How did the Vietnamese people regard the American soldiers and the American presence in their country?

   _____

   _____

Name _____ Date _____

"Who Burns for the Perfection of Paper" by Martin Espada, **"Camouflaging the Chimera"** by Yusef Komunyakaa, and **"Streets"** by Naomi Shihab Nye

Open-Book Test

Short Answer *Write your responses to the questions in this section on the lines provided.*

1. In "Who Burns for the Perfection of Paper," Espada's distinctive voice is evident in the following lines: "Then the glue would sting, / hands oozing / till both palms burned / at the punchclock." What message about physical labor emerges from the poet's voice in these lines?

   _____

   _____

2. What implicit belief of Espada's is evident in these lines from "Who Burns for the Perfection of Paper"?

   I knew . . . . that every open lawbook / was a pair of hands / upturned and burning.

   _____

   _____

   _____

3. Often the title of a poem can provide important clues to its meanings. The title "Who Burns for the Perfection of Paper" implies what about the relationship between the finished product and the people who produce it?

   _____

   _____

4. In "Camouflaging the Chimera," Komunyakaa uses language in an original way to give voice to his battlefield experiences in Vietnam. What kind of atmosphere does Komunyakaa's voice create with this passage?

   . . . But we waited / til the moon touched metal, / till something almost / broke inside use. VC struggled / with the hillside, like black silk. . . .

   _____

   _____

5. Poems often convey the poet's implicit beliefs. Does "Camouflaging the Chimera" convey to you the author's feelings about the Vietnam War in particular or about war in general? Why or why not?

   _____

   _____

   _____

6. What seems to be the speaker's attitude toward the VC in "Camouflaging the Chimera"? Does the speaker hate the VC? Give details from the poem to support your answer.

_____

_____

_____

_____

7. What aspect of the poet's voice is evident in these lines from "Streets"?

> Overhead lout grackles are claiming their trees / and the sky which sews and sews, tirelessly sewing, / drops her purple hem.

_____

_____

_____

8. In the second half of "Streets," in which the narrator speaks of people who "dream thickly, who dream double," what implicit belief about life can be inferred from the poet's words?

_____

_____

_____

9. Each of the poets in this section uses words, phrases, even sound devices to convey a particular voice. Use this chart to record words from the poems that identify the poet's voice.

Poem	Words that Describe Voice

_____

_____

10. If you were walking down the street and suddenly found yourself seeking *refuge*, is it likely that the weather would suddenly have turned stormy or sunny? Explain your answer, basing it on the definition of *refuge* as it is used in "Camouflaging the Chimera."

_____

_____

Essay

Write an extended response to the question of your choice or to the question or questions your teacher assigns you.

11. Of the three poems in this section—"Who Burns for the Perfection of Paper," "Camouflaging the Chimera," and "Streets"—which speaks to you the most strongly? Why? State your opinion in an essay supported by details from the poem of your choice.

12. The language of each of the three poems in this grouping—"Who Burns for the Perfection of Paper," "Camouflaging the Chimera," and "Streets"—conveys the distinctive and original voice, or literary personality, of the poet. Compare and contrast the voice that emerges from two of the poems in this grouping, identifying specific examples of language and devices that help create the poet's voice.

13. Often a poet conveys his or her implicit beliefs about a political or social reality through his or her work. In an essay, compare and contrast the implicit author beliefs that emerge from "Who Burns for the Perfection of Paper" and "Camouflaging the Chimera." What are Espada's implicit beliefs about factory labor? What implicit beliefs about war and combat are evident in "Camouflaging the Chimera"? In which poem are the author's beliefs clearer and more strongly communicated? Develop your thoughts in an essay supported by details from the two poems.

14. **Thinking About the Essential Question: Does literature shape or reflect society?** Each of the poems in this section—"Who Burns for the Perfection of Paper," "Camouflaging the Chimera," and "Streets"—comments on an important social issue: respectively, the exploitation of labor, attitudes toward war, and feelings about death. Do these poems reflect social attitudes on these subjects or seek to shape attitudes in the reader? Develop your thoughts in a brief essay.

Oral Response

15. Go back to question 1, 2, or 9 or to the question your teacher assigns you. Take a few minutes to expand your answer and prepare an oral response. Find additional details in one of the poems in this section that support your points. If necessary, make notes to guide your oral response.

Poems by Martín Espada, Yusef Komunyakaa, and Naomi Shihab Nye
Selection Test A

MULTIPLE CHOICE

Critical Reading *Choose the answer that best answers the question or completes the statement.*

____ 1. In "Who Burns for the Perfection of Paper," what is the connection between the poet's high-school job and his lataer experience in law school?
   A. He now goes to law school.
   B. He worked with legal pads in both places.
   C. He worked in the courtroom.
   D. He got paper cuts in both places.

____ 2. What does the poet feel toward those who are still making legal pads in "Who Burns for the Perfection of Paper"?
   A. annoyance   C. misunderstanding
   B. sympathy   D. curiosity

____ 3. In "Who Burns for the Perfection of Paper," phrases such as "Yellow paper," "seven feet high," "red glue," "sharp paper," "hands oozing," and "palms burned" show that the poet creates his voice using
   A. vivid, descriptive language   C. dialogue.
   B. plain, stark images   D. reflection

____ 4. The author of "Who Burns for the Perfection of Paper" believes that
   A. hard jobs make you a better person.
   B. hard labor is behind many endeavors.
   C. legal pads are poorly made.
   D. students use too much paper in law school.

____ 5. Where is the speaker in the poem "Camouflaging the Chimera"?
   A. at home in the United States
   B. on a vacation in Bangkok
   C. in a doorway
   D. at war in Vietnam

____ 6. In "Camouflaging the Chimera," why does the poet compare the army to a fire-breathing dragon?
   A. Fighting in the jungle is very hot.
   B. Armies are destructive forces.
   C. Soldiers in uniform look like monsters.
   D. Armies are often found in myths.

____ **7.** In "Camouflaging the Chimera," the poet's voice is so personal because
   A. he describes his experiences in great detail.
   B. he talks about a story he once heard.
   C. he blocks out the horrors of war.
   D. he presents a complicated opinion about the army.

____ **8.** Which of these passages in "Camouflaging the Chimera" suggests the idea of soldiers becoming one with their environment?
   A. "We weren't there."
   B. "The river ran through our bones."
   C. "we held our breath"
   D. "VC struggled / with the hillside"

____ **9.** The atmospherr of "Streets" created by the poet's voice is
   A. slow and dreamlike   **C.** happy and bouncy
   B. frenetic and loud   **D.** dark and forboding

____ **10.** At the begining of "Streets," the poet is referring to someone who has
   A. moved away.   **C.** gotten married.
   B. died.   **D.** gone to sleep.

____ **11.** The poet in "Streets" believes which of the following about the death of a loved one?
   A. People who are left behind turn to each.
   B. People who are gone can leave behind a strong presence.
   C. Death takes people away forever.
   D. Sleep is the same thing as death.

____ **12.** What is the setting of "Streets"?
   A. a country road   **C.** an apartment building
   B. a city   **D.** a bedroom

____ **13.** In "Streets," which of the following image is used to describe a person's death?
   A. "One more window dark"
   B. "the figs on his branches"
   C. "Overhead loud grackles are claiming their trees"
   D. "Each thing in its time"

Vocabulary

___ **14.** Which word best replaces *crevices* in this sentence: The *crevices* in the ice made it dangerous to walk on"?

    A. machines   **C.** cracks

    B. lines   **D.** snow

___ **15.** In which sentence is *refuge* used correctly?

    A. We took refuge from the rain by standing inside the doorway.

    B. Because we took refuge from the rain, we got soaking wet.

    C. We wanted to take refuge from the mosquitoes, because we loved being with them.

    D. Our refuge was the exposed field with no trees or structures in sight.

Essay

16. In "Who Burns for the Perfection of Paper," a law student remembers making the legal pads he is now using in law school. He recalls how painful the process was. What feelings does he express? Write a brief essay to address the connection between his high-school job and his life as a law student.

17. In "Camouflaging the Chimera," the poet describes how U.S. soldiers in Vietnam had to camouflage themselves to blend in with the countryside, just as the Vietnamese soldiers did. When the "moon touched metal," the soldiers knew they were looking at a weapon, not at part of the natural world. Why? Write a brief essay to address this question.

18. **Thinking About the Essential Question: Does literature shape or reflect society**? Each of the poems in this section—"Who Burns for the Perfection of Paper," "Camouflaging the Chimera" and "Streets"—comments on an important social issue. Identify the social issue that is the focus of each poem. In a brief essay, explain what each poet thinks about the issue raised in his or her poem.

Poems by Martín Espada, Yusef Komunyakaa, and Naomi Shihab Nye

Selection Test B

MULTIPLE CHOICE

Critical Reading *Choose the answer that best answers the question or completes the statement.*

_____ 1. In "Who Burns for the Perfection of Paper," why must the speaker use fingertips with no gloves when at work in the printing plant?
   A. because he must feel the paper to get it perfectly straight
   B. because gloves would damage the paper
   C. because the expense of providing gloves for workers would be large
   D. because he must feel the paper to make sure the ink has dried

_____ 2. In "Who Burns for the Perfection of Paper," why do the paper cuts hurt so badly?
   A. The cuts are wide and deep.   C. The paper has ragged edges.
   B. The glue on the cuts causes a sharp   D. The stack of paper crushes the
      sting.   skin.

_____ 3. In "Who Burns for the Perfection of Paper," what pattern of sounds contributes to the poet's voice in these lines: "Sluggish by 9 PM, the hands / would slide along suddenly sharp paper."
   A. the sound of numbers   C. use of the hard *g* sound
   B. embedding the letter *a*   D. repetition of sound *s*

_____ 4. When the poet in "Who Burns for the Perfection of Paper" says that "every open lawbook / was a pair of hands / upturned and burning," to whom or what does the phrase "pair of hands" refer?
   A. Hthe law students   C. the workers who made the legal
                                                          pads
   B. the laborers who work at the   D. the front and back covers of the
      university   books

_____ 5. In "Who Burns for the Perfection of Paper," what is the poet's implicit belief about manual labor?
   A. The work of laborers supports the work of others.
   B. People who work with their hands do not work hard.
   C. The best results occur when everyone works together.
   D. He would rather do physical labor than practice law.

_____ 6. In "Camouflaging the Chimera," what was the goal behind the soldiers' activities described in these lines?

   We tied branches to our helmets.
   We painted our faces & rifles
   with mud from a riverbank,
   blades of grass hung from the pockets
   of our tiger suits.

   A. They wanted to be noticed.   C. They wanted to play a game.
   B. They wanted to examine their   D. The wanted to blend in with nature.
      natural surroundings.

___ 7. In "Camouflaging the Chimera," which of the following contributes to the creation of the poet's voice?
A. images from the jungle and natural world
B. detailed descriptions of the VC
C. dialogue centered on the poet's fellow soldiers
D. impersonal description of the environment

___ 8. In "Camouflaging the Chimera," why is the poet in a jungle in Vietnam?
A. He is on vacation.
B. He is fighting a war.
C. He is looking for lost relatives.
D. He is negotiating a peace treaty.

___ 9. In "Camouflaging the Chimera," what runs through the soldiers' bones?
A. the river
B. rain
C. love of nature
D. excitement

___ 10. In "Camouflaging the Chimera," who are the "women left in doorways / reaching in from America," the "ghosts" who travel with the soldiers?
A. the military nurses
B. the dead family members of the soldiers
C. the wives, mothers, and sisters left behind
D. the enemies' families

___ 11. Which detail in "Streets" suggests that life goes on even when someone dies?
A. "A man leaves the world"
B. "the figs on his branches / will soften for birds"
C. "it would be nice to think the same about people"
D. "Some people do."

___ 12. In "Streets," the poet's implicit belief is that
A. no one notices when someone dies.
B. only birds are affected by death.
C. people sleep and dream for hours before they die.
D. the death of one person can be felt by many.

___ 13. In "Streets," the poet's calm voice is created by
A. short lines
B. a quiet tone
C. long words
D. a tragic attitude

___ 14. In "Streets," the poet's voice is partially based on images of
A. sporting events
B. bright sunshine
C. people's clothes
D. nature

_____ **15.** In "Streets," the people who "sleep twice" dream about the present and
    A. the past.
    B. the future.
    C. nothing else.
    D. ways to remember things they forget.

Vocabulary

_____ **16.** In which sentence is *crevices* used correctly?
    A. The crevices in the ice caused the ice to break apart.
    B. The crevices in the ice made the frozen surface of the pond solid.
    C. It was cold outside because of the crevices in the ice.
    D. We made snowmen out of the crevices in the ice.

_____ **17.** An appropriate word to describe the land over which the soldiers move is
    A. terrain   **C.** target
    B. desert   **D.** shadow

_____ **18.** In which sentence is refuge used correctly?
    A. We took refuge from the rain by standing inside the doorway.
    B. Because we took refuge from the rain, we got soaking wet.
    C. We wanted to take refuge from the mosquitoes, because we loved being with them.
    D. Our refuge was the exposed field with no trees or structures in sight.

Essay

19. In "Who Burns for the Perfection of Paper," a law student remembers making the legal pads he is now using in law school. He recalls how painful the process was. What feelings does he express? Write a brief essay to address the connection between his high-school job and his life as a law student.

20. In "Camouflaging the Chimera," the poet describes how U.S. soldiers in Vietnam had to camouflage themselves to blend in with the countryside, just as the Vietnamese soldiers did. When the "moon touched metal," the soldiers knew they were looking at a weapon, not at part of the natural world. Why? What was the soldiers' relationship to the natural world? Write a brief essay to address this question.

21. In "Streets," the poet reflects on death and whether things are different when someone "leaves the world." In a brief essay, identify and discuss at least three reactions people and the natural world can have when a person dies. Do things change of stay the same/

22. **Thinking About the Essential Question: Does literature shape or reflect society?** Each of the poems in this section—"Who Burns for the Perfection of Paper," "Camouflaging the Chimera," and "Streets"—comments on an important social issue: respectively, the exploitation of labor, attitudes toward war, and feelings about death. Do these poems reflect social attitudes on these subjects or seek to shape them in the reader? Develop your thoughts in a brief essay.

Vocabulary Warm-up Word Lists

Study these words from the selections. Then, complete the activities.

Word List A

coarse [KAWRS] *adj.* having a rough surface
  His unshaven cheek felt like <u>coarse</u> sandpaper.

flannel [FLAN uhl] *n.* a soft fabric, often used for warm nightwear
  It was cold enough for father to wear his <u>flannel</u> robe to breakfast.

scolded [SKOHLD ed] *v.* reprimanded; rebuked or chided
  My mother <u>scolded</u> me for leaving all the lights on.

steal [STEEL] *v.* move silently or secretly
  You can't <u>steal</u> through the house wearing those heavy boots.

Word List B

scarcely [SKAIRS lee] *adv.* barely; hardly
  We had <u>scarcely</u> started dancing when the power went out.

sprawled [SPRAWLD] *v.* spread out awkwardly
  Bert <u>sprawled</u> in his seat, his leg sticking out into the aisle.

proclaiming [proh KLAYM ing] *v.* announcing loudly
  <u>Proclaiming</u> that she had heard enough, Marlee stormed out of the show.

repent [ri PENT] *v.* feel bad enough about past behavior or mistakes to change one's life
  Bonita apologized, but she clearly did not <u>repent</u> her action.

"Halley's Comet" by Stanley Kunitz
Vocabulary Warm-up Exercises

Exercise A *Fill in the blanks, using each word from Word List A only once.*

When Michael and Sara were children, they invented a game that they played only when their parents had company. They would say goodnight and get all ready for bed in their plaid [1] _____ pajamas. Then, when their parents thought they were asleep, they would silently [2] _____ down the hall and peek into the dining room. In their bare feet, they could feel the [3] _____ texture of the hall rug. The goal was to watch the grown-ups without getting caught, but that never happened. Usually after only a few moments, their mother would sense their presence. It was not often that she [4] _____ them for the game. Usually a stern glance was all it took to send them running for bed.

Exercise B *Find a synonym for each of the following words. Then, use each synonym in a sentence that makes the word's meaning clear. Refer to a thesaurus if you need help finding a synonym.*

1. scarcely   synonym: _____

   _____

2. sprawled   synonym: _____

   _____

3. proclaiming   synonym: _____

   _____

4. repent   synonym: _____

   _____

"Halley's Comet" by Stanley Kunitz
Reading Warm-up A

Read the following passage. Then, complete the activities.

Although they all began their lives as children, few adults remember how powerful their words can be. One offhand remark from a teacher about ogres or fire or strangers can <u>steal</u> its way into a child's imagination and set off months of anxiety. A parent's casual statement about the state of world affairs can creep into a child's head and take up residence there, leading to nightmares. Even the comfort of soft <u>flannel</u> pajamas is no protection from the monsters in the mind.

For each generation of children, there are new dangers lurking around every corner. Some of these are based in reality and some not. For those who were children during the Cuban Missile Crisis of the 1960's, the danger was imminent nuclear attack. To prepare children for the possibility of this disaster, schools held drills in which everyone had to "duck and cover." That meant that when the alarm sounded, they had to duck under the desk or a nearby table and cover their heads. It was the rare child who questioned the value of this exercise. Certainly if one did, he or she would have been promptly <u>scolded</u> by a teacher, and then perhaps sent to the principal for further disciplinary action.

More sensitive children spent those moments under the desk facing the terror of nuclear war. Supposing, for example, the bright flash of the bomb went off while they were walking home from school? Should they crouch on the <u>coarse</u> pavement, hoping for the best? Would that rough surface be their last contact with the Earth? Fortunately, it never came to that. Now a new generation of children has its own worries.

1. Circle the word that has the same meaning as <u>steal</u>. Explain what this definition of *steal* means in your own words.

2. Underline the words that hint at the meaning of <u>flannel</u>. What else can be made out of *flannel*?

3. Circle the words that explain the meaning of <u>scolded</u>. Give an antonym for *scolded*.

4. Underline the words that have nearly the same meaning as <u>coarse</u>. Name something else that is *coarse*.

"Halley's Comet" by Stanley Kunitz
Reading Warm-up B

Read the following passage. Then, complete the activities.

In London's Hyde Park, there is a famous area known as "Speakers' Corner." There, for over a century, people have stood on platforms loudly <u>proclaiming</u> their opinions on everything from politics to religion. These orators declare their views to any passing person who will listen. Their usual goal is to bring an issue that they think is important to the attention of a wider audience. For those who are preaching their ideas on the Bible, the purpose may be somewhat more specific. They may be hoping that they can convince their listeners to <u>repent</u> before it is too late. Then, in the preacher's view, their atonement for past sins will make them eligible for salvation.

Hyde Park, which is located in the center of the city, has also been the setting for larger exercises in free speech. These include demonstrations in earlier eras supporting women's right to vote or protesting whichever war is currently taking place. Concerts have also been held there, including some that have drawn almost a quarter-million people. <u>Scarcely</u> a day goes by that there isn't some event in the park, so there is hardly any time that visitors would find themselves bored there.

The 350-acre park is next to Kensington Gardens and, between the two, there is room for all kinds of activities for Londoners and tourists alike. There are places for sports, and there are lakes, trees, and benches. There are also open areas where families, <u>sprawling</u> on the grass after their picnic lunches, can grab a few moments of peace in a hectic world just by lying on a blanket in the sunshine.

1. Underline the phrase that helps explain the meaning of <u>proclaiming</u>. Use the word *proclaiming* in a new sentence.

2. Circle the phrase that gives a synonym for <u>repent</u>. Then underline the phrase that explains why some preachers want people to *repent*.

3. Underline the word that means the same as <u>scarcely</u>. Then give an antonym for *scarcely*.

4. Underline the phrase that gives a clue to the meaning of <u>sprawling</u>. Can a person be *sprawling* when standing? Explain your answer.

Name _____ Date _____

"Halley's Comet" by Stanley Kunitz
Literary Analysis: Free Verse

Free verse is poetry without regular meter or rhyme. Nevertheless, free verse does contain many formal elements. The poet recreates the cadences of natural speech—or cadences that reflect meaning—by using line lengths crafted in one of the following ways.

- **End-stopped lines** are lines that end just where a speaker would pause:

    So mother scolded me
    and sent me early to my room.

    Such lines are used to create a conversational mood or to mimic a storytelling voice.

- **Enjambed** lines are lines that do not end with a grammatical break and that do not make full sense without the line that follows:

    At supper I felt sad to think
    that it was probably
    the last meal I'd share
    with my mother and sisters. . . .

Enjambed lines help the poet emphasize important words and hint at double meanings. In the lines above, for example, the poet emphasizes the key words and phrases *think, share,* and *mothers and sisters,* which call attention to what and whom he is thinking about.

Use the chart below to identify two examples of end-stopped lines and two examples of enjambed lines. In each case, briefly discuss the poet's purpose in using these devices.

End-stopped line 1:	Poet's Purpose:
End-stopped line 2:	Poet's Purpose:
Enjambed line 1:	Poet's Purpose:
Enjambed line 2:	Poet's Purpose:

Name _____ Date _____

"**Halley's Comet**" by Stanley Kunitz

Reading Strategy: Identify Changes in Tense and Tone

When writing in free verse, poets do not have the benefit of strong rhythm and rhyme to draw the reader's attention to important details. Instead, they must use more subtle techniques. As you read Halley's Comet, try to **identify changes in verb tenses and tone.** Then ask yourself whether these changes signal a shift in meaning, a shift in perspective, or both. Use a chart like the one shown to record your ideas.

Type of Change	
Where It Occurs	
Possible Meaning	
Type of Change	
Where It Occurs	
Possible Meaning	

"Halley's Comet" by Stanley Kunitz
Vocabulary Builder

Word List

proclaiming   repent   steal

A. DIRECTIONS: *Think about the meaning of the underlined World List word in each sentence. Then, answer the question.*

1. The red-bearded preacher in the public square was <u>proclaiming</u> that he was sent by God to save everyone. Was he saying this in a whisper? How do you know?

   _____

   _____

2. The red-bearded preacher in the public square urged all the sinners to <u>repent</u>. Was he passing any kind of judgment on the sinners? How do you know?

   _____

   _____

3. Late at night the narrator of the poem decided to <u>steal</u> into the stairwell and climb onto the roof. Did he tell his mother and sister what he was doing? How do you know?

   _____

   _____

B. DIRECTIONS: *On each line, write the letter of the word or phrase that is closest in meaning to the Word List word.*

1. proclaiming
   A. whispering
   B. declaring
   C. lying
   D. questioning

2. repent
   A. confirm
   B. deny
   C. feel sorry
   D. think about

3. steal
   A. sneak
   B. tumble
   C. race
   D. soar

"Halley's Comet" by Stanley Kunitz
Support for Writing

The poem "Halley's Comet" evokes the confusions and distortions that a young boy's mind can bring to an event such as the arrival of Halley's Comet. As part of your preparation for writing a reflective essay about something you misunderstood or misinterpreted when you were a child, use the following chart to sketch out preliminary ideas and notes. Fill in each category of the chart as completely as you can.

Which childhood memory do I wish to write about? What did I misunderstand about it?	
Should I recount events in the past tense or the present tense? Why?	
What key words and images will help me to create a certain mood?	
Which details are most strongly related to my chosen memory?	

Using the notes you made in the chart, write a first draft of your essay on a separate page.

"Halley's Comet" by Stanley Kunitz
Enrichment: Astronomy

In the poem "Halley's Comet," the narrator recalls the hopes and fears he attached as a child to the impending arrival of Halley's Comet. The comet is named for the man who discovered it: the English astronomer Edmond Halley (1656–1742).

The science of astronomy has made giant strides since the eighteenth century, relying on ever more powerful telescopes, advanced mathematics, and the laws of physics and chemistry. Today's astronomers can avail themselves of the supermagnifying powers of eyes into the skies such as radio telescopes, and, more recently, an eye *in* the sky: the orbiting Hubble telescope, which enables scientists to capture images of the planets and stars free of the distorting film of the earth's atmosphere. With these powerful instruments, astronomers can range billions of light years into space to investigate the origins and movements of planets and stars.

Instead of peering into outer space directly through a lens, as scientists did for centuries, today's astronomers attach photographic equipment to telescopes to collect distant light and turn it into digital images on a computer. Hot-air balloons, rockets, and satellites are all part of the array of high-tech marvels with which astronomers seek ever clearer views of outer space. The astronomer decides what to observe and what methods of observation to use. He or she then analyzes the results of these observations and explains their significance or relevance to an existing theory, often publishing the findings in a scientific journal.

Because astronomy is a very competitive field, more opportunities exist for those who have a master's or doctor's degree in astronomy or in a related field, such as mathematics or physics. Most opportunities are in the government or education sectors.

DIRECTIONS: *Answer each of the following questions.*

1. What high school courses would best help you prepare for a career in astronomy?

   _____

   _____

   _____

2. How have an astronomer's tools of observation changed over the years?

   _____

   _____

   _____

3. Why are critical thinking and writing skills probably important for an astronomer?

   _____

   _____

   _____

4. In what way does astronomy connect our smaller world with the larger universe?

   _____

   _____

   _____

"Halley's Comet" by Stanley Kunitz
Open-Book Test

Short Answer *Write your responses to the questions in this section on the lines provided.*

1. What is the narrator's reaction to the way in which his teacher describes the course of the comet through space in the poem, "Halley's Comet"? Cite two examples of words or phrases that give evidence of the narrator's reaction.

   _____

   _____

2. What tense does the poet use throughout the entire first stanza of "Halley's Comet"?

   _____

   _____

3. Often in free verse enjambment is used to emphasize certain words or ideas that cannot be emphasized by traditional techniques of rhyme and meter. What word and idea are emphasized by the enjambed ending at line 13 of "Halley's Comet"?

   _____

   _____

   _____

4. In "Halley's Comet," why do you think the poet chose an end-stopped cutoff for line 16 of the poem? What effect or image is enhanced by the use of the end–stopped line here?

   _____

   _____

   _____

5. In the first stanza of "Halley's Comet," the narrator seems to have mixed feelings about a possible collision of Halley's Comet with the earth. How would you characterize those mixed feelings at the prospect of this event? Cite details from the poem to support your answer.

   _____

   _____

   _____

6. Line 27 of "Halley's Comet" uses enjambment to emphasize the last word of the line, "steal." What meaning or meanings of the word *steal* does the poet wish to underscore in this fashion?

   _____

   _____

   _____

7. What is the change in tense that occurs with line 30 of "Halley's Comet"? What change in tone accompanies this change in tense? Support your answer with information from the poem.

_____

_____

_____

_____

8. At the beginning of the second stanza of "Halley's Comet," the narrator says, "Look for me, Father, on the roof / of the red brick building / at the foot of Green street—. . ." Whom do you think the narrator is addressing in these lines?

_____

_____

_____

9. Poems that are written in free verse, such as "Halley's Comet," often use a combination of enjambed lines—lines that do not end with a grammatical break and that do not make full sense without the line that follows—and end-stopped lines. Use the chart below to give two examples of each kind of line ending from "Halley's Comet."

Examples of Enjambed Lines	Examples of End-Stopped Lines

10. If you decided that you needed to *repent* for something you had done, does that mean that you probably feel guilty about having done it? Why or why not? Base your answer on the meaning of *repent* as it is used in "Halley's Comet."

_____

_____

Essay

Write an extended response to the question of your choice or to the question or questions your teacher assigns you.

11. Halley's Comet" recalls the poet's understanding—or misunderstanding—of the significance of Halley's Comet when he learned about it in his first–grade class. In what respect are the young boy's perceptions of Halley's Comet accurate? In what respect are his perceptions inaccurate or exaggerated? Develop your thoughts in an essay supported by details from the poem.

12. Halley's Comet" evokes an event in nature—the approach of Halley's Comet to the planet earth—in a way that touches on both scientific and religious issues. In an essay, discuss how the poem moves from the mention of an astronomical event to a consideration of religious issues that are important to the poet. Support your response by citing details from the poem.

13. "The deepest thing I know is that I am living and dying at once," Stanley Kunitz once wrote. In the poem "Halley's Comet" the arrival of Halley's Comet, as envisioned in the mind of a first–grade boy, is going to cause the end of the world. As such, the poem can be seen as a meditation on death. In an essay, explain how the poem treats the boy's perception of the arrival of the comet as a symbol of the mystery of death. Support your answer with details from the poem.

14. **Thinking About the Essential Question: What is the relationship between place and literature?** In "Halley's Comet," a number of specific places are visited in the speaker's memory. In an essay, describe these places and explain their importance to the overall impact and meaning of the poem. What do these places show about the overall significance of place in the poet's work?

Oral Response

15. Go back to question 1, 3, or 7 or to the question your teacher assigns you. Take a few minutes to expand your answer and prepare an oral response. Find additional details in "Halley's Comet" that support your points. If necessary, make notes to guide your oral response.

Name _____ Date _____

Halley's Comet, by Stanley Kunitz
Selection Test A

MULTIPLE CHOICE

Critical Reading *Identify the letter of the choice that best answers the question.*

____ 1. Which of the following correctly defines free verse, as this form is used in Stanley Kunitz's poem "Halley's Comet"?
   A. peotry on ordinary, everyday subjects
   B. poetry witholut regular meter or rhyme
   C. poetry with striking figurative language
   D. poetry that deals with political themes

____ 2. When the speaker in "Halley's Comet" was in first grade, what did his teacher Miss Murphy say about Halley's Comet?
   A. that it was discovered by an astronomer named Halley
   B. that it was roaring through the Milky Way at frightening speed
   C. that it was beautiful
   D. that it would never strike planet Earth

____ 3. Read the following lines that report Miss Murphy's prediction in "Halley's Comet":

> . . . and if it wandered off its course
> and smashed into the earth,
> there'd be no school tomorrow.

   What does Miss Murphy suggest might happen?
   A. There would be a holiday at school.
   B. The students might like to do a report on Halley's Comet.
   C. The world might come to an end.
   D. The comet would not be visible in the night sky.

____ 4. In "Halley's Comet," what did the red-headed preacher from the hills urge the people in the public square to do?
   A. sing   B. repent   C. write a letter   D. go home

____ 5. In "Halley's Comet," which of the following line groups is end-stopped, rather than enjambed?
   A. Miss Murphy in first grade / wrote its name in chalk
   B. and if it wandered off its course / and smashed into the earth
   C. Look for me, Father, on the roof / of the red brick building·
   D. searching the starry sky, / waiting for the world to end.

____ 6. In "Halley's Comet," the first two scenes portray the schoolteacher Miss Murphy
and the red-headed preacher in the public square. How are these characters
similar?

   A. They both reassure the speaker.

   B. They both know a lot about comets.

   C. They both hint that the world may end soon.

   D. They both talk about religion.

____ 7. When the speaker in "Halley's Comet" describes how supper at his house, what
were his feelings like?

   A. calm

   B. angry

   C. frightened

   D. sad but also excited

____ 8. After the speaker is sent to his room in "Halley's Comet," the speaker says in
lines 26-27, "The whole family's asleep/except for me." What change do you
notice in the poet's use of verb tenses?

   A. from past to present

   B. from present to future

   C. from future to present

   D. from present to past

____ 9. In poems such as "Halley's Comet," enjambed lines are lines that do not end
with a grammatical break and that do not make full sense without the line that
follows. One reason that poets use enjambed lines is

   A. to make the meter of a line more regular.

   B. to emphasize important words.

   C. to produce rhyming sounds.

   D. to establish an informal tone.

____ 10. In the final scene in "Halley's Comet," the speaker is on the roof. Whom does he
directly address in this scene?

   A. Father   C. the red-headed prwacher

   B. Mother   D. the reader

____ 11. How does the tone in "Halley's Comet" change in the last section of the poem
(lines 30–37)?

   A. The tone becomes more frightened.

   B. The tone becomes angrier.

   C. The tone becomes sadder and gentler.

   D. The tone becomes more humorous.

___ **12.** What is Stanley Knnitz's poem "Halley's Comet" mostly about?

    A. a rare event in the night sky

    B. a boy's experiences at school

    C. the speakrer's reflections on childhood and loss

    D. the speaker's observations of superstition

Vocabulary

___ **13.** Which of the following is a synonym for *proclaiming* in this sentence: "The candidates were *proclaiming* victory in the election"?

    A. announcing

    B. doubting

    C. predicting

    D. pretending

___ **14.** If you *repent* an action, how do you feel?

    A. proud   **B.** sorry   **C.** doubtful   **D.** joyful

___ **15.** If you *steal* away from a party in order to be by yourself, which of the following verbs would best describe the way you move?

    A. stroll   **B.** creep   **C.** run   **D.** prance

Essay

16. How does Stanley Kunitz use end-stopped lines and enjambed lines in the free verse of "Halley's Comet"? In a brief essay, identify two examples of each type of line. Then discuss why you think Kunitz used a particular type of line in each context.

17. Consider the ways in which the speaker in "Halley's Comet" reveals his personality in childhood. Write an essay in which you create a character sketch of the speaker. In your essay, consider questions such as the following: What emotions does the speaker feel during the experience he narrates? What does he notice or observe about the people and scenes around him? What do we learn about his state of mind? Support your main ideas with specific references to the poem.

18. **Thinking About the Essential Question: What is the relationship between place and literature?** In an essay, compare and contrast the description in the final scene in "Halley's Comet" with the three preceding scenes: the classroom, the public square, and suppertime with the speaker's family. What features in the description make the final scene stand out? How does the final scene relate to the poem's overall message? Support your ideas with specific references to the text.

Halley's Comet, by Stanley Kunitz
Selection Test B

MULTIPLE CHOICE

Critical Reading *Identify the letter of the choice that best answers the question.*

____ 1. Poetry without regular meter or rhyme, such as the poem "Halley's Comet" by Stanley Kunitz, is called which of the following?
A. narrative poetry
B. free verse
C. enjambed lines
D. dramatic poetry

____ 2. In "Halley's Comet" by Stanley Kunitz, how did Miss Murphy describe the comet when the speaker was in first grade?
A. It was roaring down the Milky Way at frightful speed.
B. It could be seen right after sunset in the western sky.
C. It was not a threat to planet Earth.
D. It was discovered by a man named Halley.

____ 3. Read the following lines from "Halley's Comet" by Stanley Kunitz:
and if it wandered off its course
and smashed into the earth
there'd be no school tomorrow.

Which of the following best describes the effect produced by the last line in this passage?
A. comic exaggeration
B. surprise ending
C. internal conflict
D. ironic understatement

____ 4. In "Halley's Comet," what did the red-headed preacher from the hills ask his listeners to do?
A. seek shelter
B. sing a hymn
C. repents
D. stare at the sky

____ 5. In "Halley's Comet," which of the following line groups is end-stopped, as opposed to enjambed?
A. and wrote its name in chalk/across the board and told us
B. to save every one of us,/even the little children
C. At supper I felt sad to think/that it was probably
D. The whole family's asleep/except for me. They never heard me steal

____ 6. In Stanley Kunitz's poem "Halley's Comet," how are Miss Murphy and the red-headed preacher similar?
A. They both believe devoutly in God.
B. Neither of them knew very much about science.
C. They both suggested that the world might end.
D. They both waved their hands and had a wild look.

____ 7. In "Halley's Comet," how did the speaker feel that night at supper?
A. angry
B. both sad and excited
C. fearful
D. calm and confident

____ 8. Read the following passage from "Halley's Comet":

. . . that it was probably

the last meal I'd share

with my mother and sisters . . .

What does the word *probably* suggest about the speaker's situation?
A. He was so inexperienced that he believed the comet might destroy Earth.
B. He found himself in conflict with his mother and sisters.
C. He did not believe either Miss Murphy or the red-headed preacher.
D. He wondered if he would get to see Halley's Comet.

____ 9. In the narrative in "Halley's Comet," what change in verb tense occurs after the speaker is sent to his room?
A. from past perfect to past
B. from past to present
C. from present to future
D. from present to past

____ 10. In "Halley's Comet," Stanley Kunitz uses a number of enjambed lines. Which of the following correctly identifies enjambment?
A. lines that do not end with a grammatical break
B. lines that end just where a speaker would pause
C. lines that are split by a full stop
D. rhyming lines

____ 11. In the last section of "Halley's Comet" (lines 30–37), whom does the speaker directly address?
A. his father, and possibly also God   C. Miss Murphy
B. his mother   D. the red-headed preacher

____ 12. Considering the details that Stanley Kunitz includes in the last section of "Halley's Comet," what might the "white flannel gown" that the boy wears symbolize?
A. his misunderstanding of Halley's comet
B. the innocence of an angel
C. his love for his father
D. his ability to repent

____ 13. How does the tone of Stanley Kunitz's poem "Halley's Comet" change in the last section, when the speaker describes himself on the roof?
A. The semi-humorous understatement of the earlier scenes gives way to a tone of poignant longing.
B. The speaker recognizes that his earlier fears were groundless.
C. The speaker's fears become rapidly more intense.
D. The speaker is able to feel more relaxed about the end of the world.

____ 14. Stanley Kunitz's poem "Halley's Comet" is mostly about which of the following?
A. the rash assumptions that people make about the future
B. the conflicts posed by the speaker's home life
C. the speaker's inability to have faith in the future
D. the speaker's reflections on childhood innocence and loss

Vocabulary

___ 15. Which of the following would be the best substitute for the word *proclaiming* in this sentence: "The headlines today are *proclaiming* the mayor's re-election to another term in office"?
A. criticizing
B. announcing
C. predicting
D. praising

___ 16. In which of these sentences is the word *repent* used correctly?
A. The burglars apologized to their victim and promised to repent.
B. We were so happy with our vacation that we decided to repent it next year.
C. If you repent for that crime, you will almost surely never be forgiven.
D. Their cheerful laughter was a sign that they were willing to repent.

___ 17. Which one of the following is closest to the meaning of the word *steal* in this sentence: "Even during busy periods at the office, Mom would *steal* away to spend an hour or so of quiet time by herself."
A. snatch
B. *dash*
C. creep
D. glide

Essay

18. In free verse, end-stopped lines can be used to create a conversational mood or to imitate a storyteller's voice. Enjambed lines, by contrast, help a poet emphasize important points and may hint at double meanings. In a brief essay, discuss Stanley Kunitz's use of these different types of lines in "Halley's Comet." Focus on two examples of end-stopped lines and two examples of enjambed lines in your discussion.

19. In "Halley's Comet," Stanley Kunitz structures his poem as a sequence of four scenes of approximately equal length: the speaker's first-grade classroom, the public square, the supper table, and the concluding scene on the roof. In an essay, discuss each of these scenes briefly, indicating how you think each one contributes to the poem as a whole and its underlying theme or message. Support your main ideas with specific references to the text.

20. In "Halley's Comet," Stanley Kunitz's speaker recalls a childhood event from the perspective of adulthood. In an essay, discuss how Kunitz vividly portrays the personality of this speaker. In particular, focus on the delicate balance Kunitz establishes between excitement, curiosity, and fear on the one hand, and longing and loneliness on the other. Support your main ideas with specific references to the poem.

21. **Thinking About the Essential Question: What is the relationship between place and literature?** In "Halley's Comet," a number of specific places are visited in the speaker's memory. In an essay, describe these places and explain their importance to the overall impact and meaning of the poem. What do these places show about the overall significance of place in the poet's work?

Vocabulary Warm-up Word Lists

Study these words from the selections. Then, complete the activities.

Word List A

aisles [Y uhlz] *n.* passages
The <u>aisles</u> of the store were so crowded that I gave up and left.

gaze [GAYZ] *v.* stare; look at for a long time
Jonathan's <u>gaze</u> was fixed on the target before he shot his arrow in the archery competition.

magnetized [MAG nuh tyzd] *v.* having properties of attraction, like a magnet
Current flowing through the metal caused it to become <u>magnetized</u>.

maternal [muh TER nuhl] *adj.* motherly
Winston's big sister is so <u>maternal</u> towards him that it drives him crazy.

patroness [PAY truh nis] *n.* woman who is a benefactor, protector, or supporter
Lady Astor was the <u>patroness</u> of many worthy causes.

plump [PLUMP] *adj.* having a full, rounded form
I ate so much last winter when it was cold that I became a little <u>plump</u>.

portrait [PAWR trit] *n.* a pictorial representation of a person
Rasheed had his <u>portrait</u> painted by his friend Wilson.

votive [VOHT iv] *adj.* designed to express a special intention, like a wish, vow or thanks
The tribe members made <u>votive</u> offerings, which they thought would insure a successful hunt.

Word List B

disillusions [dis i LOO zhuhns] *n.* disenchantments; disappointments
During the course of his long life, he had experienced many <u>disillusions</u>.

formica [fawr MY kuh] *n.* plastic-like surface used mostly for counters
They decided to redo the kitchen because the <u>formica</u> was so worn.

lyrically [LIR i kuh lee] *adv.* expressive in the manner of song or poetry
He always spoke so <u>lyrically</u> that it was easy to believe he was a poet.

memories [MEM uh reez] *n.* recollections; things or times remembered
My grandmother has many <u>memories</u> of her childhood that she has shared with us.

perfecting [per FEK ting] *v.* improving; making more nearly excellent and flawless
She practiced for hours, <u>perfecting</u> her piano technique.

register [REJ is ter] *n.* a machine for recording fares, money, etc.
There was a crisis at the store, as the <u>register</u> broke down during the big sale.

stale [STAYL] *adj.* tasteless or tough from age
He forgot to seal the bag, and by the next day the bread was <u>stale</u>.

trade [TRAYD] *v.* engage in commerce; buy and sell goods
My father owns several businesses that <u>trade</u> with other countries.

"Ars Poetica" by Judith Ortiz Cofer
Vocabulary Warm-up Exercises

Exercise A *Fill in the blanks, using each word from Word List A only once.*

Walking down the [1] _____ of the local mega-mart, her [2] _____
was drawn to the amazing variety of goods on display. She still remembered the days
when all you could buy at a grocery store were groceries. Now, her town had such a
diverse population that the stores were stocked with all sorts of goods. There were
[3] _____ candles decorated with the image of the [4] _____
of Mexico. There were Polish baked goods decorated with a [5] _____ of a
[6] _____ blond woman with a vaguely [7] _____ air. There
were giant [8] _____ figures that were the pieces on a life-size metal
chessboard and there was furniture imported from Bali and Thailand. There were even
groceries!

Exercise B *Without changing the meaning of the sentence, replace each underlined word or
group of words with a word from Word List B. Use each word only once.*

Example: The two countries <u>engage in commerce</u> with each other.
       The two countries trade with each other.

1. The <u>dried and tasteless</u> bread is good for feeding to the birds.

    _____

2. The customers pulled their chairs up to the <u>colored plastic</u> counter.

    _____

3. It took her a long time to learn to deal with her <u>disappointments</u> when people let
her down.

    _____

4. Mary rang up their purchases on the old <u>machine that keeps track of sales</u> in the
general store.

    _____

5. That cabin held so many <u>recollections</u> of family vacations.

    _____

6. James recited poetry so <u>expressively</u> that people love to listen to him.

    _____

7. Randolph spent hours <u>improving</u> his golf swing.

    _____

"Ars Poetica" by Judith Ortiz Cofer
Reading Warm-up A

Read the following passage. Then, complete the activities.

A mother and child have been among the principle subjects of art through the ages. For centuries, most art was religious art. As a result, for centuries the Virgin Mary and Christ Child were the most common subjects in a <u>portrait</u> that pictured <u>maternal</u> devotion. This mother and child have remained popular subjects. Today, if you visit churches you will often still see many paintings of the Madonna and Child. They adorn altars in side <u>aisles</u>, and the passageways lined with numerous <u>votive</u> candles burning before them. Believers kneel and <u>gaze</u> upon the portraits. They light the candles to express their wishes as they look up at the Madonna and pray to her.

Paintings of Madonna and Child also make up a large portion of the art in museums. Artists from many periods chose this subject.

The way in which the Madonna and Child have been represented has changed across the ages. Each country in Latin America, as well as Spain and the United States, has a special image of the Virgin Mary recognized as the protector and <u>patroness</u> of that country. In Mexico, for example, it is Our Lady of Guadalupe. This special version of the Madonna first appeared as an image on a cloth in 1531. Now, the image of the Lady of Guadalupe has entered popular culture in Mexico and the border states of the U.S. The Virgin is depicted alone, standing, a robe of turquoise dappled with stars covering her slightly rounded and <u>plump</u> body. Today, that image decorates everything from the back windows of pickup trucks to plastic tablecloths, from elaborate oil paintings to <u>magnetized</u> refrigerator art. Once purely a religious figure, the motherly image of Lady of Guadalupe now serves as a cultural icon.

1. Underline the nearby word that helps explain the meaning of <u>portrait</u>. Have you ever seen a *portrait* of anyone? If so, who was the subject?

2. Circle the words that give clues to the meaning of <u>maternal</u>. Give the male version of the word *maternal*.

3. Underline the words that tell what was in the <u>aisles</u>. Give a word or phrase that means the same as *aisles*.

4. Underline the word that tells what <u>votive</u> describes. Use *votive* in an original sentence.

5. Circle the words that tell what it is that people <u>gaze</u> at. Give a word that means the same as *gaze*.

6. Underline the word that gives a clue to the meaning of <u>patroness</u>. What is the masculine version of the word *patroness*?

7. Underline the word that helps determine the meaning of <u>plump</u>. Give a word that is the opposite of *plump*.

8. Underline the word in the sentence that tells what is <u>magnetized</u>. Explained what *magnetized* means in your own words.

"Ars Poetica" by Judith Ortiz Cofer
Reading Warm-up B

Read the following passage. Then, complete the activities.

The corner store had been a part of the neighborhood forever as far as Pablo was concerned. He and his friends referred to it as the *bodega*, the Spanish word for small store. It stocked many of the items that their parents and grandparents loved. These products evoked <u>memories</u> of their childhoods, recalling the Latin American countries of their birth. Even the pink <u>formica</u> counter, with its worn plastic top, and the ancient manual cash <u>register</u>, which had only recently been replaced by a computerized one, reminded the older generation of what they still called "home."

The bodega owners were also immigrants but they were not from any place that Pablo had heard of until he started school and studied geography. When the bodega owners had opened the store, many years ago, people from the same part of Europe that they came from had populated the neighborhood. Over the last decades, that had changed but they continued to <u>trade</u> with customers, now selling their goods to a different group of immigrants. Their stock had also changed along with their shoppers.

Every once in a while, the bodega would get in a new product that Pablo's mom remembered fondly and would insist that he try. These situations were almost always the causes of disappointments and <u>disillusions</u> for Pablo. The tastes never lived up to what he had been led to expect. His parents would speak longingly and <u>lyrically</u> of certain items, which made him think that they would taste great. However, to Pablo, they just tasted strange, old and tough, as though they were <u>stale</u>. However, he had spent time improving and <u>perfecting</u> his response so that his parents would not be disappointed. His face would register delight while "yuck!" was going through his mind.

1. Underline the words that help explain the meaning of <u>memories</u>. Give another word that means the same as *memories*.

2. Circle the words that tell what was made of <u>formica</u>. Use *formica* in a sentence.

3. Underline the words that describe <u>register</u>. Use the word *register* in a sentence.

4. Underline the words that give a clue to the meaning of <u>trade</u>. What are some countries that *trade* with the United States?

5. Circle the word that gives a hint to the meaning of <u>disillusions</u>. What things were the sources of *disillusions* for Pablo?

6. Underline the words that give a hint as to the meaning of <u>lyrically</u>. What is something you might speak of *lyrically*?

7. Underline the words that hint at the meaning of <u>stale</u>. Give a word that means the opposite of *stale*.

8. Underline the word in the sentence that gives a clue to the meaning of <u>perfecting</u>. Tell a skill that you are working on *perfecting*.

"The Latin Deli: An Ars Poetica" by Judith Ortiz Cofer
Literary Analysis: Imagery

Poets use **imagery** to give body to their ideas. Imagery is language that uses **images**—words or phrases that appeal to the one or more of the five senses of sight, smell, touch, sound, or taste. Images can draw readers into a literary work by creating the sensations of actual experience—for example: "the heady mix of smells from the open bins / of dried codfish, the green plantains / hanging in stalks like votive offerings . . ." As they accumulate over the course of a poem, the images combine to express a central idea or feeling.

DIRECTIONS: *Use the chart below to give four examples images from "The Latin Deli: An Ars Poetica." In the middle column, state the sense or senses to which the image appeals. Then, in the right-hand column, briefly state how the image contributes to the meaning of the poem.*

Image	Sense to Which the Image Appeal	How the Image Contributes to the Meaning of the Poem

Name _____ Date _____

Reading: Analyzing Sensory Details

Some poems present a one main idea. Others present a large collection of concrete details from which you must infer the meaning. To read and understand this kind of poem, follow two steps:

- First, clearly picture in your mind each separate detail.

- Second, ask yourself what the details have in common and what overall feeling or idea they are trying to express.

Use a graphic organizer like this one to **analyze sensory details** as you read "The Latin Deli: An Ars Poetica." Choose four such details, tell what they have in common, and then state what overall feeling or idea they are trying to express.

Sensory Detail 1:	Sensory Detail 2:	Sensory Detail 3:	Sensory Detail 4:

What details have in common:

Overall feeling or idea expressed by details:

"The Latin Deli: An Ars Poetica" by Judith Ortiz Cofer
Vocabulary Builder

Word List

ample   disillusions   divine   heady

A. DIRECTIONS: *Write whether each statement is true of false. Then, explain your answer using the meaning of the word in italics.*

1. A *heady* mix of smells from open bins would be barely noticeable.

     _____

2. If you discovered that you had *ample* supplies in the refrigerator for the next week, you would need to make an urgent trip to the supermarket.

     _____

3. Experiencing a number of *disillusions* would leave you with fewer false notions about life.

     _____

4. If you had studied thoroughly for a test and had mastered all the material, there would be no need for you to *divine* the answers.

     _____

B. DIRECTIONS: *Circle the letter of the word that is closest in meaning to the word in CAPITAL LETTERS.*

1. HEADY
   A. egotistical
   B. smart
   C. cautious
   D. intoxicating

2. AMPLE
   A. sufficient
   B. excessive
   C. random
   D. luxurious

3. DISILLUSIONS
   A. confusions
   B. realities
   C. difficulties
   D. memories

4. DIVINE
   A. pray
   B. restore
   C. guess
   D. accept

"The Latin Deli: An Ars Poetica" by Judith Ortiz Cofer
Support for Writing

A person in exile is someone who has been forced by circumstances to leave his or her homeland. Write an essay in which you explore the ideas of exile and home in this poem. As part of your preparation, answer the questions that appear below:

1. Who is exiled in this poem? From where? Why?

   _____

   _____

   _____

   _____

2. Which does the deli represent—exile, home, or both?

   _____

   _____

   _____

   _____

3. Why is the deli owner referred to as "the Patroness of Exiles"? What does she represent to the customers of the deli?

   _____

   _____

   _____

   _____

4. What larger, more universal kind of "exile" might be symbolized by the places and events of the poem?

   _____

   _____

   _____

   _____

After reflecting on your answer to these questions, write a rough draft of your essay. Be sure to include a clear thesis statement, details from the poem to support your assertions, and a conclusion.

"The Latin Deli: An Ars Poetica" by Judith Ortiz Cofer
Enrichment: Geography

"The Latin Deli: An Ars Poetica" is about Latinos who find in a local deli their North American home away from home. The poem mentions several of the native countries of these customers: Mexico, Puerto Rico, and Cuba. Many Latino immigrants to the United States come from these and many other Caribbean, Central American, and South American nations. The following map shows all three of the nations mentioned in the poem and several others.

FPO

DIRECTIONS: *Answer each of the following questions based on the map on this page.*

1. Which is the largest island nation in the area of the Caribbean Sea?

   _____

2. What are the names of the two nations of the only island in the Caribbean Sea that is divided into two countries?

   _____

3. What major body of water lies to the northwest of the Caribbean Sea?

   _____

4. Which country has the longest coastline that faces the Caribbean Sea?

   _____

5. What is the capital of Puerto Rico?

   _____

6. Which two nations have coastlines that face both the Caribbean Sea and the Gulf of Mexico?

   _____

Name _____ Date _____

"The Latin Deli: An Ars Poetica" by Judith Ortiz Cofer
Open-Book Test

Short Answer *Write your responses to the questions in this section on the lines provided.*

1. Poets use **imagery** to give body to their ideas. Imagery is language that uses **images**—words or phrases that appeal to one or more of the senses: sight, smell, touch, sound, or taste. Using the chart below, give examples of four images from "The Latin Deli: An Ars Poetica" in the first column. In the middle column, state the sense or senses to which the image appeals. And, in the right-hand column, briefly state how the image contributes to the meaning of the poem.

Image	Sense(s) to which it appeals	Contribution to meaning of poem

2. The first line of "The Latin Deli: An Ars Poetica" is "Presiding over a formica counter, . . ." What atmosphere and tone does the sensory detail of the formica counter help establish in the poem? Give details about the atmosphere and tone.

_____

_____

_____

3. Lines 3–4 of "The Latin Deli: An Ars Poetica" mentions a "plastic Mother and Child magnetized / to the top of an ancient register." What meaning is established by combining the images of the plastic Mother and Child and the "ancient register"? How does this meaning express the overall theme of the poem? Explain how this is accomplished.

_____

_____

_____

4. Who is the "Patroness of Exiles" mentioned in line 7 of "The Latin Deli: An Ars Poetica"? What is her significance in the poem?

_____

_____

Unit 6 Resources: New Voices, New Frontiers
© Pearson Education, Inc. All rights reserved.
127

5. In line 8 of "The Latin Deli: An Ars Poetica," the "Patroness of Exiles" is described as "a woman of no-age who was never pretty." What do these sensory details tell the reader about this woman and her significance to her customers?

_____

_____

_____

6. As described in lines 9–17 of "The Latin Deli: An Ars Poetica," what is the main activity of the customers of the deli? What does this tell the reader about the function of the deli in the community? Use details to support your answer.

_____

_____

_____

7. Lines 19–20 of "The Latin Deli: An Ars Poetica" use these words to describe the owner of the deli: "family portrait of her plain wide face . . ." How does this image help to explain the importance of the owner and her business to the people who come there? Provide details that demonstrate this.

_____

_____

_____

8. Line 23 of "The Latin Deli: An Ars Poetica" tells of the customers' "dreams and disillusions." What does this phrase imply about the experience in North American of the Latinos who patronize the store? Use details to support your answer.

_____

_____

_____

9. In "The Latin Deli: An Ars Poetica," the reader learns that the coffee or sandwiches at the deli are more expensive than those at the supermarket. What does this fact tell the reader about the customers' feelings about the deli?

_____

_____

_____

10. If you went on a camping trip with *ample* supplies, would you expect to have enough to last for the entire trip? Why or why not? Base your answer on the meaning of *ample* as it is used in "The Latin Deli: An Ars Poetica."

_____

_____

Unit 6 Resources: New Voices, New Frontiers
128

Essay

Write an extended response to the question of your choice or to the question or questions your teacher assigns you.

11. In "The Latin Deli: An Ars Poetica," the deli is much more than a place of business—it is a kind of community/social/cultural center where Latino immigrants from various countries come to experience a sense of "home" in what is for them the often alien environment of North America. Is there a place like that in your community—either a store, a community center, a friend's house, or a place of worship —that serves a similar purpose? Describe the place in an essay that is supported by specific descriptive details.

12. "The Latin Deli: An Ars Poetica" tells the reader a good deal about the woman who presides over the deli, "the Patroness of Exiles." In an essay, explain why this woman is so important to the deli and to the people who come there for various reasons—comfort, conversation, a reminder of their homeland. Support your answer with details from the text.

13. In describing the deli customers in "The Latin Deli: An Ars Poetica," the narrator speaks of "places that now exist only in their [the customers'] hearts." What kinds of feelings do most of the deli customers seem to have about their adopted homeland of North America vs. their original homeland? How do these feelings help explain the significance of the deli in their lives? Develop your thoughts in an essay supported by details from the poem.

14. **Thinking About the Essential Question: What is the relationship between place and literature?** Much of "The Latin Deli: An Ars Poetica" evokes the homesickness Latino emigrants feel for their homeland. Which place does the poem evoke most strongly—the place that is the deli of their adopted North American home, or the place that was the country of the characters' birth? Develop your thoughts in a brief essay.

Oral Response

15. Go back to question 2, 3, or 4 or to the question your teacher assigns you. Take a few minutes to expand your answer and prepare an oral response. Find additional details in "The Latin Deli: An Ars Poetica" that support your points. If necessary, make notes to guide your oral response.

The Latin Deli: An Ars Poetica, by Judith Ortiz Cofer
Selection Test A

MULTIPLE CHOICE

Critical Reading *Identify the letter of the choice that best answers the question.*

_____ 1. In the subtitle of Judith Ortiz Cofer's poem "The Latin Deli," the phrase "Ars Poetica" means

    A. a poem in free verse.   C. a poem about present-day life.

    B. the art of poetry.   D. the rhyme scheme of a poem.

_____ 2. Read these lines from Judith Ortiz Cofer's "The Latin Deli":

    . . . plastic Mother and Child magnetized

    to the top of an ancient register

    To what two senses does the imagery in this passage appeal?

    A. sight and hearing   C. touch and sight

    B. taste and smell   D. thearing and smell

_____ 3. In "The Latin Deli," which of the following adjectives best describes the woman who presides over the counter?

    A. jolly   B. sad   C. patient   D. shy

_____ 4. In "The Latin Deli," what do all the deli customers have in common?

    A. They are all from Puerto Rico.

    B. In a certain sense, they are all exiles.

    C. They all hope to return to their native land one day.

    D. They all like candy.

_____ 5. In "The Latin Deli," the customers could buy their items more cheaply elsewhere. Why do they still come to the deli?

    A. The deli is closer to where they live.

    B. The customers are related to the deli owner.

    C. The quality of the items is better than at the A&P.

    D. The deli reminds them of their homeland.

_____ 6. According to the speaker in "The Latin Deli," what do the Cuban customers look forward to doing?

    A. They want to earn as much money as they can.

    B. They look forward to a "glorious return" home.

    C. They hope that more delis will spring up in the neighborhood.

    D. They want to learn to speak English well.

_____ 7. What "comfort" does the speaker in "The Latin Deli" say that the deli provides the customers?

    A. cheaper prices

    B. a place to sit down

    C. availability of newspapers in Spanish

    D. spoken Spanish

_____ 8. Read the following lines from "The Latin Deli":

    when they walk down the narrow aisles of her store
    reading the labels of packages aloud, as if
    they were the names of lost lovers . . .

    What overall feeling do the sensory details and the comparison to "lost lovers" suggest?

    A. longing   **C.** satisfaction

    B. joy   **D.** anger

_____ 9. In "The Latin Deli," the speaker describes a "fragile old man lost in the folds of his winter coat." What does the old man read to the woman at the deli counter?

    A. his lists of items to purchase   **C.** a newspaper article

    B. a poem about his native land   **D.** a speech about Havana, Cuba

_____ 10. What is the most likely reason that Judith Ortiz Cofer included some spanish words and phrases in her poem "The Latin Deli"?

    A. There are no English equivalents for the meaning of these words and phrases.

    B. Spanish words and phrases help to rienforce the poem's overall theme.

    C. Cofer wanted English-speaking readers to learn a little Spanish.

    D. The deli customers could speak no English.

_____ 11. Which of the following is Ortiz Cofer's poem "The Latin Deli" mainly about?

    A. the deli woman's struggle to make a living

    B. the immigrants' longing for their native culture

    C. the competition between the deli and other stores

    D. the poetry written by the fragile old man

_____ 12. Overall, what seems to be the woman's attitude toward her customers in "The Latin Deli"?

    A. understanding and sympathetic

    B. cold and uncaring

    C. picky and impatient

    D. detahced and objective

Vocabulary

_____ **13.** If you described the smell of a restaurant dish as *heady*, which of the following words would come closest to your meaning?

    A. intense

    B. disagreeable

    C. unfamiliar

    D. offbeat

_____ **14.** Which word best replaces *ample* in this sentence: "The *ample* living room of their new house was so spacious that they had room for a grand piano."

    A. airy   **B.** large   **C.** luxurious   **D.** long

_____ **15.** In which of the following sentences is the word *disillusions* used correctly?

    A. They spoke cheefully about their disillusions.

    B. Disillusions usually satisfy people.

    C. Over the years, their disillusions made them sadder and sadder.

    D. Everyone enjoys disillusions occasionally.

Essay

16. In an essay, discuss the sensory imagery used by Judith Ortiz Cofer in "The Latin Deli." Choose three images from the poem that you find especially vivid. Identify the sense to which each image appeals, and then explain how the images relate to the poem's overall theme, or main idea.

17. In "The Latin Deli," Judith Ortiz Cofer uses images and descriptive details to suggest the emotions of the deli customers. Write an essay in which you discuss these emotions. In your essay, answer such questions as the following: How do the customers feel about shopping at the deli? How do they feel about their native culture? How have they adjusted, or failed to adjust, to life in their new surroundings? Support your main ideas with specific references to the poem.

18. Thinking About the Essential Question: Does a sense of place shape literature or does literature shape a sense of place? Why do you think Judith Ortiz Cofer titled her poem "The Latin Deli"? How important is this setting to the poem as a whole? In an essay, discuss some of the ways in which the setting of the poem is closely tied to the mood and overall message of the work.

The Latin Deli: An Ars Poetica, by Judith Ortiz Cofer
Selection Test B

MULTIPLE CHOICE

Critical Reading *Identify the letter of the choice that best answers the question.*

____ 1. In Judith Ortiz Cofer's poem "The Latin Deli: An Ars Poetica," who is said to "preside" over the deli counter?
   A. the poem's speaker
   B. a woman called the Patroness of Exiles
   C. an old man wearing a winter coat
   D. a Mexican who wants to make *dólares* in El Norte

____ 2. Read these lines from Judith Ortiz Cofer's poem "The Latin Deli":
   the heady mix of smells from the open bins
   of dried codfish, the green plantains
   hanging in stalks like votive offerings . . .

   A. sight and hearing
   B. hearing and touch
   C. touch and taste
   D. sight, smell, and taste

____ 3. In "The Latin Deli" by Judith Ortiz Cofer, some of the customers are said to complain about the prices there. Why do they still come to the store?
   A. They are related to the owner.
   B. They seek the comfort of spoken Spanish.
   C. They cannot obtain coffee anywehere else.
   D. They cannot speak English.

____ 4. In "The Latin Deli," Judith Ortiz Cofer refers to the deli items as "canned memories." How does this phrase hint at the poem's central subject and theme?
   A. It suggests that the items are inexpensive.
   B. It suggests that the items symbolize nostalgia for a culture that the customers have left behind.
   C. It suggests that the memories are not real.
   D. It suggests that the deli items are overpriced.

____ 5. What do the customers in Judith Ortiz Cofer's "The Latin Deli" all have in common?
   A. They love candy.
   B. They talk about the deli owner.
   C. They come from Spanish-speaking backgrounds.
   D. They drink coffee, rather than tea.

____ 6. Read Ortiz Cofer's description of the Cubans in "The Latin Deli":
   . . . and to Cubans perfecting their speech
   of a "glorious return" to Havana—where no one
   has been allowed to die and nothing to change until then . . .

   A. They are unrealistic.
   B. They are likely to come true.
   C. They deserve the reader's sympathy.
   D. They are supported by the Patroness of Exiles.

____ 7. In Ortiz Cofer's poem "The Latin Deli," the speaker describes the customers "when they walk down the narrow aisles of her store/reading the labels of packages aloud, as if/they were the names of lost lovers . . . "(lines 25-27). What overall feeling or atmosphere do the sensory details in these lines suggest?
   A. joy   **B.** anger   **C.** longing   **D.** regret

____ 8. On the whole, what seems to be the woman's attitude toward the deli customers in "The Latin Deli"?
   A. resignation   **B.** hopr   **C.** sympathy   **D.** scorn

____ 9. Read the following lines from "The Latin Deli":
   > She spends her days
   > slicing *jamón y queso* and wrapping it in wax paper
   > tied with string . . .

   Which of the five senses do the images in these lines appeal to?
   A. sight, taste, and touch
   B. sight, hearing, and smell
   C. hearing, touch, and smell
   D. hearing, touch, and taste

____ 10. Why would ham and cheese from the A&P not satisfy the fragile old man's hunger in "The Latin Deli"?
   A. because it would be too expensive
   B. because it would not be nutritious
   C. because he would not enjoy the cultural surroundings of the deli
   D. because the old man wanted something else to eat

____ 11. In "The Latin Deli," Cofer says that the old man reads lists of items to the woman "lik poetry." How does this phrase relate to the poem's main idea as a whole?
   A. The poem is basically about poetry.
   B. The deli items symbolize their Hispanic heritage for the customers.
   C. The old man has fallen in love with the woman.
   D. The woman finds her work boring and needs a romantic distraction.

____ 12. In the final lines of Ortiz Cofer's poem "The Latin Deli," the woman is compared to a trader who must deal with "closed ports." What does Cofer imply with this comparison?
   A. The deli items are hard to obtain.
   B. The customers are picky and hard to deal with.
   C. The woman has no other way to make a living.
   D. The deli items symbolize homrelands that have been left behind.

____ 13. Judith Ortiz Cofer's poem "The Latin Deli" is mainly about
   A. how to write poetry.
   B. the longing of immigrants for their homeland and native culture.
   C. how to run a deli.
   D. the deli owner's relationship with her customers.

____ 14. Considering Cofer's use of sensory details in "The Latin Deli: An Ars Poetica," in what way might the poem and the deli be compared?
  A. Soanish words and phrases are present in both the poem and the deli.
  B. The poem describes a deli in great detail.
  C. Both the poem and the deli serve to conjure up a cultural heritage.
  D. Both the poem and the deli deal with people's unhappiness.

Vocabulary

____ 15. In which sentence is the word *heady* used correctly?
  A. The poem was arranged in heady stanzas.
  B. The students couldn't understand the professor's heady lecture.
  C. There was a heady mix of smells wafting from the kitchen.
  D. The yowls of the cats were sharp and heady.

____ 16. Which word best replaces *ample* in this sentence: "The restaurant customers kept returning because of the reasonable prices and *ample* portions"?
  A. generous   B. scanty   C. decroative   D. sweet-smelling

____ 17. Which of the following is the best synonym for *disillusions* in this sentence: "The sad look on Maria's face unmistakably expressed the *disillusions* that had piled up over the years."
  A. expenditures   C. lost dreams or ideals
  B. woes   D. illnesses

____ 18. In which sentence is the verb *divine* used correctly?
  A. We had to divine his intentions from the look on his face.
  B. Everyone divined the colorful floats at the parade.
  C. When you divine a march in music, keep a steady rhythm.
  D. They divined to go to the lake over the weekend.

Essay

19. In "The Latin Deli: An Ars Poetica," Judith Ortiz Cofer uses imagery appealing to all the five senses to present vivid impressions of the deli, its owner, and its customers. Choose three of the five senses. In an essay, identify and discuss an image in the poem that appeals to each of these senses. Explain how each image makes an especially vivid impression.

20. In an essay, discuss Judith Ortiz Cofer's purpose and theme in writing "The Latin Deli: An Ars Poetica." Why do you think Cofer selected this subject to write about? What is her over-all message in the poem? In answering these questions, support your points with specific references to the selection.

21. The subtitle of Judith Ortiz's poem "The Latin Deli" is "An Ars Poetica"—a reference to a statement about the art and purpose of poetry. Cofer echoes this allusion when she refers to the lists of deli items that the fragile old man reads to the deli owner "like poetry" (line 35). In an essay, discuss what you think Cofer is suggesting about the nature and purpose of poetry in "The Latin Deli." Support your main ideas with specific references to the text.

22. **Thinking About the Essential Question: Does a sense of place shape literature or does literature shape a sense of place?** Much of "The Latin Deli: An Ars Poetica" evokes the homesickness Latino immigrants feel for their homeland. Which place does the poem evoke most strongly—the place that is the deli of their adopted North American home, or the place that was the country of the characters' birth? Discuss your thoughts in a brief essay.

Unit 6: New Voices, New Frontiers
Benchmark Test 11

MULTIPLE CHOICE

Literary Analysis and Reading Skills

Read the passage. Then, answer the questions that follow.

(1) "Dear Jen," I typed. I was trying to write an email. I was worried that my friendship with Jennifer was slipping away.

(2) It was a friendship that began last year. I was reading a book between practices at soccer camp. This skinny girl with a big smile plopped down next to me. "I liked that book a lot. When you're done, let's talk. I don't want to ruin the surprise ending for you."

(3) "Surprise ending?" I asked. It didn't seem to be that kind of book.

(4) "Won't say another word. Except that I'm Jen. Hi! Well, bye! See you on the field!" and she sprinted off.

(5) We spent a lot of time together at camp that summer and became good friends. When we went home, we expected to keep in close touch. We did, for a while. But we live far apart, she is in the city and I'm out in the country. The train fare into the city is too expensive for me to see her often. She's offered to pay, but I'd be embarrassed if she did that. She's always been welcome to visit me out here in Oakdale, but she usually says, "Natalie! Oakdale?" As though it's Mars or a desert or something. She doesn't mean to, but it always hurts my feelings.

(6) I finished my email to Jen. It took a long time. But when I read it over, it seemed to buzz with anger and hurt. So I took a breath and deleted all my harsh words and sent her a much calmer note. Now I'm waiting to hear back from her. But I want to send a P.S. I want to tell her, "Let's be friends, no matter what. I don't want *us* to have a surprise ending—at least not a sad one."

1. Which of the following plot elements begins in paragraph 2?
   - A. climax
   - B. resolution
   - C. denouement
   - D. flashback

2. What plot element is represented in Jen's comment in paragraph 2 about "the surprise ending"?
   - A. denouement
   - B. climax
   - C. foreshadowing
   - D. *in media res*

3. Which is the best description of Jen's character, as presented in the narrative?
   - A. shy, introverted, sensitive
   - B. outgoing, lively, impulsive
   - C. unhappy, aggressive, envious
   - D. mature, compassionate, caring

4. What quality does Natalie reveal about herself in paragraph 5?
   - A. her sensitivity
   - B. her sense of humor
   - C. her loneliness
   - D. her envy

5. Which word best describes the author's style in the passage?
   A. scholarly
   B. conversational
   C. formal
   D. poetic

6. Which sentence could replace the first sentence of the passage and retain the same style as the author's?
   A. Dear Jen, It is with great regret that I write to you to convey my hurt and concern.
   B. Hi Jen, Sorry to write a serious email, but I think we need to talk.
   C. Yo Jen, Im feeling dissed, bff. RU 2?
   D. Jen: It is abundantly clear to me that we need to take a serious look at our friendship.

7. Which statement most accurately contrasts the two characters in this selection?
   A. They became friends because they have similar backgrounds.
   B. One enjoys reading, while the other does not.
   C. One character seems to be more sensitive than the other.
   D. One character tends to gossip, while the other does not.

8. Why is this passage not a frame story?
   A. It takes place within a year or less.
   B. The story gives only one point of view.
   C. I has a flashback, but not a true story within a story.
   D. It takes place in modern times and is not a classic story.

Answer the following questions.

9. What is a frame story?
   A. a narrative told from several different points of view
   B. a narrative that is enclosed by another narrative
   C. a plot that uses chronological order
   D. a story told in the form of letters between two or more characters

10. Which of the following is not a characteristic of a lyric poem?
    A. It tells a story.
    B. It reflects one character's viewpoint.
    C. It primarily expresses emotion.
    D. It uses beautiful figurative language.

11. Which of the following lines of poetry most likely come from a lyric poem?
    A. Listen my children and you shall hear/Of the midnight ride of Paul Revere.
    B. The Soul selects her own Society—/Then— shuts the Door— . . . .
    C. That's my last Duchess painted on the wall,/Looking as if she were alive.
    D. Whenever Richard Cory went down town,/We people on the pavement looked at him.

12. To what does an epiphany refer?
  A. a character's sudden insight, which is the story's climax
  B. the incident that first presents the main conflict in a story
  C. a religious ceremony
  D. any part of the narration in which the narrator comments on a character

13. Which of the following incidents from a fairy tale could be regarded as an epiphany?
  A. the evil queen being told by the mirror that Snow White is fairer than she
  B. the three bears' finding Goldilocks in their house
  C. Beauty's sudden realization that she loves the Beast
  D. the prince's discovery of the glass slipper that Cinderella left at the ball

Read this poem by Carl Sandburg. Then, answer the questions that follow.

1	Give me hunger,
2	O you gods that sit and give
3	The world its orders.
4	Give me hunger, pain and want,
5	Shut me out with shame and failure
6	From your doors of gold and fame,
7	Give me your shabbiest, weariest hunger!
8	But leave me a little love,
9	A voice to speak to me in the day end,
10	A hand to touch me in the dark room
11	Breaking the long loneliness.
12	In the dusk of day-shapes
13	Blurring the sunset,
14	One little wandering, western star
15	Thrust out from the changing shores of shadow.
16	Let me go to the window,
17	Watch there the day-shapes of dusk
18	And wait and know the coming
19	Of a little love.

14. What is the theme of this poem?
  A. With a little love, a person can survive many daily hardships.
  B. Hunger, pain, and want cannot hurt proud and hard-working people.
  C. Always look on the bright side, even during dark times and suffering.
  D. People should take the time to come together whenever they can.

15. Which lines best convey the poem's theme?
  A. lines 1–3, 5–7   **C.** 1, 8
  B. 1, 7, 19   **D.** 16–17

16. In Sandburg's poem, what quality do you hear in the speaker's voice in lines 4 through 7?
   A. joy
   B. grief
   C. hope
   D. defiance

17. How does the speaker's voice change from the first stanza to the second stanza?
   A. It changes from challenging to hope.
   B. It changes from hope to despair.
   C. It changes from grief to resignation.
   D. It changes from joy to solemnity.

18. What does the speaker hope to do at the window in line 16?
   A. to see shadows outside
   B. to get in touch with his loneliness
   C. to see a western star in the sky
   D. to see the possibility of love

19. What belief is implied by the poet in the first stanza of this poem?
   A. that love will always come to us in the end
   B. that humans have little power against fate
   C. that most people are treated unfairly by the rich and successful
   D. that life is terrible in every way

20. Which question would be the most helpful to ask yourself as you read the poem?
   A. Do gods control human fate?
   B. Does line 14 refer to an actual western star, and, if so, which one?
   C. How can love compensate for hunger and failure?
   D. Why do the adjectives *shabbiest* and *weariest* apply to hunger in this poem?

Answer the following question.

21. How would background knowledge of an author's life and works enable you to make predictions prior to reading a story written by the author?
   A. You could assume that the story's plot was based on real events and people.
   B. The main character would probably have personality traits similar to the author's.
   C. The story might explore problems treated in the author's other works.
   D. The story might be set in the author's home town.

Vocabulary

22. The Spanish word *corral* has come into the English language. It contains the root *corro*, which means "circle or ring." Based on the meaning of the root, what does *corral* mean in this sentence?

    To protect themselves against attack, the settlers decided to *corral* their wagons.

    A. put them into a barn or shed   C. drive them around a fenced-in area

    B. drive them into a circle formation   D. strengthen the wheels

23. Based on the meaning of the Latin root *-doc-*, choose the definition of *docudrama*.
    A. a play about doctors in a hospital
    B. a textbook article about real people and events
    C. a fictional play based on real people or events
    D. a dramatic work originally written in Latin

24. What is the meaning of the adjective *doctrinal*, based on the Latin root *-doct-*?
    A. intelligent
    B. pertaining to beliefs
    C. unnatural
    D. pertaining to medicine

25. What is the best synonym for the word *exhaust* in the following sentence?

    We tried to exhaust all of our other options before taking this unpleasant action.

    A. tire out
    B. use up
    C. analyze
    D. improve

26. Which line contains a transitional word or phrase that indicates a contrast between related ideas?
    A. After dinner we told stories around the campfire.
    B. Most of the stories were very exciting and full of suspense.
    C. The last one, however, was very long and boring.
    D. As a result, most of us slept well that night.

27. Which of the following transitional words or phrases might be used to show chronological order?
    A. meanwhile
    B. as an example
    C. similarly
    D. nevertheless

ESSAY

28. Boo! Turn a story, movie, or television show that you know well into a spooky tale. For example, you might transplant the characters from a television series into a suspenseful, frightening setting. Decide on the events of your scary plot. Adapt the personality traits and behavior patterns of the characters to the new setting and situation. Be sure to heighten the suspense and scary mood by including vivid details that appeal to the senses of sight, hearing, touch, taste, and smell.

29. Choose two songs or poems that express strong feelings about life. Then in an essay, analyze the relationship between the title and meaning of each song or poem. Be sure to include whether the title directly or indirectly points to the song or poem's meaning. Then compare the relationships between the titles and meanings of both songs or poems. State and defend your opinion on which title seems more effective in communicating the meaning.

30. Write an essay exploring the theme of a story, television show, play, or movie. In your essay, analyze how that theme represents a comment on life. Discuss the following questions: Does the work express an optimistic or pessimistic view of experience? Does it convey a message or a lesson that can be applied to real life, and how does it convey that message?

Vocabulary Warm-up Word Lists

Study these words from the selections. Then, complete the activities.

Word List A

eloquence [EL uh kwuhns] *n.* persuasive, graceful and forceful speech
   Sharon is known for her <u>eloquence</u> when she speaks on any topic.

icebreaker [YS brayk er] *n.* a ship that has a strong bow to force its way through ice
   The movie showed the <u>icebreaker</u> thrusting its way through the frozen channel.

imitative [IM i tayt iv] *adj.* mimicking
   He did such a good job of making an <u>imitative</u> sound that everyone was fooled.

paralyzing [PAIR uh lyz ing] *v.* stunning; rendering unable to move
   The inhabitants of the forest were rumored to use a dart gun that delivered a <u>paralyzing</u> liquid.

rhetorical [ri TAWR i kuhl] *adj.* relating to the skill of using language effectively and well
   The politician's <u>rhetorical</u> powers were so great that he could convince anyone of anything.

superpowers [SOO per pow ers] *n.* the most powerful nations in the world
   At a meeting of the <u>superpowers</u>, global warming was an important topic of discussion.

theories [THEE uh reez] *n.* generally possible ideas or principles based on some evidence
   There are many <u>theories</u> about what happened to the dinosaurs.

upend [up END] *v.* to affect or disturb to the point of being upset
   The new discovery threatened to <u>upend</u> everyone's ideas.

Word List B

columnists [KAHL uhm nists] *n.* people who write regular pieces for a magazine or newspaper
   My dad had his favorite newspaper <u>columnists</u> whose work he tried to read every day.

denoting [dee NOHT ing] *v.* meaning; designating
   The restaurant received an "A" rating, <u>denoting</u> that it meets the highest standards.

dictator [DIK tayt er] *n.* someone who behaves like a tyrant or absolute ruler
   I had a fight with my friend because she tried to be the <u>dictator</u> of our group.

lexicographers [lek suh KAHG ruh ferz] *n.* authors and editors of a dictionary
   A convention of <u>lexicographers</u> was held in my town, and they spent days talking about words.

mavens [MAY vuhns] *n.* people who are experienced and knowledgeable; experts
   The fashion <u>mavens</u> have declared that high heel boots are out this year.

obsession [uhb SESH un] *n.* a totally absorbing interest in something
   When he was young, he had an <u>obsession</u> with trains.

originated [uh RIJ uh nayt ed] *v.* started or began
   She had always wondered where her family <u>originated</u>.

watchful [WAHCH fuhl] *adj.* carefully observant or attentive
   The cat was very <u>watchful</u> the whole time the dog was in the room with her.

"ONOMATOPOEIA" by William Safire
Vocabulary Warm-up Exercises

Exercise A *Fill in the blanks, using each word from Word List A only once.*

The movie is one of my favorites. It is the story of warring _____ and the secret agents who work for them. The good guy is handsome and speaks with _____. His _____ skills are exceeded only by his _____ abilities, which allow him to disguise his voice when he assumes other identities. The bad guy, on the other hand, relies on high-tech devices like an umbrella with a point that dispenses _____ serum. During the final scene, the good guy is trapped on an _____ in the Arctic Sea. The bad guy laughs at him and spouts his _____ of how the world works, saying that his masters plan to _____ the world order. Of course, our hero has an answer for that, as well as a plan to escape this predicament. But I'll let you discover it for yourself!

Exercise B *Revise each sentence so that the underlined vocabulary word is used in a logical way. Be sure to keep the vocabulary word in your revision.*

Example: Because the offer was so *advantageous*, we declined it firmly.
Because the offer was so <u>advantageous</u>, *we eagerly accepted it.*

1. She received several ribbons *denoting* that she was a terrible gymnast.
   _____

2. He was such a *dictator* that everyone enjoyed working with him.
   _____

3. People who are *columnists* have poor writing skills and don't like to share their opinions.
   _____

4. Mothers are never *watchful* when their young children are playing in the park.
   _____

5. The letters to Santa Claus *originated* from Santa.
   _____

6. She had an *obsession* with the television star and never watched any show he was on.
   _____

7. *Lexicographers* never spend their time reading and studying words.
   _____

8. Sports *mavens* never know what they are talking about when they discuss games.
   _____

"ONOMATOPOEIA" by William Safire
Reading Warm-up A

Read the following passage. Then, complete the activities.

Buck was a huge science fiction fan. Perhaps that wasn't surprising, since his father had named him after an early hero of the genre, Buck Rogers.

People made fun of his passion. But Buck defended his interest with surprising <u>eloquence</u> and persuasiveness. Early practitioners of the art of science fiction writing had often been no more than hacks churning out similar stories for the masses. <u>Imitative</u> and poorly written examples certainly existed.

However, Buck claimed, some of the most intellectual modern writers had turned their <u>rhetorical</u> gifts and language skills to science fiction. These works dealt with the clash of <u>superpowers</u>, for example, by writing about warring empires on distant planets. After World War II, these works put forth <u>theories</u> and concerns about the advancing nuclear age. Authors tried to disturb or <u>upend</u> usual ways of thinking. By setting their tales in the future, they were able to address universal issues in a less threatening way.

Science fiction attempts to speculate about the future of known concepts of science and technology. Such trappings as a <u>paralyzing</u> gun that stunned its victims, or a nuclear-powered <u>icebreaker</u> smashing the way through the ice for the ship to reach its goal, seemed fantastic when writers used them. But eventually they became reality.

What is known as modern science fiction dates from the early 1960s. An important milestone was the publication of a book called *Dune*. Even people who didn't generally enjoy science fiction found it fascinating. It dealt with what at the time were unfamiliar ideas about scarce resources and concern for the environment. As in the best science fiction, issues brought up in *Dune foreshadowed* major concerns in the real world. As Buck would say, science fiction entertains but also makes us think about where technology might take us.

1. Underline the word that helps explain the meaning of <u>eloquence</u>. Use *eloquence* in a sentence of your own.

2. Underline the word in the previous sentence that helps explain the meaning of <u>imitative</u>. Give another word or phrase that means the opposite of *imitative*.

3. Circle the words that give a clue to the meaning of <u>rhetorical</u>. What kind of job might a person with *rhetorical* skills be good at?

4. Underline the words that give a clue to the meaning of <u>superpowers</u>. Name some *superpowers*.

5. Circle the words that tell what writers had <u>theories</u> about. Give a synonym for *theories*.

6. Underline the word in the sentence that gives a clue to the meaning of <u>upend</u>. Give a word or phrase that means the same as *upend*.

7. Underline the word that tells what was <u>paralyzing</u>. Use the word *paralyzing* in an original sentence.

8. Break <u>icebreaker</u> into the two words that make its meaning clear. Where might this kind *icebreaker* be used?

"ONOMATOPOEIA" by William Safire
Reading Warm-up B

Read the following passage. Then, complete the activities.

Who decides what words get in the dictionary? And, for that matter, who decides when a word is removed? <u>Lexicographers</u> are people who compile dictionaries. They spend a lot of time researching and thinking about words and the way they are used; for some, it is an <u>obsession</u>. They are the ones who decide which words are in and which words or out.

There are many kinds of dictionaries, though most people using the term are referring to a volume dedicated to <u>denoting</u> the spelling, pronunciation, meaning, and examples of usage of words in a given language.

Most language <u>mavens</u> involved with dictionaries today are experts who believe that all living languages change and evolve, and that it is not their job to be the <u>dictator</u> making tyrannical rules about what is and isn't a word. It is rather to research and record the way words are being used at a given point in time. They spend their time reading everything, from print magazines to scholarly journals, from the writings of respected <u>columnists</u> in the nation's top newspapers to the rantings of online bloggers. (There's a perfect example: "blogger," a word that an online dictionary states <u>originated</u> in 1999. It does not appear in a published dictionary until 2007.)

When their <u>watchful</u> perusal locates a new word like blogger that has entered the language, lexicographers propose it for inclusion in a dictionary. Of course, now that many dictionaries are published online, the process of adding words goes much faster. And online publication means that there is no longer worry about a book becoming too big to handle and too expensive to produce. So now there is no reason not to add every word the lexicographers decide should be included.

1. Underline the words that explain the meaning of <u>lexicographers</u>. Use the word *lexicographers* in an original sentence.

2. Circle the words that help explain the meaning of <u>obsession</u>. Give a word or phrase that means the same as *obsession*.

3. Underline the words that tell what the volume was <u>denoting</u>. Give a word with a meaning similar to *denoting*.

4. Underline the word that gives a hint to the meaning of <u>mavens</u>. Give a word that is the opposite of *mavens*.

5. Circle the words that tell what a <u>dictator</u> does. Use *dictator* in an original sentence.

6. Underline the words that give a hint as to the meaning of <u>columnists</u>. Where might you read the work of *columnists*.

7. Underline the words that give a hint to the meaning of <u>originated</u>. Give a word that means the same as *originated*.

8. Underline the word in the sentence that tells what is being done in a <u>watchful</u> manner. Give a synonym for *watchful*.

"Onomatopoeia" by William Safire
Literary Analysis: Expository Essay

In an **expository essay,** the writer provides information about a topic, discusses ideas, or explains a process. In "Onomatopoeia," Safire explains the origin, meaning, pronunciation and uses of onomatopoeia.

Like other forms of nonfiction, expository essays can vary widely in tone, according to the nature of the subject and the author's purpose. Safire chooses to take a light, humorous approach to his subject, especially in his frequent use of idioms, common or expressions that have acquired meanings different from their literal meaning. For example, if you say that someone "has an axe to grind," that is an informal way of saying that he or she has a grievance or resentment. Or if you say that someone "gets your goat," it means that someone is able to annoy you easily.

A. DIRECTIONS: *Use the chart below to list four examples of idioms that Safire uses to establish an informal tone for his expository essay. In each case, provide a standard English definition of the idiomatic word or phrase you have identified.*

Safire's Idiom	Standard English Meaning

B. DIRECTIONS: *On the lines below or on a separate sheet of paper, write a brief explanation of some simple topic (for example, how to send an e-mail, how to record a DVD, how to hard-boil an egg, etc.). In your explanation, use at least two idioms to establish an informal, humorous tone.*

_____

_____

_____

_____

"**Onomatopoeia**" by William Safire
Reading Strategy: Paraphrase

To help you determine the main ideas in an essay, take time to **paraphrase,** or restate in your own words, any passages that require clarification. By helping you clarify meaning, paraphrasing allows you to identify and understand the author's main points.

A. DIRECTIONS: *Use the chart below to paraphrase passages from Safire's essay "Onomatopoeia."*

Original Passage	My Paraphrase
1. "He pointed out that one speculation about the origin of language was the *bow-wow theory,* holding that words originated in imitation of natural sounds of animals and thunder."	
2. "Thus we can see another way that the human mind creates new words: imitating what can be heard only in the mind's ear."	
3. "The coinage filled a need for an unheard sound and—*pow!*—slammed the vocabulary right in the kisser."	

B. Directions: *On the lines below, briefly paraphrase the main points of "Onomatopoeia" in no more than four sentences.*

_____

_____

_____

_____

"**Onomatopoeia**" by William Safire
Vocabulary Builder

Word List

coinage   derive   speculation   synonymous

A. DIRECTIONS: *Think about the meaning of the underlined World List word in each sentence. Then, answer the question.*

1. The teacher asked us to think of a word that is <u>synonymous</u> with the word *stubborn*. Does that mean she was asking for a word that means the opposite of *stubborn* ? How do you know?

_____

_____

2. Safire writes that you can <u>derive</u> the meaning of the word onomatopoeia from a Greek word meaning "word making." Does that mean that Safire is discussing the origin of *onomatopoeia*? How do you know?

_____

_____

3. Safire writes that the bow-wow theory of language is <u>speculation</u>. Does that mean that the theory is well grounded in facts? How do you know?

_____

_____

4. Safire speaks of the <u>coinage</u> of the word zap. Is he talking about the way the word came into being? How do you know?

_____

_____

B. DIRECTIONS: *On each line, write the letter of the word or phrase that is* closest *in meaning to the Word List word.*

1. synonymous
   A. original
   B. imaginary
   C. linguistic
   D. similar

2. derive
   A. trace
   B. steer
   C. theorize
   D. question

3. speculation
   A. conjecture
   B. significance
   C. attempt
   D. conclusion

4. coinage
   A. pronunciation
   B. trial
   C. invention
   D. novelty

Name _____ Date _____

Support for Writing

Use the chart below to help you prepare to write an essay on a word or phrase in English that you find interesting, odd or funny. Fill in the blanks in the chart to help you organize the results of your research on the word you have chosen.

The word I have chosen to write about is _____.

Why I find the word odd, interesting, or funny	
Origins of the word	
Earliest known appearance or usage in English	
Changes in meaning over the years	

Now, on a separate piece of paper, use the results of your research to write a rough draft of your essay on the origin and evolution of the word you have chosen. Try to use idiomatic language to help to create an informal tone of the kind Safire uses in his essay.

Name _____ Date _____

Enrichment

In "Onomatopoeia," William Safire explains the Greek origins of the word *onomatopoeia*. Many much more commonly used English words come from ancient Greek words or word parts as well. Knowing some of these common Greek word origins can help you to figure out the meanings of many English words.

DIRECTIONS: *The following chart lists English words derived from ancient Greek words or parts of words. In a dictionary, look up the meaning and derivation of each word, and fill in the information on the chart.*

Word	Ancient Greek Origin	Present-Day English Meaning
allegory		
barbarian		
nemesis		
narcissist		
hector		
mentor		

Name _____ Date _____

"Onomatopoeia" by William Safire
Open-Book Test

Short Answer *Write your responses to the questions in this section on the lines provided.*

1. Based on Safire's definition of the term *onomatopoeia*, give your own example of this kind of word.

   _____

   _____

2. There are several kinds of essays. In "Onomatopoeia," Safire explains how writers use onomatopoeia in their work. What kind of essay is "Onomatopoeia"?

   _____

   _____

3. In your own words, paraphrase Safire's definition of the word *onomatopoeia*.

   _____

   _____

4. In "Onomatopoeia," what special quality of the word *zap* interests Safire so much?

   _____

   _____

5. By mentioning the words *imitative* and *echoic* in the first paragraph of "Onomatopoeia," Safire is using what technique to help explain the meaning of *onomatopoeia*?

   _____

   _____

6. In an expository essay, an author explains a topic. In "Onomatopoeia," Safire explains the origin, meaning, and significance of onomatopoeia through several techniques: He states a main point and then gives reasons, facts, and examples to support or explain that point. Use the chart below to give three examples of how Safire uses this expository technique in his essay. (You may not have to fill in every box in the chart to do a thorough job.)

	Main Point:	**Main Point:**
Reasons		
Facts		
Examples		

7. Paraphrase the "pooh-pooh theory" of language as presented by Safire in the third paragraph of "Onomatopoeia."

_____

_____

_____

8. What two examples of onomatopoeia does Safire use in the following sentence from "Onomatopoeia"?

> The verb will live long after superpowers agree to ban ray guns; no sound thunders or crackles like an imaginary sound turned into a new word.

_____

_____

_____

9. In your own words, state the meaning of *zap* as it is used in the last paragraph of "Onomatopoeia," in which Ellen Goodman describes how she zaps commercials while watching television.

_____

_____

_____

10. If you based your answer to a social-studies essay question on *speculation*, would you have a good grasp of the subject matter? Why or why not? Base your answer on the meaning of *speculation* as it is used in "Onomatopoeia."

_____

_____

_____

Essay

Write an extended response to the question of your choice or to the question or questions your teacher assigns you.

11. "Onomatopoeia" is an expository essay. In a brief essay of your own, explain what an expository essay is and how "Onomatopoeia" fulfills the criteria of that kind of essay. Support your answer with examples from "Onomatopoeia."

12. Write a brief expository essay on a topic of your choice in which you make liberal use of onomatopoeia to make your point (use at least three examples in your essay). Your essay should clearly identify a main topic and explain it with appropriate examples, facts, and logic.

13. In "Onomatopoeia," William Safire discusses two theories of the origin of language: the "bow-wow theory" and the "pooh-pooh theory." In an essay, paraphrase each of these theories, and then give your opinion about which theory offers a more likely and persuasive account of the origin of language. Support your opinion with clear reasoning and specific examples.

14. **Thinking About the Essential Question: What Makes American Literature American?** In "Onomatopoeia," William Safire reflects on the origins and contemporary uses of onomatopoeia. Does his essay make this device seem like a uniquely American mode of expression or one that is more universal? What role does his analysis of the word *zap* play in this discussion? Develop your thoughts in an essay supported by clear reasoning and relevant details and examples.

Oral Response

15. Go back to question 1, 3, or 5 or to the question your teacher assigns you. Take a few minutes to expand your answer and prepare an oral response. Find additional details in "Onomatopoeia" that support your points. If necessary, make notes to guide your oral response.

Onomatopoeia, by William Safire
Selection Test A

MULTIPLE CHOICE

Critical Reading *Identify the letter of the choice that best answers the question.*

____ 1. What kind of essay is William Safire's "Onomatopoeia," which explains how writers use onomatopoeia in their work?

    A. an analytical essay that breaks down a topic into separate parts

    B. a satirical essay that uses humor to comment on a topic

    C. a personal essay that shares the author's feelings

    D. an expository essay that explains a topic

____ 2. What is the meaning of the word *onomatopoeia,* according to William Safire's essay of the same name?

    A. words that rhyme, such as "jail" and "fail".

    B. words used in comic books, such as "Batman"

    C. words that sound like what they mean, such as "crunch"

    D. words used in historical times, such as "thee" and "thou"

____ 3. Which of these words is an example of onomatopoeia?

    A. language   **C.** crackle

    B. poetry   **D.** animal

____ 4. In his essay "Onomatopoeia," with which of these writers does Safire associate the onomatopoetic word *hurlyburly?*

    A. Ellen Goodman   **C.** Henry Peacham

    B. Edgar Allan Poe   **D.** Gertrude Stein

____ 5. In his essay "Onomatopoeia," the word *zap* interests Safire because it

    A. imitates an imaginary noise.

    B. sounds like the action of a ray gun.

    C. is a relatively new example of onomtopoeia.

    D. has many different uses.

____ 6. Read the following sentence from Willam Safire's essay "Onomatopoeia":

> The coinage filled a need for an unheard sound and—*pow!*—slammed the vocabulary right in the kisser.

Which of the following word groups in the sentence is an example of an idiom?

    A. the coinage filled a need

    B. for an unheard sound

    C. the vocabulary

    D. right in the kisser

154

___ 7. In his essay "Onomatopoeia," what is the most likely reason that Safire includes mention of the *bow-wow theory* and the *pooh-pooh theory?*

    A. He wants readers to evaluate both theories

    B. He wants to entertain readers.

    C. He wants to persuade readers to take both theories seriously.

    D. He wants to satirize Edgar Allan Poe.

___ 8. Which of the following is the best paraphrase of the *pooh-pooh theory,* as it is explained by Safire in "Onomatopoeia"?

    A. Language began with interjections like *oof!*

    B. Language began with the imitation of animal sounds.

    C. There is no way we can tell how onomatopoetic words developed.

    D. Gertrude Stein was obsessive in her interest in onomatopoetic words.

___ 9. According to Safire in his essay "Onomatopoeia," how many pronunciations do the letters *poe* have?

    A. 1   **C.** 3

    B. 2   **D.** 4

___ 10. According to Safire, all the following words are usual examples of onomatopoeia *except*

    A. hiss   **C.** buzz

    B. babble `   **D.** chaos

___ 11. Based on the discussion of onomatopoeia in Safire's essay, which of the following words is onomatopoetic?

    A. murmur   **C.** lovely

    B. funny   **D.** stroll

___ 12. Which of the following correctly defines "idioms," as they are used in Safire's essay "Onomatopoeia"?

    A. similes that include words such as "like" or "as"

    B. symbols that stand for both themselves and something outside themselves

    C. informal expressions that mean something other than their literal meaning

    D. words borrowed from foreign languages

___ 13. In William Safire's essay "Onomatopoeia," what is the main idea of the concluding quotation from Ellen Goodman?

    A. The word *zap* has no precise meaning.

    B. Zapping TV commercials gives a person satisfaction.

    C. There are too many commericls on TV.

    D. Zapping commercials may mean the end of the TV industry.

_____ **14.** Judging from Safire's discussion in his essay, to which of the senses do ono-matopoetic words appeal most?

    A. hearing   **C.** touch

    B. sight   **D.** taste

_____ **15.** In the essay "Onomatopoeia," how would you describe the writer's overall tone, or attitude toward the subject matter and the audience?

    A. satirical   **C.** humorous

    B. pessimistic   **D.** scholarly

Vocabulary

_____ **16.** Which of the following is the best substitute for the word *derive* in this sen-tence: "We *derive* the word 'poetry' from an ancient Greek word"?

    A. get from a source   **C.** symbolize

    B. interpret   **D.** quote

_____ **17.** A *coinage* is a word or expression that has been

    A. often quoted.   **C.** interpreted as a symbol.

    B. classified as an idiom.   **D.** made up or invented.

Essay

18. Why can William Safire's essay "Onomatopoeia" be considered an expository piece of writing? In a brief essay of your own, define the term "expository essay." Then, use details from the selection to explain why it is a piece of expository writing.

19. In an essay, discuss William Safire's use of idioms in his essay "Onomatopoeia" to entertain the reader and to give his essay a certain tone. Begin by defining the term "idiom." Then identify and discuss at least two idioms in the selection, explaining the tone that these expressions create.

20. **Thinking About the Essential Question: What makes American literature American?** In "Onomatopoeia," William Safire reflects on the meaning and uses of onomatopoeia. Does his essay make this device seem uniquely American, or does Safire portray onomatopoeia as more universal? Consider particularly his remarks about the onomatopoetic word *zap*. Develop your thoughts in an essay supported by clear reasoning and relevant details and examples.

Onomatopoeia, by William Safire
Selection Test B

MULTIPLE CHOICE

Critical Reading *Identify the letter of the choice that best answers the question.*

____ 1. William Safire begins his essay "Onomatopoeia" with which of the following?
  A. a literary allusion   **C.** a timeline
  B. a definition   **D.** a paraphrase

____ 2. The main purpose of an expository essay is to inform readers. Another likely purpose of Safire's "Onomatopoeia" is to
  A. evaluate   **C.** entertain
  B. persuade   **D.** reflect

____ 3. According to William Safire, the first person to use and define the word *onomatopoeia* in English was which of the following?
  A. Ellen Goodman   **C.** Edgar Allan Poe
  B. Willard Espy   **D.** Henry Peacham

____ 4. According to Safire in "Onomatopoeia." the onomatopoetic word *hurlyburly* means
  A. uproar   **C.** circle
  B. problem   **D.** postponement

____ 5. Which of the following is the best paraphrase of the *bow-wow theory* described by Safire in "Onomatopoeia"?
  A. Words took shape in imitation of natural sounds.
  B. Words originated in nonsense speech.
  C. Words imitated imaginary noises.
  D. We cannot tell how words originally took shape.

____ 6. According to Safire in his essay "Onomatopoeia," how many pronunciations do the letters *poe* have?
  A. 1   **B.** 2   **C.** 3   **D.** 4

____ 7. Read the following sentence from William Safire's essay "Onomatopoeia":
  The coinage filled the need for an unhead sound and—*pow!*—slammed the vocabulary right in the kisser.

  Which of the following best describes the phrase "right in the kisser"?
  A. metaphor   **C.** hyperbole
  B. simile   **D.** idiom

____ 8. Read the following passage from Safire's "Onomatopoeia":
  . . . in the crunch (a word imitating the sound of an icebreaker breaking through ice) Gertrude Stein turned into an *onomatomaniac.*

  Which of the following is the best equivalent for the idiom "in the crunch"?
  A. from time to time
  B. at the scene of the accident
  C. going to extremes
  D. in a manner of speaking

____ 9. In "Onomatopoeia," why does William Safire find the word *zap* so interesting?
   A. It has an unusual spelling.
   B. It imitates an imaginary noise.
   C. It was invented in the 1600s.
   D. It was borrowed from an ancient language.

____ 10. What is the most likely reason for William Safire's use of idioms in "Onomatotopoeia"?
   A. to create a breezy, informal tone
   B. to show connections between literal and figurative language
   C. to prove that most idioms are onomatopoetic
   D. to confuse the reader

____ 11. According to Safire, all the following words are usual examples of onomatopoeia *except*
   A. hiss   **C.** buzz
   B. babble   **D.** chaosl

____ 12. What is the most likely reason that Safire includes the quotation from Ellen Goodman at the end of "Onomatopoeia"?
   A. Ellen Goodman is a well-known linguistic expert.
   B. Ellen Goodman offers specific support for Safire's analysis.
   C. The quotation serves to end the essay on a humorous note.
   D. Ellen Goodman uses a variety of onomatopoetic words in the quotation.

____ 13. Which of the following words is an example of onomatopoeia?
   A. language   **C.** crackle
   B. poetry   **D.** animal

____ 14. What organizational method does William Safire use in the body of his essay, "Onomatopoeia"?
   A. spatial order
   B. comparison-and-contrast order
   C. chronological order
   D. cause-and-effect organization

____ 15. How would you describe the writer's overall tone, or the attitude toward the subject matter and the audience, in "Onomatopoeia"?
   A. scholarly   **C.** critical
   B. humorous   **D.** tentative

____ 16. Judging from the discussion of Safire in his essay, to which of the senses do onomatopoetic words appeal most?
   A. taste   **C.** hearing
   B. sight   **D.** touch

____ 17. Which of the following sources did William Safire most likely consult to research the information he includes in his essay?
   A. dictiomnary   **C.** almanac
   B. newspaper article   **D.** interview

Vocabulary

____ 18. In which sentence below is the word *synonymous* used correctly?
   A. The word *contemptuous* is synonymous with *scornful.*
   B. Words with opposite meanings can be called synonymous.
   C. The word *prudent* is synonymous with *reckless.*
   D. Onomatopoetic words are usually synonymous.

____ 19. Which of the following is the best substitute for the word *speculation* in this sentence: "How words originally took shape is a matter of much *speculation* among language experts"?
   A. emphasis   C. humor
   B. thought or conjecture   D. irrational theory

Essay

20. In a brief essay, explain why "Onomatopoeia" by William Safire can be classified as expository writing. Begin by defining the term "expository essay." Then, support your main points by citing specific details from the selection.

21. In an essay, discuss the ways in which William Safire uses idioms in his essay "Onomatopoeia," both to convey his own ideas and to entertain the reader. Support your main ideas with specific references to the essay, citing at least three idioms from the text.

22. William Safire clearly believes that language can be fun. In an essay, discuss some of the ways that Safire reveals unexpected features of language in "Onomatopoeia" and makes his subject entertaining. Be sure to support your main ideas with specific references to the selection.

23. **Thinking About the Essential Question: What makes American literature American?**
   In "Onomatopoeia," William Safire reflects on the origins and contemporary uses of onomatopoeia. Does his essay make this device seem like a uniquely American mode of expression or one that is more universal? What role does his analysis of the word zap play in this discussion? Develop your thoughts in an essay supported by clear reasoning and relevant details and examples.

Study these words from the selections. Then, complete the activities.

Word List A

combustion [kuhm BUS chuhn] *n.* the act or process of burning
Combustion requires a combination of oxygen and fuel.

detonation [det uhn AY shuhn] *n.* explosion
The soldiers heard the detonation of the bomb from a mile away.

detriment [DE truh muhnt] *n.* disadvantage; damage; harm
To the detriment of many people, the country's borders were sealed shut.

disintegration [dis in tuh GRAY shuhn] *n.* falling or coming apart into tiny bits that cannot be put back together
Ten families moved, resulting in the disintegration of our neighborhood.

liability [ly uh BIL uh tee] *n.* responsibility for loss and damage
The judge determined that Jack's employer had liability for the accident.

nonexistent [nahn eg ZIS tuhnt] *adj.* not present; not existing now
We looked for pots and pans, but they were nonexistent; there were none.

silhouette [sil uh WET] *n.* the outline of a thing, or person
The artist quickly and accurately drew Juan's silhouette.

veered [VEERD] *v.* shifted direction
Thank goodness Isabel veered right to avoid the oncoming car.

Word List B

affixed [uh FIXT] *v.* fastened; attached
Gerald affixed postage stamps to the enormous box before mailing it.

compressed [kuhm PREST] *adj.* made smaller by the use of pressure
A compressed sponge has been squashed to a fraction of its original size.

eligible [EL i juh buhl] *adj.* qualified for
The school said Kim's good grades made her eligible to play athletics.

encumbered [en KUM berd] *v.* burdened by; laden with; hindered by
Janice was encumbered by three heavy suitcases.

implications [im pli KAY shuhns] *n.* things indicated or suggested
With dark clouds overhead, the implications are that a storm is imminent.

premature [pree muh CHOO(lig)R] *adj.* too early; arriving or occurring before a thing is ready
His thank-you speech was premature, since he had not yet been elected.

subsequently [SUB si kwent lee] *adv.* following afterwards
Jack fell down and, subsequently, Jill tumbled after him.

virtual [VER choo uhl] *adj.* essentially equivalent to; in effect; almost the same thing as
Luis took care of the Whites' dog so often that he was its virtual owner.

Name _____ Date _____

Native American Origin Myths from the Onondaga, Modoc, Navajo, and Iroquois
Vocabulary Warm-up Exercises

Exercise A *Fill in the blanks, using each word from Word List A only once.*

Millie was always tinkering in the garage with her chemistry set. One unfortunate after-noon, to the [1] _____ of the garage door that became singed, she mixed several chemicals by mistake. They exploded, and the loud [2] _____ could be heard up and down her street. Mr. Smith, who was in his car at the time, [3] _____ off the road and smashed into the Pickering's garbage cans. Luckily, a few seconds before the [4] _____ of the chemicals, Millie had walked back inside her house to search for an extra glass jar. She rushed back to the garage with a fire extinguisher. There was so much smoke that, when the fire depart-ment arrived, only Millie's [5] _____ was outlined in the smoke. The acci-dent resulted in the [6] _____ of most of Millie's equipment, which lay in tiny pieces all over. The fire chief soon declared that the danger of further explosions was [7] _____. He reminded Millie of her [8] _____ for the damage done to her house, and she agreed to restrict her further experiments to a well-appointed laboratory.

Exercise B *Decide whether each statement below is true or false. Circle T or F, and explain your answer.*

1. If you have <u>compressed</u> a pile of laundry, you have enlarged it.
   T / F _____

2. A person who is <u>eligible</u> to vote is allowed to cast a ballot.
   T / F _____

3. If a baby is <u>premature</u>, it has been born too late.
   T / F _____

4. If you <u>subsequently</u> write a note, it means you write the note afterwards.
   T / F _____

5. If the <u>implications</u> are that it will snow, that means it is certain to happen.
   T / F _____

6. A label that has been <u>affixed</u> to a jar has been removed from it completely.
   T / F _____

7. A meeting <u>encumbered</u> by speakers has too many of them on its schedule.
   T / F _____

8. A <u>virtual</u> cat is the same as a real cat.
   T / F _____

"Coyote v. Acme" by Ian Frazier
Reading Warm-up A

Read the following passage. Then, complete the activities.

When Uncle Oscar retired, he looked around for a part-time occupation. A company that made electronic toys offered him a two-month trial job as a field tester. They also mailed him a stack of forms to sign, basically saying the company assumed no <u>liability</u>, or responsibility, if he were to become injured during the toy testing process.

Everyone in the family told Uncle Oscar he would be nuts to sign forms like that but he waved us all off impatiently, insisting he could think of no <u>detriment</u> or disadvantage to signing. As far as he was concerned, the dangers to him were <u>nonexistent</u>. Nothing would happen to him and, in the unlikely event that anything did, he had excellent health insurance.

The company shipped him ten copies of their new remote-controlled car. Uncle Oscar knew I loved these and invited me to help out. My mother agreed, but only if I stood at least twenty feet away while the cars were in motion. After we got everything ready in Uncle Oscar's back yard, we chuckled as I followed my mother's wishes and stood back.

The loud "boom" sound of the <u>detonation</u> shook the windows in Uncle Oscar's house. He had <u>veered</u> away as the first test car exploded; he must have dived onto the grass. He was so covered with soot that all I could see was the outline of his gray <u>silhouette</u>.

It was unclear how a chemical reaction like <u>combustion</u> could have occurred in a battery-operated car. But its <u>disintegration</u> was complete, as the car had broken into a thousand pieces.

Uncle Oscar, who escaped with only cuts and bruises, spent little time wondering how it all happened. He packed up the remaining cars and shipped them back to the company with his resignation.

1. Circle the word that gives a clue to the meaning of <u>liability</u>. Explain why the toy company would want Uncle Oscar to sign forms saying they it had no *liability* if he was injured.

2. Underline the word that is a synonym for <u>detriment</u>. Write another synonym for the word *detriment*.

3. Circle the phrase that hints at the meaning of <u>nonexistent</u>. Write an antonym for the word *nonexistent*.

4. Circle the word in a nearby sentence that has a meaning similar to <u>detonation</u>. What did the *detonation* do to Uncle Oscar's house?

5. Underline the phrase that tells what Uncle Oscar must have done when he <u>veered</u>. What is the opposite of *veered*?

6. Circle the word that helps to explain the meaning of <u>silhouette</u>. Write a sentence using the word *silhouette*.

7. Underline the words that tell what <u>combustion</u> is. Give an example of *combustion* that is useful in everyday life.

8. Underline the words that help to explain the meaning of <u>disintegration</u>. Write your own definition for the word *disintegration*.

"Coyote v. Acme" by Ian Frazier
Reading Warm-up B

Read the following passage. Then, complete the activities.

People who practice law in the United States are called attorneys-at-law or, more commonly, 'lawyers.' They advise clients about legal matters and can also act on their clients' behalf in any situation that has to do with the laws governing our country.

Have you ever thought about becoming a lawyer? People pick their careers at all ages, and some people switch careers when they are well into adulthood. However, it is not necessarily <u>premature</u>, or too early, to think about the <u>implications</u> of making the choice to pursue a career in law.

One thing to consider is whether or not you might feel <u>encumbered</u> by the prospect of many years of study. Does the idea of attending both college and graduate school seem like a burden? If so, it may be best to seek a different line of work. The time it takes to learn the law thoroughly cannot be easily shortened or <u>compressed</u>. In this country, anyone who has <u>affixed</u> the letters J.D. to his or her name, for 'Juris Doctor,' had to graduate from both college and law school.

<u>Subsequently</u>, after obtaining a law degree, a young lawyer must pass exams and be certified as having good moral character in order to become <u>eligible</u> to practice. The main test is called the bar exam. Lawyers qualify to practice by passing the bar exam in the state where they intend to work.

Some people consider a law degree a <u>virtual</u> passport to other fields of work, like politics and business. In fact, legal training can be helpful to people who wish to become investment bankers, entrepreneurs, journalists, or administrators. A thorough knowledge of the law is useful in a multitude of exciting professions.

1. Circle the words that are a synonym for <u>premature</u>. Write a sentence using the word *premature*.

2. Underline the phrase referred to by the word <u>implications</u>. Name one of the *implications* of studying law mentioned in this passage.

3. Circle the word in a nearby sentence that has a meaning similar to <u>encumbered</u>. Write an antonym for the word *encumbered*.

4. Circle the word that gives a clue to the meaning of <u>compressed</u>. Write an *antonym* for the word *compressed*.

5. Underline the words that tell what a person who has graduated from law school may have <u>affixed</u>. Write a synonym for the word *affixed*.

6. Underline the phrase referred to by the word <u>subsequently</u>. Write your own definition for the word *subsequently*.

7. Circle the word in a nearby sentence that has a meaning similar to <u>eligible</u>. Write a sentence telling about something you hope to become *eligible* for.

8. Underline the word described by <u>virtual</u>. Write a sentence using the word *virtual*.

"Coyote v. Acme" by Ian Frazier
Literary Analysis: Parody

A **parody** is a humorous piece of writing that mocks the characteristics of a literary form, a specific work, or the style of a certain writer. Through the use of exaggeration, a parody calls attention to ridiculous elements of the original, particularly those that have become clichés.

DIRECTIONS: *On the lines following each of the passages from "Coyote v. Acme," explain what is exaggerated and/or ridiculous in the passage and how those elements add to the humor of the parody.*

1. My client, Mr. Wile E. Coyote, a resident of Arizona and contiguous states, does hereby bring suit for damages against the Acme Company. . . ."

_____

_____

_____

2. "Such injuries sustained by Mr. Coyote have temporarily restricted his ability to make a living in his profession of predator. Mr. Coyote is self-employed and thus not eligible for Workmen's Compensation."

_____

_____

_____

3. "As Mr. Coyote gripped the handlebars, the Rocket Sled accelerated with such sudden and precipitate force as to stretch Mr. Coyote's forelimbs to a length of fifty feet."

_____

_____

_____

4. "The sequence of collisions resulted in systemic physical damage to Mr. Coyote, viz., flattening of the cranium, sideways displacement of the tongue, reduction of length of the legs and upper body, and compression of vertebrae from base of tail to head."

_____

_____

_____

5. "Mr. Coyote respectfully requests that the Court regard these larger economic implications and assess punitive damages in the amount of seventeen million dollars. In addition, Mr. Coyote seeks actual damages (missed meals, medical expenses, days lost from professional occupation) of one million dollars. . . ."

_____

_____

_____

Name _____ Date _____

"Coyote v. Acme" by Ian Frazier
Reading Strategy: Cause and Effect

As a parody of a legal argument, this essay is organized using **cause-and-effect text structure.** To analyze cause and effect, look for words and phrases that signal those relationships, such as *subsequently, as a result,* and *resulted in.*

DIRECTIONS: *Use the chart below to analyze examples of cause-and-effect text structure in "Coyote v. Acme." For each example given, identify the key word or phrase that signals the cause/effect relationship, the cause(s), and the effect(s).*

Example	Key Word or Phrase	Cause(s)	Effect(s)
1. "Mr. Coyote is self-employed and thus not eligible for Workmen's compensation."			
2. "Mr. Coyote vigorously attempted to follow this maneuver but was unable to, due to poorly designed steering system on the Rocket Sled and a faulty or nonexistent braking system."			
3. "The force of this impact then caused the springs to rebound, whereupon Mr. Coyote was thrust skyward."			
4. The sequence of collisions resulted in systemic physical damage to Mr. Coyote, viz., flattening of the cranium, sideways displacement of the tongue. . . .			

Name _____ Date _____

"Coyote v. Acme" by Ian Frazier
Vocabulary Builder

Using the Latin Root Word *Corpus*

A. DIRECTIONS: *Knowing that the Latin root word corpus means "body," circle the letter of the best synonym for each word*

1. *corpulent*　　A. official　　B. competent　　C. fat　　D. distant
2. *corpse*　　A. cadaver　　B. officer　　C. precedent　　D. ground
3. *corporate*　　A. combined　　B. light　　C. profitable　　D. risky

Using the Word List

contiguous　emit　incorporated　precipitate　punitive　systemic

B. DIRECTIONS: *For each of the following items, choose the Word List word that best completes the meaning of the sentence. Circle the letter of your choice.*

1. The United States has a large _____ contiguous border with Canada.
   A. incorporated　　B. contiguous　　C. precipitate　　D. punitive

2. In addition to compensation for the flaws in the product, the plaintiff sought _____ damages as well to deter the company from making shoddy products in the future.
   A. incorporated　　B. contiguous　　C. precipitate　　D. punitive

3. I was so angry with my boss that I was tempted to give him a piece of my mind, but my colleague wisely advised me to cool down and avoid any _____ actions that I might regret later.
   A. incorporated　　B. contiguous　　C. precipitate　　D. punitive

4. The electric-generating plant seemed to _____ a strange odor at night.
   A. incorporated　　B. contiguous　　C. systemic　　D. emit

5. After receiving my rough draft back from the teacher, I _____ all her suggestions in my final draft.
   A. incorporated　　B. contiguous　　C. systemic　　D. emit

6. My doctor advised me that my symptoms were not serious and were not due to any _____ disorder.
   A. incorporated　　B. contiguous　　C. systemic　　D. emit

"**Coyote v. Acme**" by Ian Frazier
Support for Writing

In his satirical essay "Coyote v. Acme," Frazier parodies aspects of the legal profession. Working in groups as teams of attorneys defending the Acme Company, develop a response to the arguments presented in "Coyote v. Acme."

Prewriting   Work together to come up with effective responses to the main arguments presented in the essay. Use the following suggested starting points as an aid in organizing your thoughts.

1. The plaintiff Coyote misused Acme's products in the following ways:

   _____

   _____

   _____

   _____

   _____

2. Acme's products are reliable when used as recommended because . . .

   _____

   _____

   _____

   _____

   _____

3. Acme's products have a record of being used safely and effectively by . . .

   _____

   _____

   _____

   _____

   _____

After you have gathered and thought out your best counterarguments to Coyote's brief, Prepare an **opening statement** for the defense. Use your most convincing response to address each of the essay's main arguments. Mimic the exaggerated style of the original piece to add humor and irony.

Name _____ Date _____

"**Coyote v. Acme**" by Ian Frazier

Enrichment: Social Studies

As in many modern nations, the legal system of the United States consists of two main branches of law—criminal and civil. Criminal law involves offenses considered detrimental to society, such as murder, armed robbery, rape, arson, and kidnapping. Civil law determines wrongs individuals commit against one another, including disputes over contracts or property or intentional or accidental injuries.

A civil case begins when the plaintiff, either an individual or organization, files a complaint against another individual or organization, known as the defendant. A complaint states the wrong the defendant has committed against the plaintiff and asks for a certain amount of money in damages. The following flow chart shows the general process of a civil court case.

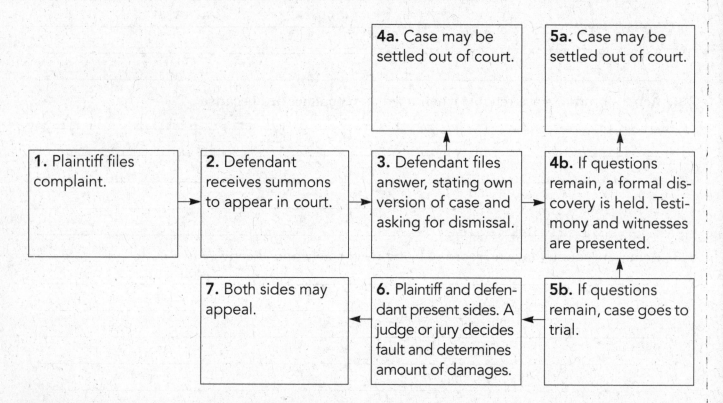

DIRECTIONS: *Use the information on this page and details from "Coyote v. Acme" to answer the following questions.*

1. Is Coyote v. Acme a criminal or civil case? Why?

_____

2. What stage in the case proceedings does the essay "Coyote v. Acme" represent?

_____

3. What answer might the defendant have given in Coyote v. Acme?

_____

_____

Name _____ Date _____

"**Coyote v. Acme**" by Ian Frazier
Open-Book Test

Short Answer *Write your responses to the questions in this section on the lines provided.*

1. "Coyote v. Acme" is a parody of a well-known formal kind of document. What kind of formal document is parodied in this selection?

   _____

   _____

2. According to the opening paragraph of "Coyote v. Acme," what is the direct cause of Wile E. Coyote's "personal injuries, loss of business income, and mental suffering"?

   _____

   _____

3. A satirical essay uses parody to make its points. In the second paragraph of "Coyote v. Acme," what two details describing Wile E. Coyote's professional status make clear the satirical nature of the selection?

   _____

   _____

   _____

4. The third paragraph of "Coyote v. Acme," uses elements of parody to detail the injuries Coyote sustained from the use of the supposedly defective Rocket Sled. Use the chart to record some of these details. Then tell what elements of parody Frazier used.

Detail From the Parody	Element of Parody used

5. In paragraph six of "Coyote v. Acme," how does the author's use of language heighten the satirical effect of the description of Coyote's mishaps with Acme's explosive devices?

   _____

   _____

   _____

6. What disadvantage in his pursuit of Road Runner does Wile E. Coyote seek to over-come with his use of Acme Products? What character flaw of Wile E. Coyote is evident in his repeated use of these products despite the constant disastrous results?

_____

_____

7. As part of a cause-and-effect analysis of the lawyer's case in "Coyote v. Acme," explain what purpose is served by the presentation of exhibits?

_____

_____

8. After describing a horrific series of injuries caused by Coyote's use of the Acme Spring-Powered Shoes near the end of the essay, the brief states Mr. Coyote now emits "an off-key accordion-like wheezing with every step." According to the brief, because of this condition Mr. Coyote can no longer pursue a "normal social life." What characteristic of satire is evident in this last statement? Explain your answer.

_____

_____

_____

_____

9. What characteristic of contemporary lawsuits is parodied in the last paragraph of "Coyote v. Acme"?

_____

_____

_____

10. If the map showed that two countries were *contiguous*, would they be right next to each other? Why or why not? Explain your answer, based on the meaning of *contiguous* as it is used in "Coyote v. Acme"

_____

_____

Essay

Write an extended response to the question of your choice or to the question or questions your teacher assigns you.

11. "Coyote v. Acme" is a parody of a legal complaint by Wile E. Coyote against the Acme Company because of the many disastrous malfunctions of the products he has purchased from them in his quest to capture Road Runner. Have you ever owned something that did not work to your satisfaction—a TV, a telephone, a piece of athletic equipment, a tool? Write an essay in which you lay out your legal complaint against the company that makes the product. Use facts, examples, and clear reasoning in your legal brief, which can take the form of a serious complaint or a parody.

12. "Coyote vs. Acme" details the spectacular and hilarious disasters that befall Wile E. Coyote in his chronic use and abuse of the products of the Acme Company during his futile attempts to capture Road Runner. The legal brief, of course, takes the form of a parody. In an essay, write a responding brief from the Acme Company, challenging the validity of the complaints and arguments of the lawyer for Wile E. Coyote. In your response—which can adopt a serious or satirical tone—you should address the specific details and line of reasoning used in Wile E. Coyote's legal brief. Feel free to use your imagination if you wish to make up "facts" to counter the details used in the selection.

13. "Coyote v. Acme" is a satirical essay. A satirical essay uses irony, ridicule, parody, or sarcasm to comment on a topic. In an essay, explain the topic or topics that are targeted in "Coyote v. Acme." Does the essay refer just to the Road Runner cartoon series or to serious issues in the real world? If so, how does it address these issues? Explain your answer in an essay based on details from the selection, facts, and clear reasoning.

14. **Thinking About the Essential Question: How does literature shape or reflect society?** "Coyote v. Acme" aims its satire at a number of social targets. In particular, what does this satire reflect about the state of the American legal system? Does it merely seek to reflect and parody a set of problems, or does the satire imply that there are other ways to behave? Explain your answer in an essay supported by specific examples and clear reasoning.

Oral Response

15. Go back to question 2, 5, or 6 or to the question your teacher assigns you. Take a few minutes to expand your answer and prepare an oral response. Find additional details in "Coyote v. Acme" that support your points. If necessary, make notes to guide your oral response.

Coyote v. Acme, by Ian Frazier
Selection Test A

MULTIPLE CHOICE

Critical Reading *Identify the letter of the choice that best answers the question.*

____ 1. In "Coyote v. Acme," Ian Frazier uses parody to create satire. Which of the following correctly defines *parody?*
  A. a humorous imitation
  B. a figure of speech
  C. exaggeration
  D. a reflective essay

____ 2. Much of Ian Frazier's "Coyote v. Acme" consists of descriptions of products that have not worked well or that have injured Coyote. Which of the following best describes the text structure of the selection?
  A. comparison-and-contrast   C. cause-and-effect
  B. spatial order   D. chronological order

____ 3. In "Coyote v. Acme," which of the following is the basis for Mr. Coyote's lawsuit?
  A. The Acme company ruined Mr. Coyote's reputation.
  B. The Acme Company sold Mr. Coyote defective priodcts.
  C. The Acme Company overcharged Mr. Coyote for his purchases.
  D. The Acme Company claimed that the warranty on the products had expired.

____ 4. In "Coyote v. Acme" by Ian Frazier, which of the following serves as the speaker or narrator in the selection?
  A. Mr. Coyote
  B. Judge Joan Kujava
  C. the president of the Acme Company
  D. Harold Schoff, the attorney for Mr. Coyote

____ 5. Read the following passage from "Coyote v. Acme":
  Such injuries sustained by Mr. Coyote have temporarily restricted his ability to make a living in his profession as predator.

  Satire is writing that r idicules or holds up to contempt the faults of individuals or groups. What is satirical about this passage?
  A. the identification of Mr. Coyote, who claims to have been a victiim, as a predator
  B. the idea that Mr. Coyote sustained injuries
  C. the idea that Mr. Coyote has a profession
  D. the concept that Mr. Coyote was temporarily restricted

____ 6. In "Coyote v. Acme," Exhibits A-D consist of sales slips, a doctor's report, the Acme mail order catalogue, and the remains of a pair of shoes. What is the purpose of these exhibits?

    A. They summarize the different incidents involving Acme products.

    B. They suppoert the attorney's line of reasoning.

    C. They illustrate Mr. Coyote's injuries.

    D. They emphasize the seriousness of the lawsuit.

____ 7. In "Coyote v. Acme," Mr. Coyote is said to have made 85 different purchases from the Acme Company. Many of the products sold to Mr. Coyote have injured him, however. According to his lawyer, why has Mr. Coyote continued to buy products from Acme?

    A. He has no other source of the goods he needs for his "profession" as predator.

    B. He is always eager to try a new product.

    C. Acme's telephone marketing staff has persuaded him to keep buying new products.

    D. Acme's prices are so low as to be appealing to Mr. Coyote.

____ 8. According to his attorney in "Coyote v. Acme," what does Mr. Coyote want the court to do?

    A. shut down the Acme Company

    B. award him $38,750,000 in damages

    C. Tsend the president of Acme to jail

    D. fine Acme $1 million

____ 9. Whom or what is the author satirizing in "Coyote v. Acme," in which a cartoon character sues a company?

    A. "Roadrunner" cartoons   **C.** the legal profession

    B. doctors   **D.** poorly made products

____ 10. What reason is given in "Coyote v. Acme" to justify the lawsuit?

    A. Coyote has paid too much for Acme products.   **C.** Coyote has been unable to catch the Roadrunner.

    B. Coyote has been repeatedly injured by Acme products.   **D.** Coyote has been overcharged by his lawyers.

____ 11. Since "Coyote v. Acme" is based on "Roadrunner" cartoons, in which the coyote is always getting hurt, what conclusion can you draw about these cartoons?

    A. They are not very funny.   **C.** They are old-fasioned.

    B. They are violent.   **D.** They are well animated.

___ 12. Read the following passage from "Coyote v. Acme":

> Encumbered by his heavy casts, Mr. Coyote lost control of the Rocket Skates soon after strapping them on, and collided with a roadside billboard so violently as to leave a hole in the shape of his full silhouette.

Which of the following techniques does Frazier use in this passage?

A. flashback　　　B. foreshadowing　C. exaggeration　　D. simile

___ 13. In "Coyote v. Acme," Ian Frazier uses parody to create satire. Which of the following is most likely the purpose of the author's satire in the selection?

A. to poke fun at the legal profession and at unreasonablel awsuits

B. to show that the legal profession needs reform

C. to satirize cartoons like the "Roadrunner" series

D. to suggest that companies like Acme are poorly organized

___ 14. The tone of a selection is the author's overall attitude toward the subject matter, the characters, or the audience. Which of the following best describes the tone of "Coyote v. Acme"?

A. sad　　　　　B. humorous　　　C. angry　　　　　D. neutral

Vocabulary

___ 15. Which of the following is the best substitute for the word *emit* in this sentence: "The heart monitor machine was set to *emit* regular beeping sounds"?

A. send out　　　B. register　　　C. circulate　　　D. sustain

___ 16. In which of the following sentences is the word *systemic* used correctly?

A. *Systemic* injuries affected the hospital patient's entire body.

B. The highway was crowded with *systemic* traffic.

C. The math test was so *systemic* that Luke knew he had not studied enough.

D. Clare's oral report was *systemic* in its approach.

Essay

17. In "Coyote v. Acme," Coyote demands damages for several easons. He says that the company's products do not work well; that he has been injured by the products; that Acme is the only company that makes these products, so he cannot buy elsewhere; and that he has many medical bills to pay. In a brief essay, choose one of Coyote's demands, and explain why it is humorous or unreasonable.

18. Much of the humor in "Coyote v. Acme" depends on a striking contrast between the absurd and exaggerated incidents described and the stiff, formal language that Coyote's attorney employs. Choose one paragraph from the selection that you especially enjoyed. In an essay, analyze the contrast between absurd exaggeration and the formal language used to describe the incident.

Coyote v. Acme, by Ian Frazier
Selection Test B

MULTIPLE CHOICE

Critical Reading *Identify the letter of the choice that best answers the question.*

____ 1. Which of the following correctly defines *parody*, as this mode of writing is exemplified
in "Coyote v. Acme" by Ian Frazier?
   A. a figure of speech
   B. a humorous or mocking imitation
   C. a reflective essay
   D. a persuasive argument

____ 2. In "Coyote v. Acme" by Ian Frazier, the text is structured as which of the
following?
   A. a ruling by a judge
   B. a cross-examination by a defense attorney
   C. an opening statement by the attorney for the plaintiff
   D. a statement by a witness

____ 3. In "Coyote v. Acme," which of the following is the basis for Mr. Coyote's lawsuit?
   A. product liability
   B. slander and defamation of
      character
   C. blackmail
   D. breach of contract

____ 4. Read the following passage from "Coyote v. Acme":
   Such injuries sustained by Mr. Coyote have temporarily restricted his ability to make a living
   in his profession as predator. Mr. Coyote is self-employed and thus not eligible for Workmen's Compensation.

   Which of the following literary techniques does this passage illustrate?
   A. metaphor
   B. exaggeration
   C. irony
   D. foreshadowing

____ 5. In "Coyote v. Acme," what is the purpose of Exhibits A–D?
   A. They summarize the different incidents involving Acme products.
   B. They support the attorney's line of reasoning.
   C. They illustrate Mr. Coyote's injuries.
   D. They emphasize the seriousness of the lawsuit.

____ 6. According to the text in "Coyote v. Acme," why does Mr. Coyote continue to buy prod-
ucts from Acme, despite the unexpected outcome of these purchases?
   A. He has no other source of the goods he needs for his "profession" as predator.
   B. He is always eager to try a new product.
   C. Acme's telephone marketing staff persuades Coyote to buy products.
   D. Acm's prices are very competitive.

____ 7. Which sentence is an example of the main line of reasoning in "Coyote v. Acme"?
   A. "In an instant, the fuse burned down to the stem, causing the bomb to detonate."
   B. "Mr. Coyote is self-employed and thus not eligible for Workmen's Compensation."
   C. "Adjacent to the boulcder was a path which Mr. Coyote's prey was known to
      frequent."
   D. "The sequence of collisions resulted in systemic physical damage to Mr. Coyote."

____ 8. According to his attorney in "Coyote v. Acme,", what does Mr. Coyote want the court to do?
   A. shut down Acme
   B. award him $38,750,000 in damages
   C. send the president of Acme to jail
   D. fine Acme $1 million

____ 9. "Coyote v. Acme" is a satirical essay because it
   A. uses irony and humor to criticize a topic.
   B. paints an amusing picture of its topic.
   C. imitates legal language to make its main point.
   D. explores different aspects of a topic.

____ 10. What is the author satirizing in "Coyote v. Acme," in which a cartoon character sues a company?
   A. "Roadrunner" cartoons
   B. doctors
   C. the legal profession
   D. poorly made products

____ 11. What reason is given in "Coyote v. Acme" to justify the lawsuit?
   A. Coyote has paid too much for Acme products.
   B. Coyote has been injured reepeatedly by Acme products.
   C. Coyote has been unable to catch the Roadrunner.
   D. Coyote has been overcharged by his lawyers.

____ 12. Since "Coyote v. Acme" is based on "Roadrunner" cartoons, in which the coyote is always getting hurt, what conclusion can you draw about these cartoons?
   A. They are funny.
   B. They are old-fashioned
   C. They are violent.
   D. They are well animated.

____ 13. Read the following passage from "Coyote v. Acme":

   Encumbered by his heavy casts, Mr. Coyote lost control of the Rocket Skates soon after strapping them on, and collided with a roadside billboard so violently as to leave a hole in the shape of his full silhouette.

   Which of the following techniques does Ian Frazier use in the passage?
   A. flashback
   B. exaggeration
   C. metaphor
   D. foreshadowing

____ 14. What was most likely Ian Frazier's purpose in writing "Coyote v. Acme"?
   A. to satirize the legal profession and frivolous damage claims
   B. to show that the legal profession needs reform
   C. to satirize cartoons like the "Roadrunner" series
   D. to suggest that companies indulge frequently in false advertising

Vocabulary

____ 15. In which of the following sentences is the word *contiguous* used correctly?
   A. Yesterday, the thunderstorms were contiguous, and our area had four inches of rain.
   B. Our property is contiguous with that of the Willards, and we share a side-yard fence.
   C. A contiguous lawsuit may catch you off-guard.
   D. The baseball eam played contiguous games and won them both.

____ 16. Which of the following is the best substitute for *precipitate* in this sentence: "The mist rolled in all at once, and there was a *precipitate* traffic jam on the freeway"?
    A. huge
    B. very sudden
    C. annoying
    D. desperate

____ 17. Which of the following is the best substitute for the word *emit* in this sentence: "The heart monitor machine was set to *emit* regular beeps"?
    A. send out
    B. register
    C. calculate
    D. sustain

____ 18. In which sentence is the word *punitive* used correctly?
    A. Mario proposed an ingenious, punitive solution to the math problem.
    B. Teresa's report was punitive, and she added to its interest by presenting a brilliant slide show.
    C. The jury's verdict awarded the plaintiff $3 million in punitive damages.
    D. The candidate conducted a punitive campaign, reassuring the voters that there would be no tax increase.

Essay

19. In "Coyote v. Acme," Coyote demands damages for several reasons. He says that the company's products do not work well; that he has been injured by the products; that Acme is the only company that makes these products, so he cannot buy elsewhere; and that he has many medical bills to pay. In a brief essay, choose one of Coyote's demands and explain why it is humorous or unreasonable.

20. In "Coyote v. Acme," Frazier uses exaggeration or overstatement to add to his satirical humor. In an essay, identify three examples of exaggeration, and explain how they contribute to the essay's satirical humor.

21. Why does Ian Frazier choose Wile E. Coyote for his satire? Write an essay in which you explore Frazier's use of the cartoon and draw conclusions about its satiric qualities. In your essay, translate the cartoon incidents into the real-life circumstances Frazier is criticizing.

22. **Thinking About the Essential Question: How does literature shape or reflect society?** "Coyote v. Acme" aims its satire at a number of social targets. In particular, what does this satire reflect or show about the state of the American legal system? Does it merely seek to reflect and parody a set of problems, or does the piece imply alternative models of behavior? Explain your answer in an essay supported by specific examples and clear reasoning.

"Urban Renewal" by Sean Ramsay
"Playing for the Fighting Sixty-Ninth" by William Harvey

Primary Sources: Oral History and E-mail

An **oral history** is a spoken account of an event by an eyewitness. It is usually unrehearsed, and combines factual information with impressions, feelings, and memories. An oral history can help bring a major event to life for those who were not present. An e-mail (short for "electronic mail") is a message sent through a computer network. Though **e-mails** often contain informal, unimportant messages, they have also proved to be an important source of communication during times of crisis.

As you read these primary sources, you might find it useful to **apply background knowledge** based on what you have already read, learned, or witnessed about the events of 9–11. You might also wish to **draw conclusions** about the speakers: their thoughts and feelings, and their relationship to larger events.

DIRECTIONS: *Read each question about the primary sources presented in this group and answer the questions.*

1. Based on your own reactions to the events of 9–11 or the reactions of people you know, what conclusions can you draw about Sean Ramsay's motivation in walking along the promenade in Brooklyn Heights, across from the scene of the collapse of the Twin Towers in "Urban Renewal"?

   _____

   _____

2. Based on the actions of the sanitation workers as recounted in "Urban Renewal," what can you conclude about the feelings and attitudes of all New Yorkers in the immediate aftermath of the events of 9-11?

   _____

   _____

3. What advantages of an oral history as a primary source—as opposed to other sources such as print and broadcast journalism accounts, photographs, and so on—are evident in "Urban Renewal"?

   _____

   _____

4. Based on your background knowledge of the events of 9-11, what can you conclude about how humans react to emergencies based on Harvey's account of his own extraordinary services and those of the soldiers he played for in "Playing for the Fighting Sixty-Ninth."

   _____

   _____

5. What aspect of Harvey's written account in "Playing for the Fighting Sixty-Ninth" shows a possible advantage of an e-mail as a primary source as opposed to an oral account of the kind provided in "Urban Renewal"?

   _____

   _____

Unit 6 Resources: New Voices, New Frontiers
178

"Urban Renewal" by Sean Ramsay
"Playing for the Fighting Sixty-Ninth" by William Harvey
Vocabulary Builder

Word List

accosted   cadence   casualties   condolences   fatigues
homages   intently   intonation   memorials   regiment

A. DIRECTIONS: *For each of the following items, choose the Word List word that best completes the meaning of the sentence.*

1. The city of Washington, D.C., is notable for its many prominent ——————— that honor the achievements of past great presidents of the United States.

     A. memorials   B. condolences   C. casualties   D. fatigues

2. Judging by the low, simmering ——————— of my teacher's voice, she was none too pleased with the effort I had made on my oral report.

     A. regiment   B. cadence   C. intonation   D. homages

3. At the town ceremony on Memorial Day, many of the speakers delivered moving ——————— to the brave men and women who had made the ultimate sacrifice for their country in wartime.

     A. regiment   B. cadence   C. intonation   D. homages

4. I was nervous and wary as a strange man ——————— me on a dark, deserted street late at night.

     A. intently   B. accosted   C. intonation   D. intently

5. Everyone in the audience listened ——————— as the speaker told of his experiences flying on the space shuttle.

     A. intently   B. intonation   C. regiment   D. intently

6. After the tornado devastated the town, a ——————— of the National Guard quickly appeared to help survivors and restore order.

     A. intently   B. intonation   C. regiment   D. intently

7. Many of the officers kindly offered their ——————— to grieving residents who had lost family members to the tornado.

     A. memorials   B. condolences   C. casualties   D. fatigues

8. Dressed in their battle ———————, the soldiers set about giving first aid to survivors, clearing debris, and restoring essential services.

     A. cadence   B. condolences   C. casualties   D. fatigues

9. Speaking in a slow, mournful ———————, the minister paid tribute to the memory of those who had fallen victim to the tornado.

     A. cadence   B. condolences   C. casualties   D. fatigues

10. Despite the terrible toll taken by the tornado, the ——————— could have been much worse if the twister had taken a more direct path through the residential area of the town.

     A. memorials   B. condolences   C. casualties   D. fatigues

Primary Sources: "Playing for the Fighting Sixty-Ninth" by Wiliam Harvey and **"Urban Renewal"** by Sean Ramsay

Selection Test

MULTIPLE CHOICE

Critical Reading *Identify the letter of the choice that best completes the statement or answers the question.*

_____ 1. Why does Ramsay get upset at the sanitation workers?

   A. He thinks they have taken too long to clean up the walkway.

   B. He thinks they should be working at Ground Zero, not in Brooklyn.

   C. He thinks they are cleaning up the tributes to those killed in the 9/11 attacks.

   D. He thinks they are doing a poor job of cleaning up since there are many objects still on the walkway.

_____ 2. Why does Ramsay like the tributes that he sees on the walkway?

   A. They are valuable works of art.

   B. They show that people are ready to go to war.

   C. They distract people from the horror of the 9/11 attacks.

   D. They help him and others to grieve and to remember what happened.

_____ 3. Ramsay's story is an oral history transcript. This means that

   A. Ramsay read the story out loud.

   B. It was sent by e-mail to many other people.

   C. It was originally spoken rather than written.

   D. It was never meant to be heard or read by anyone.

_____ 4. Why is Ramsay's story valuable?

   A. It is an example of great literature and should be preserved as such.

   B. It persuades people not to take down tributes to victims of a tragedy.

   C. It is a first-person historical record of important events as they happened.

   D. It requires the listener or reader to have background knowledge about the event.

_____ 5. What background knowledge does a listener or reader need to have in order to understand and appreciate Ramsay's story?

   A. the full schedules of Brooklyn's sanitation workers

   B. that Ramsay won a story slam contest with this story

   C. the names of the people pictured in the walkway tributes

   D. that almost 3,000 people died in the 9/11 attacks on the World Trade Center

_____ 6. From "Urban Renewal" and your own background knowledge, you can conclude that Ramsay's feelings

A. are mild in comparison to most people's following 9/11

B. represent those of a great many people in New York following 9/11

C. are unusually intense and do not represent most people's reactions to 9/11

D. have been shut off as he tries to process events as unemotionally as possible

_____ 7. In Playing for the Fighting Sixty-Ninth," how does the Colonel reward Harvey for his efforts at the armory?

A. He pays him in cash.

B. He solemnly salutes him.

C. He gives him the coin of the regiment.

D. He makes him an honorary member of the Fighting Sixty-Ninth

_____ 8. Why does Harvey consider his hours playing at the armory to be the most meaningful time he has ever had as a musician?

A. because he was able to use his music to help people feel better during a terrible tragedy

B. because he played the most technically perfect music he has ever played before in his life

C. because he played for more hours straight and more difficult pieces than he has ever played before

D. because he realizes that he no longer wants to be a professional musician and would rather join the National Guard instead

_____ 9. What form of primary source is William Harvey's account "Playing for the Fighting Sixty-Ninth"?

A. an e-mail   C. an oral history

B. a transcript   D. a journal entry

_____ 10. Who was the original intended audience for Harvey's story about his time with the Fighting Sixty-Ninth?

A. his family   C. his instructors at Juilliard

B. the Colonel of the 69th   D. a major New York newspaper

_____ 11. Based on Harvey's account as well as your background knowledge about 9/11 and how people deal with grief, what conclusion can you draw about how people at the armory felt while listening to Harvey's violin music that day?

A. angry at his intrusion on their grief

B. somewhat soothed and grateful for his presence

C. completely overwhelmed by the beauty of his playing

D. critical of his frequent errors but entertained by is efforts

Study these words from the selections. Then, complete the activities.

Word List A

embodiment [em BAHD i muhnt] *n.* a physical expression of an idea
   Jackson is the <u>embodiment</u> of what it means to have integrity.

motivation [MOHT uh vay shuhn] *n.* a reason or inspiration for action
   Getting into college was Jamal's <u>motivation</u> for excelling in high school.

optimists [AHP tuh mists] *n.* hopeful people
   The <u>optimists</u> are sure Jim can rebuild his house after the fire.

personified [per SAHN uh fyd] *adj.* symbolized
   The happy atmosphere of the party was <u>personified</u> by the funny clown.

pessimists [PES uh mists] *n.* people who expect the worst outcome
   The <u>pessimists</u> in his town doubt Jim will ever rebuild his house.

psyche [SY kee] *n.* the human soul; the mind
   His favorite activity, fishing, is the key to understanding his <u>psyche</u>.

realists [REE uh lists] *n.* people focused on practical, real things
   The <u>realists</u> think Jim can rebuild since he has the money and time for it.

reflexively [ree FLEK siv lee] *adv.* automatically
   He backed out of the driveway, steering <u>reflexively</u> around the hedge.

Word List B

coincidence [koh IN suh duhns] *n.* events or ideas that occursimultaneously by accident, although it seems as if they may have happened at the same time for a reason
   By <u>coincidence</u>, Mark and his girlfriend gave each other the same gift.

indelible [in DEL uh buhl] *adj.* permanent; cannot be erased
   The trip to Cairo left <u>indelible</u> memories in Diego's mind.

legacy [LEG uh see] *n.* ideas or property passed from one generation to the next; something that is handed down
   Mr. Smith's <u>legacy</u> to his son included a tradition of public service.

monotonous [muh NAHT uhn uhs] *adj.* boring because it is unchanging
   At the <u>monotonous</u> meeting, people repeated the same ideas for hours.

muting [MYOOT ing] *adj.* softening; quieting; subduing
   There were extra ceiling panels <u>muting</u> the sounds from the music room.

obsessed [uhb SESD] *v.* hugely preoccupied by something or someone
   Chelsea was <u>obsessed</u> with playing guitar and practiced six hours a day.

trance [TRANS] *n.* daze; stupor; an altered, dreamy state of mind
   After Steve received the terrible news, he walked around in a <u>trance</u>.

transformations [trans fawr MAY shuhnz] *n.* changes; alterations
   When the <u>transformations</u> were complete, both lots had become gardens.

"One Day, Now Broken in Two" by Anna Quindlen
Vocabulary Warm-up Exercises

Exercise A *Fill in the blanks, using each word from Word List A only once.*

Mr. Ferntree was the [1] _____ of a good teacher. He could give you inspiration and the [2] _____ to achieve your goals. If you felt negative, like one of the [3] _____ who could only see bad things up ahead during exam week, Mr. Ferntree [4] _____ found a way to cheer you up; it was just his habit. "I must be a member of the [5] _____ club," he'd say, "Because I can't help feeling hopeful about *you*." And then he would tell you why he knew you would do well on those exams, and the reasons that his idea of a good student was [6] _____ by you in particular. "All of us are practical [7] _____ to some extent," he'd say. "We have to work with the abilities we have. But we can't lose our hope. That's just part of the human mind, part of the [8] _____ as far as I'm concerned." By the time he finished pepping you up, you would be ready to face a hundred exams.

Exercise B *Decide whether each statement below is true or false. Circle T or F, and explain your answer.*

1. When you make an appointment to see someone, you meet by <u>coincidence</u>.
   T / F _____

2. If a woman dies and leaves her daughter a thousand dollars, that money is a <u>legacy.</u>
   T / F _____

3. <u>Transformations</u> are a type of radio.
   T / F _____

4. A man <u>obsessed</u> with golf hopes he will never play the game again.
   T / F _____

5. A person you meet once but never forget has left an <u>indelible</u> impression.
   T / F _____

6. A <u>monotonous</u> trip offers something new to see every day.
   T / F _____

7. It would probably be difficult to converse with a person in a <u>trance</u>.
   T / F _____

8. If the walls are <u>muting</u> the sound of an argument, they are making it harder to hear.
   T / F _____

Name _____ Date _____

"One Day, Now Broken in Two" by Anna Quindlen
Reading Warm-up A

Read the following passage. Then, complete the activities.

Here's a familiar riddle: If a glass is filled to its mid-line with water, is the glass half-full, or half-empty? The water in that glass is the <u>embodiment</u> of another question, giving a physical representation to "Are you a pessimist or an optimist?"

Tradition says that <u>optimists</u> will answer that the question about the water glass by saying it is half-full. That is because optimists are <u>reflexively</u>, or habitually, hopeful. The 18th-century German philosopher Gottfried Leibniz famously explained a philosophy of optimism. He reasoned that we live in the best of all possible worlds.

Tradition also says that <u>pessimists</u> will answer the question by saying that the glass is half-empty. That is because pessimists have a tendency to think that bad things may happen, or will certainly happen. The English word "pessimism" comes from a Latin word, *pessimus*, which means "worst."

Perhaps this split between optimism and pessimism is <u>personified</u> by that glass of water. The glass is a symbol for the idea that you can look at one object and have two very different reactions to it.

However, in daily life, optimism and pessimism may not result from philosophical ideas. These tendencies may come from something in a person's <u>psyche</u>, or soul, that predisposes a person to think positively or negatively. Many scholars will argue that both are necessary. They will say that people usually have some of each. After all, both hope and worry provide <u>motivation</u> for us, inspiring us to take action to improve our lives and the lives of others.

<u>Realists</u> are practical and focused on what actually seems possible. Perhaps it is the realists who can set aside the extremes of optimism and pessimism and simply pick up the glass of water – without thinking how full or empty it is – and drink it.

1. Underline the phrase that describes the <u>embodiment</u> of a question. Use the word *embodiment* in a sentence.

2. Circle the word in a nearby sentence that describes <u>optimists</u>. Write your own definition for the word *optimists*.

3. Circle the word that is a synonym for <u>reflexively</u>. Name something that you do *reflexively*.

4. Underline the phrase in a nearby sentence that describes <u>pessimists</u>. Describe a beautiful sunny day from the *pessimists'* point of view.

5. Circle the word in a nearby sentence that is a clue to the meaning of <u>personified</u>. Name an object that has *personified* happiness to you.

6. Circle the word that is a synonym for <u>psyche</u>. Give another synonym for the word *psyche*.

7. Underline the phrase that tells what hope and worry provide <u>motivation</u> for. Write a sentence telling what gives you *motivation*.

8. Underline the phrase that helps to explain the meaning of <u>realists</u>. Use the word *realists* in a sentence.

"One Day, Now Broken in Two" by Anna Quindlen
Reading Warm-up B

Read the following passage. Then, complete the activities.

Even though Isabel was very young on September 11, 2001, the events of that day left an <u>indelible</u> impression on her. She could not erase her memory of her teacher, Mrs. Chang, as she stood in front of the classroom television as if she were in a <u>trance</u>, or daze, unable to pull away from it to teach. For a while, the classroom became very noisy, <u>muting</u> the sound of the television. The kids did not hear what was going on because the sound of the set had been softened by the loud noise of the students.

Later, Isabel's parents explained to her what had happened in a way that a young child could understand. She and her friend Lizzie decided to set up a lemonade stand to raise money for victims' families. Isabel still had the letter of thanks they received. The letter said their contribution would aid families making <u>transformations</u>, changing their grief to healing as they rebuilt their lives after such profound losses.

By <u>coincidence</u>, almost as if they had planned it, the following year Isabel and Lizzie left each other phone messages on September 11. They each asked if the other one wanted to do the lemonade stand again. Every year since, around the anniversary of 9–11, she and Lizzie had gotten together to sell food and drink of some kind, and donated the proceeds to a charity. It was never <u>monotonous</u>, or boring and unchanging, because they planned something different each time. Maybe you could say they had become a little bit <u>obsessed</u>, since they started planning their annual project months ahead of time, but Isabel could not help thinking it was a good thing to be preoccupied by. For Isabel, this personal tradition of community service had become part of the <u>legacy</u> of 9–11.

1. Underline the phrase in a nearby sentence that helps to explain the meaning of indelible. Give an antonym for the word *indelible*.

2. Circle the word that has a meaning similar to trance. What is the opposite of being in a *trance*?

3. Underline the phrase in a nearby sentence that helps to explain the meaning of muting. Why do you think Mrs. Chang might have appreciated the fact that the noisy classroom was *muting* the sound of the television?

4. Circle the words that describe the transformations. Write your own definition for the word *transformations*.

5. Underline the phrases that describe the coincidence. Write a sentence telling about a *coincidence* you have experienced.

6. Circle the words that explain the meaning of monotonous. Give an antonym for the word *monotonous*.

7. Circle the word in a nearby sentence that has a meaning similar to obsessed. Write a sentence telling about something that has *obsessed* you or someone you know.

8. Underline the phrase that describes the legacy. Write a sentence describing another *legacy* of 9–11.

Name _____ Date _____

"One Day, Broken in Two" by Anna Quindlen

Literary Analysis: Comparison and Contrast Essay

A **comparison and contrast essay** presents differences and similarities between two or more people, topics or events. In this essay, Quindlen compares the thoughts and behaviors of Americans in the days following the events of September 11, 2001 and again one year later.

DIRECTIONS: *Use the chart below to compare and contrast various aspects of American life before and after the events of 9-11 as discussed in "One Day, Broken in Two." Briefly cite details from the essay to support your answers.*

Aspect of Life	Before 9-11	After 9-11
Personal Feelings		
Daily Routines		
Travel		
What Kind of People Are We		
What Kind of World Do We Live In		

"One Day, Broken in Two" by Anna Quindlen

Reading Strategy: Relate a Literary Work to Primary Source Documents

Primary source documents are nonfiction works that comment upon events taking place at the time the works were written. Some primary source documents, like the Declaration of Independence, speak solely of issues of public concern. Others reveal information about the private life of the writer. By providing personal reflections and first-hand accounts, primary source documents can offer insights into a literary work that would otherwise be unavailable.

DIRECTIONS: *There is a wide variety of primary source documents available on the subject of the events of 9-11. Use the chart below to list five such possible sources. In the middle column, state where such a source is likely to be found. In the right-hand column explain the advantage of that source to someone researching the events of 9-11.*

Primary Source	Where It to Find It	Advantage of Source

"One Day, Broken in Two" by Anna Quindlen
Vocabulary Builder

Word List

induce   mundane   prosperity   revelations   savagery

A. DIRECTIONS: *Read the incomplete paragraph below. On each line, write one of the words from the Word List. Think about the meaning of each word in the context of the paragraph.*

On the morning of September 11, 2001, most Americans began their day in an ordinary fashion, getting ready for another (1) _____ round of work or school. Then, as the (2) _____ of the terrible events at the World Trade Center began to hit the airwaves, they reacted with shock and disbelief. Few could believe the (3) _____ of the violent acts that were unfolding right before their very eyes on televisions across the country. Some believed that the seemingly invincible military strength of the United States, built on the foundations of a long term (4) _____, had managed to (5) _____ a false sense of security among its citizens.

B. DIRECTIONS: *On each line, write the letter of the word whose meaning is most nearly* opposite *in meaning to the Word List word.*

1. mundane
   A. worldly
   B. extraordinary
   C. temporary
   D. compassionate

2. induce
   A. dissuade
   B. surrender
   C. affirm
   D. question

3. savagery
   A. originality
   B. renewal
   C. gentleness
   D. intelligence

4. revelations
   A. cover-ups
   B. writings
   C. failures
   D. emancipations

5. prosperity
   A. sturdiness
   B. generosity
   C. elevation
   D. poverty

Name _____ Date _____

"One Day, Broken in Two" by Anna Quindlen
Support for Writing

Prepare to write a letter to Anna Quindlen in which you share your thoughts about her essay "One Day, Broken in Two." As part of your preparation, think of questions that occurred to you as you read her essay. Use the suggested questions below to get started, and add others of your own before you write a rough draft of your letter.

1. America had unprecedented sympathy throughout the world right after 9-11. Does America command the same sympathy from other countries today? Why or why not?

   _____

   _____

   _____

2. Have Americans completely resumed all of their normal routines since 9-11, or have some aspects of American life changed permanently since then? If so, which ones?

   _____

   _____

   _____

3. Have Americans regained their pre-9-11 sense of optimism and security about this country's place in the world? Why or why not?

   _____

   _____

   _____

4. Do Americans feel safer from terrorist attack now than they did in first year after 9-11? Why or why not?

   _____

   _____

   _____

5. What lessons can we as a country learn from the events of 9-11?

   _____

   _____

   _____

After you have sketched out answers to these questions and others you may have posed, begin to assemble your material into a rough draft of a letter to Anna Quindlen.

"One Day, Broken in Two" by Anna Quindlen
Enrichment: Heroes

The tragic events of 9-11 showed the worst in people—the brutality of the attackers—but also the best, as people from all walks of life rose to heroic heights of self-sacrifice to come to the aid of the victims of the attacks. Most notable were the valiant efforts of the first responders—police, fire fighters, medics, volunteer physicians—many of whom gave their lives in the effort to save the lives of others. Ordinary citizens were roused from their everyday routines to contribute whatever they could—their time, their energy, their compassion, even their blood at countless blood banks around the city.

It doesn't take major catastrophes to bring out the heroic side of people—countless unreported acts of self-sacrifice take place in all walks of life all over the globe everyday: organ donors, good samaritans rushing to the aid of those in trouble, volunteers in hospitals and hospices, and so on. Many of these heroic acts, large and small, share certain qualities. For example, most of them do extraordinary things, are particularly courageous, and think of others before themselves.

A. DIRECTIONS: *What do you think makes a hero? Write three words or phrases that you believe describe a heroic person. Then, give examples of one of more people (real or fictional) who have displayed each of these qualities. Explain how each example applies to the quality of heroism indicated.*

1. Heroic quality: _____

Example(s) of hero or heroes:

_____

_____

2. Heroic quality: _____

Example(s) of hero or heroes:

_____

_____

3. Heroic quality: _____

Example(s) of hero or heroes:

_____

_____

B. DIRECTIONS: *Choose one of the people or character you named and explain why he or she might be considered a hero by many people in modern American culture.*

_____

_____

_____

_____

"One Day, Broken in Two" by Anna Quindlen
Open-Book Test

Short Answer *Write your responses to the questions in this section on the lines provided.*

1. In the first paragraph of "One Day, Now Broken in Two," Quindlen describes how her son's birthday has become part of her experience of 9–11. What primary source plays a role in her son's encounter with police as it relates to 9–11?

   _____

   _____

2. What is Quindlen contrasting in "One Day, Now Broken in Two"?

   _____

   _____

3. In "One Day, Now Broken in Two," Quindlen writes, "Why do they hate us, some asked afterward, and many Americans were outraged at the question, confusing the search for motivation with mitigation." Why would some Americans be outraged at this question?

   _____

   _____

4. In "One Day, Now Broken in Two," Quindlen states that 9–11 prompted many Americans to wonder about the quality and meaning of their way of life. She asks, "Had we . . . become personified by oversize sneakers and KFC?" By comparing America to sneakers and fast food, what is Quindlen implying about American culture?

   _____

   _____

   _____

5. In "One Day, Now Broken in Two," Quindlen speaks about optimists and pessimists among Americans. Then she speaks of a third category of Americans that asserts that both are right. What is this third category of Americans, and what does Quindlen think of their views?

   _____

   _____

6. What general contrast in the post-9–11 American character is Quindlen portraying in the following passage from "One Day, Now Broken in Two"?

   > So we . . . hugged our kids a little tighter. And then we complained about the long lines at the airport. . . .

   _____

   _____

   _____

191

7. In "One Day, Now Broken in Two," what kind of primary source does Quindlen rely on mostly to give examples of how people's behavior has changed since 9–11?

   _____

   _____

   _____

8. In "One Day, Now Broken in Two," Quindlen writes of the ways in which the events of 9-11 "cracked our world cleanly in two," into the "mundane and the monstrous." Use the chart below to quote three passages from the essay that demonstrate each of these sides of the post-9–11 world: the mundane and the monstrous.

Mundane	**Monstrous**

9. Near the end of "One Day, Now Broken in Two," Quindlen describes a number of events she and her daughter experienced on September 10. What do these events have in common, and what is Qundllen's purpose in recounting these events?

   _____

   _____

   _____

   _____

10. If a country was going through a period of extended *prosperity*, would the stock market of that country likely be doing well or not? Explain your answer, based on the meaning of *prosperity* as it is used in "One Day, Broken in Two."

   _____

   _____

   _____

   _____

Essay

Write an extended response to the question of your choice or to the question or questions our teacher assigns you.

11. In "One Day, Now Broken in Two," Anna Quindlen writes about the ways in which the events of 9–11 changed her own life and the lives of other Americans. In an essay, describe the impact of the events of 9–11 on your own life. How did you first learn of the events? How did you react? What impact did the events of 9–11 have on your life and the lives of your friends and family? Develop your points in an essay supported by specific examples.

12. In "One Day, Now Broken in Two," Anna Quindlen characterizes three kinds of reactions to the events of 9-11: those of the pessimists, the optimists, and the realists. In an essay, summarize the views of each, and explain which one you believe comes closest to capturing the reality of the post-9-11 world. Support your response with examples from the essay and clear reasoning.

13. Many people view the events of 9-11-2001 as having brought about a permanent change in the way in which Americans view themselves and the world around them. This is the theme taken up by Quindlen in "One Day, Now Broken in Two," Do you agree that the events of 9-11 permanently changed something essential in the way Americans view themselves and the world around them? Why or why not? Develop your thoughts in an essay supported by details from Quindlen's essay, your own experience, and recent national and world events.

14. Thinking About the Essential Question: How does literature shape or reflect society? September 11, 2001, was one of the most significant days in American history. Its impact on American society was immediate, profound, and lasting. Is "One Day, Now Broken in Two" an attempt to shape how Americans should react to the aftermath of 9-11, or is it an attempt to reflect the impact that the events of that day have had on American society? Explain your views in an essay supported by details from the selection.

Oral Response

15. Go back to question 1, 2, or 3 or to the question your teacher assigns you. Take a few minutes to expand your answer and prepare an oral response. Find additional details in "One Day, Now Broken in Two" that support your points. If necessary, make notes to guide your oral response.

Quindlen - One Day Broken in Two
Selection Test A

MULTIPLE CHOICE

___ 1. What does Quindlen call feeding babies, walking dogs, and doing household jobs?

A. difficult chores

B. simple daily routines

C. well-paid occupations

D. enjoyable pastimes

___ 2. Quindlen says her son "got pulled over for pushing the pedal." What happened to him?

A. A police officer stopped him for speeding.

B. He was riding a motorcycle.

C. A high wind pulled him over while riding a bicycle.

D. He pushed the brake pedal too hard and crashed his car.

___ 3. Why does Quindlen call 9-11 the day "America's mind reeled"?

A. On that day, everyone recalled an earlier tragedy.

B. The day's events were like a reel of movie film.

C. Americans found it hard to comprehend the terrorist attacks.

D. America lost its mind.

___ 4. What details does Quindlen use in referring to the World Trade Center attacks?

A. planes, flames, falling bodies

B. explosions, bursting pipes, falling houses

C. bombs, cannons, flame throwers

D. tanks, warships, guided missiles

___ 5. After the attacks, what kinds of people vowed "to stop and smell the flowers"?

A. attackers

B. victims

C. optimists

D. pessimists

___ 6. Because of the attacks, writes Quindlen, what do pessimists say about the world?

A. It will end soon.

B. It is not so bad.

C. It is filled with sympathy for America and those who died.

D. It is a place of unimaginable cruelty and savagery.

Unit 6 Resources: New Voices, New Frontiers
194

____ 7. What group of people does Quindlen decide are "correct" in their views?

A. the optimists

B. the pessimists

C. the realists

D. those still undecided

____ 8. In describing later responses to the attacks, Quindlen divides Americans into what two groups?

A. optimists and pessimists

B. peacemakers and warmakers

C. idealists and realists

D. men and women

____ 9. Why, after the attacks, did some Americans call friends more often and hug their kids tighter?

A. They worried about more attacks.

B. Having escaped death, they clung more closely to loved ones.

C. They wanted to keep up on the news, so they called friends.

D. They had lost time during the attacks, so they were catching up.

____ 10. Quindlen writes that we are "people of two minds now." What do the two minds do?

A. feel angry and feel forgiving

B. look forward hopefully and flash back fearfully

C. love our neighbors and hate our enemies

D. ask questions and answer questions

____ 11. What change came over Americans as the attacks faded into memory?

A. We became increasingly angry and determined to take revenge on terrorists.

B. Our anger and fear gradually softened as we returned to normal routines.

C. We forgot all about the incident.

D. Many decided to resettle in a safer country.

____ 12. With what does Quindlen compare her feelings about returning to normal life?

A. a favorite dog

E. he funeral of a friend

F. an automobile accident

G. a broken bowl she had mended

___ 13. Why does Quindlen quote from a popular song?

    A. It expresses the same feelings as those she is experiencing.

    B. It expresses feelings opposite to those she is experiencing.

    C. It expresses the love she has for her children.

    D. The singer is a particular favorite of hers.

Vocabulary

___ 14. Which word best replaces *bifurcated* in this sentence?

> "The day approaching will always be bifurcated for me: part Sep\tember 11, the anniversary of one of the happiest days of my life, and part 9-11, the day America's mind reeled, its spine stiffened, and its heart broke."

    A. combined   B. unhappy   C. divided   D. memorable

___ 15. What is the relationship between the words *mundane* and *monstrous*?

    A. They have similar meanings.

    B. They have opposite meanings.

    C. They rhyme.

    D. They both contain three syllables.

___ 16. September 11 was the day of the World Trade Center attacks. Yet, the author of "One Day, Now Broken in Two" recalls that day with a certain amount of pleasure. Why?

    A. Her cat's life was saved that day.

    B. She escaped a speeding ticket.

    C. She forgets the bad news of that day.

    D. Her son's birthday is on that day.

Essay

17. In this essay, Quindlen compares her feelings about the date September 11 with the feelings experienced by all Americans. Many of her comments are about opposites, as when she says she both loves that date because it is her son's birthday and and hates it because of the terrorist attacks. What other sets of opposites can you find? In a brief essay, list at least three of them.

18. In describing the optimists, the pessimists, and the realists after 9-11, Quindlen declares that the realists are "correct" because they insist that both of the other two groups are right. In a brief essay, make the case for the realists. Using evidence from the essay, show ways in which the optimists and the pessimists are both right. (You may also discuss how they are both wrong.)

"Quindlen - One Day Broken in Two
Selection Test B

MULTIPLE CHOICE

____ 1. "One Day, Now Broken in Two" is an example of
   A. a satiric essay
   B. an expository essay
   C. an analytical essay
   D. a persuasive essay

____ 2. Quindlen's essay is mainly about
   A. how the writer has come to terms with conflicting feelings about events occurring on September 11.
   B. how the writer provided comfort to her son on his eleventh birthday.
   C. the writer's political point of view regarding the 9-11 terrorist attacks.
   D. the writer's inability to focus on her writing after the 9-11 attacks.

____ 3. Quindlen writes that two police officers, after seeing her son's birth date on his driver's license, both gave him a warning instead of a ticket. Why?
   A. They had sympathy for him because he was born on September 11.
   B. They both had children born on that date.
   C. They had orders not to issue any speeding tickets that day.
   D. They found that his license was legal and up to date.

____ 4. How can everyday routines mute the terror of a bad experience?
   A. They can make it worse by reminding us of it.
   B. Beingboring and tedious, they can make us to feel anxious all over again.
   C. They can lessen its impact by keeping our minds on other things.
   D. They provide the joy and excitement of meeting major challenges.

____ 5. When Quindlen writes "Slowly the planes filled up again," to what historical occurrence is she alluding?
   A. More terrorists boarded planes for a second attack.
   B. The airlines were shut down immediately after the 9-11 attacks.
   C. Before, long lines in airports caused slow boarding of planes.
   D. There was no security in airports before 9-11.

____ 6. According it Quindlen, what worldview is held by the realists among us?
   A. The threat of further terrorism is very real.
   B. No further attacks are likely, so we should resume our normal routines.
   C. We live in a world of unimaginable cruelty and savagery.
   D. The world is a mixture of goodness and evil.

____ **7.** In writing that the hijackers came from "a country of rubble and caves and desperate want," what does Quindlen imply about their motives?
   A. Living in poverty, the hijackers despised America as a place of decadent prosperity.
   B. The hijackers wanted to reduce America to rubble.
   C. The hijackers lived in secret locations in America while planning their scheme.
   D. Everyone living in poverty wants to be a hijacker.

____ **8.** What contrast does Quindlen suggest in saying that we are "obsessed about the stock market in lieu of soul-searching"?
   A. We are businesslike thinkers, not fuzzy-minded idealists.
   B. The hijackers threatened our economy more than our religions.
   C. We care more about money than about spiritual values.
   D. Many of us need psychological help as a result of the 9-11 attacks.

____ **9.** Quindlen writes: "Time passed. The blade dulled. The edges softened." These metaphors mean that
   A. our sorrow and anger intensified.
   B. we felt good about ourselves again.
   C. the keenness of our grieving lessened.
   D. we forgave the hijackers.

____ **10.** In suporting her theme, of what use does Quindlen put a bowl she once mended?
   A. She compares it to knowledge of a tragic event that will never go away.
   B. She contrasts it with the broken hearts of the 9-11 families.
   C. She compares it to the fragility of human life.
   D. She uses it to illustrate that time heals all wounds.

____ **11.** Quindlen says that we must learn to live broken-hearted, "or we cannot really go on living at all." She means that
   A. our hearts will be broken many times.
   B. life without feeling is not really lived.
   C. we should never recover from tragedy, or the dead will have died in vain.
   D. normal life can never return.

Vocabulary

____ **12.** To plot and scheme in secret is to engage in
   A. mitigations
   B. mechanisms
   C. munitions
   D. machinations

____ **13.** *Mundane* is to *monstrous* as *boring* is to
   A. dull   **C.** amusing
   B. interesting   **D.** horrifying

Essay

14. In a brief essay, state the theme of "One Day, Now Broken in Two" and discuss ways in which Quindlen uses comparisons or contrasts to illustrate it. Mention at least two specific examples in support of your answer.

15. In answer to the question "Is everything back to normal?", Quindlen describes her feelings about a broken bowl she had skillfully mended. What point is she making about herself? What larger meaning does it have for Americans in the post-9-11 world? Write a brief essay, making specific references to the text.

Study these words from the selections. Then, complete the activities.

Word List A

aspect [AS pekt] *n.* part; feature
   He had not considered that <u>aspect</u> of the problem before.

aspirations [as puh RAY shunz] *n.* goals; ambitions
   Cammie had <u>aspirations</u> to become a professional soccer player.

contemplating [KAHN tuhm playt ing] *v.* thinking about; considering
   Belinda has been <u>contemplating</u> quitting her job.

enticed [en TYSD] *v.* attracted; tempted
   She was <u>enticed</u> to go by the promise of a stop at the mall.

expressive [ek SPRES iv] *adj.* full of meaning or feeling
   Boyd did not say much, but his <u>expressive</u> face told us what he thought.

regrettable [ree GRET uh bul] *adj.* unfortunate
   A <u>regrettable</u> error in the newspaper led to disappointed shoppers.

tolerate [TAHL er ayt] *v.* allow; put up with
   Colin had a headache and could <u>tolerate</u> no noise.

vivid [VIV id] *adj.* full of life
   The painting's <u>vivid</u> colors brightened the whole room.

Word List B

daunting [DAWN ting] *adj.* intimidating
   Finishing this huge job by noon is a <u>daunting</u> prospect.

dazzlingly [DAZ ling lee] *adv.* excitingly; brilliantly
   The display of jewelry was <u>dazzlingly</u> beautiful.

disproving [dis PROOV ing] *v.* showing to be false
   By <u>disproving</u> the other lawyer's statements, she won the case.

enthralled [en THRAWLD] *v.* captivated; charmed
   The children stared at the storyteller, <u>enthralled</u> by every word.

forbiddingly [fawr BID ing lee] *adv.* in a way that is unwelcoming or discouraging
   The mountain trail was <u>forbiddingly</u> steep.

impeccable [im PEK uh buhl] *adj.* flawless; without errors
   Although she was American, her French was <u>impeccable</u>.

keenly [KEEN lee] *adv.* acutely; intensely
   In the darkness, Vera was <u>keenly</u> alert to the slightest noise.

passionate [PASH uh nit] *adj.* ruled by intense feelings or emotions
   The singer's <u>passionate</u> nature came through in his voice.

Unit 6 Resources: New Voices, New Frontiers
200

"Mother Tongue" by Amy Tan and **"For the Love of Books"** by Rita Dove

Vocabulary Warm-up Exercises

Exercise A *Fill in the blanks, using each word from Word List A only once.*

My friend Colin told me about his [1] _____ to become an actor. It is true that he has an [2] _____ face, and when he tells a story, he uses [3] _____ language and gestures that are very convincing. I asked him what it was about the profession that [4] _____ him, and he told me that he can't really explain it, but acting just seems to be in his blood. There was one [5] _____ of the work that he knew would be challenging, and that was the amount of rejection an actor has to learn to [6] _____. He had been [7] _____ this issue a long time, and had decided that even though rejection might be painful, it would be even more [8] _____ to pass up a chance to do what he really wanted with his life.

Exercise B *Revise each sentence so that the underlined vocabulary word is used in a logical way. Be sure to keep the vocabulary word in your revision.*

1. The <u>daunting</u> homework assignment promised to be very easy.

   _____

2. His <u>passionate</u> performance showed that he didn't understand the character.

   _____

3. Because I was <u>keenly</u> aware of my surroundings, I got lost.

   _____

4. The audience was so <u>enthralled</u> that many fell asleep during the show.

   _____

5. The scientist was pleased that others were <u>disproving</u> his main theory.

   _____

6. Her messy hair looked as <u>impeccable</u> as her old suit.

   _____

7. The alley was <u>forbiddingly</u> dark, so we walked calmly through it.

   _____

8. The reflection was <u>dazzlingly</u> bright, so we took off our sunglasses.

   _____

201

"Mother Tongue" by Amy Tan and **"For the Love of Books"** by Rita Dove
Reading Warm-up A

Read the following passage. Then, complete the activities.

Most people who become writers will tell you that long before they knew that writing was their goal, they had a special feeling about books. It may have been that feeling that gave them their career <u>aspirations</u> in the first place.

John Lithgow, for example, who is an actor and a writer, loved *Goodnight Moon* when he was a child. One feature of this famous story that may have attracted him was the gentle artwork by Clement Hurd. He was also <u>enticed</u> by another <u>aspect</u> of the book, which was author Margaret Wise Brown's deep understanding of children's thoughts and feelings.

Lois Lowry, who wrote *The Giver* and *Number the Stars*, remembers the book *The Yearling*, by Marjorie Kinnan Rawlings. Lowry she did not read it to herself, however. Lowry's mother read it aloud to her and her sister, most likely in an <u>expressive</u> voice that brought the story to life for them.

R.L. Stine, author of many scary books for children, credits his interest in books to the work of science fiction writer Ray Bradbury. With words, Bradbury's stories paint <u>vivid,</u> vibrant pictures of strange worlds and chilling situations. Some people cannot <u>tolerate</u> frightening books. Stine not only accepted them, he thrived on them.

Many writers enjoy thinking about the books that inspired them. <u>Contemplating</u> their childhoods in this way may even give them new ideas for their own work. It is <u>regrettable</u> that not all children and young people get excited about reading. We can only hope that this unfortunate circumstance will not lead to a shortage of great writers in the future.

1. Underline the word that has nearly the same meaning as <u>aspirations</u>. What is the difference between *aspirations* and *plans*?

2. Circle the word that is a synonym for <u>enticed</u>. Give a word or phrase that means the opposite of *enticed*.

3. Underline the word that has the same meaning as <u>aspect</u>. Give another synonym for *aspect*.

4. Underline the phrase that gives a clue to the meaning of <u>expressive</u>. Then circle what was *expressive* in this sentence.

5. Circle the word that explains the meaning of <u>vivid</u>. What is an antonym for *vivid*?

6. Circle the word that has nearly the same meaning as <u>tolerate</u>. Then use *tolerate* in a new sentence.

7. Underline the words that give a clue to the meaning of <u>contemplating</u>. Explain the meaning of *contemplating* in your own words.

8. Underline the word that gives a clue to the meaning of <u>regrettable</u>. Give a word or phrase that means the same as *regrettable*.

Name _____   Date _____

Reading Warm-up B

Read the following passage. Then, complete the activities.

For those who are raised in a specific cultural environment, learning how to speak, think in, and pronounce the language of that environment is, literally, child's play. But to try to learn a new language as an adult can be a <u>daunting</u> task. Sometimes it may not just *feel* discouraging, it may actually be nearly impossible as is, for example, the case with learning Japanese.

Even for an English-speaker who is <u>keenly</u> alert and pays intense attention, learning to speak flawless Japanese may be out of the question. It is not just developing an <u>impeccable</u> accent that is the problem. One thing that discourages English-speakers from learning Japanese is that the written language is <u>forbiddingly</u> complex. You may eventually memorize the almost 15,000 characters that were borrowed from Chinese, but they do not help you learn to speak. In Japanese, the written and spoken languages are two different systems.

Certainly there are people out there who are <u>passionate</u> about studying Japanese, and their love and enthusiasm may result in their <u>disproving</u> the statement that the language is too hard to learn. Consider, however, that when the U.S. government wants its workers to speak Japanese, it allows them three times longer to learn it than for learning French.

For those who do master Japanese, or any other new language, it is almost always worth the trouble. It is one thing to travel to another country and be <u>enthralled</u> by the people and scenery. But knowing the language adds a deeper level of understanding to this fascination. The <u>dazzlingly</u> beautiful neon signs of Tokyo, for example, become even more brilliant when you can appreciate what they say.

1. Circle the word that helps explain the meaning of <u>daunting</u>. Describe a task that might be *daunting* to you.

2. Circle the word that gives a clue to the meaning of <u>keenly</u>. Then give a word that means the opposite of *keenly*.

3. Underline the word that means the same as <u>impeccable</u>. Then give an example of something else that can be *impeccable*.

4. Circle the word that gives a clue to the meaning of <u>forbiddingly</u>. Use *forbiddingly* in a new sentence.

5. Underline the phrase that hints at the meaning of <u>passionate</u>. Give a word or phrase that means the opposite of *passionate*.

6. Underline the phrase that tells what people who learn Japanese are <u>disproving</u>. Define *disproving* in your own words.

7. Circle the word that hints at the meaning of <u>enthralled</u>. Then write a sentence about something that *enthralled* you.

8. Underline the word that gives a clue to the meaning of <u>dazzlingly</u>. What else can be *dazzlingly* beautiful?

"**For the Love of Books**" by Rita Dove
"**Mother Tongue**" by Amy Tan
Literary Analysis: Reflective Essay

In a **reflective essay,** the writer uses an informal tone to explore and identify the meaning of personal experience or pivotal event. This type of essay can reveal the writer's feeling about these experiences as well as his or her values and personality.

DIRECTIONS: *Write your answers to the following questions.*

1. What books and writers does Dove remember reading as a child?

   _____

   _____

2. What do Dove's reading tastes reveal about her values?

   _____

   _____

3. What do Dove's recollections about reading reveal about her childhood?

   _____

   _____

4. What was significant about Dove's meeting with the professional writer/poet John Ciardi when she was a high school student?

   _____

   _____

5. What do Tan's experiences with her mother reveal about her personality?

   _____

   _____

6. What do Tan's experiences with her mother reveal about her values?

   _____

   _____

7. What is the reason that Tan believes she did not do as well on standardized English tests as she did on standardized math tests?

   _____

   _____

8. How did Tan's perception of her mother's imperfect, "broken" English change from her adolescence to her adulthood?

   _____

   _____

"For the Love of Books" by Rita Dove
"Mother Tongue" by Amy Tan
Reading Strategy: Outlining

To clarify your understanding of each essay, it may be useful to create an **outline** of the author's main points. Outlining can also help you make comparisons between the essays. A key to mastering outlining skills is practicing your ability to identify an author's main ideas and the details—facts, examples, or reasons—that support those ideas. The graphic organizer below will help you to work on identifying main ideas and supporting details.

DIRECTIONS: *Identify a main idea from each of the essays in this section: "For the Love of Books" by Rita Dove and "Mother Tongue" by Amy Tan. Then identify the supporting details that support each main idea.*

"For the Love of Books"

Main Idea:	
Supporting Details:	

"Mother Tongue"

Main Idea:	
Supporting Details:	

"For the Love of Books" by Rita Dove
"Mother Tongue" by Amy Tan
Grammar and Style: Parallel Structure

    Parallel structure is the expression of similar ideas in similar grammatical forms. Writers often use parallel structure to emphasize important ideas. One of the most famous examples is Julius Caesar's declaration, "I came, I saw, I conquered." Here's an example from "The Love of Books" by Rita Dove: "I loved to feel their heft in my hand . . .; I loved the crisp whisper of a page turning. . . ."

    When the items in a sentence are joined by coordinating conjunctions (*and, but, yet, or*) or correlative conjunctions (*either/or, neither/nor*), the items must be parallel. Read the following examples:

Faulty: People in the classroom were talking of poetry, hauling books, and they read aloud.

Parallel: People in the classroom were talking of poetry, hauling books, and reading aloud.

Faulty: They were either reading aloud or they listened.

Parallel: They were either reading aloud or listening.

A. PRACTICE: *Find and list four examples of parallel structure in "For the Love of Books" and/or "Mother Tongue." Underline the parallel elements in each example.*

_____

_____

_____

_____

B. WRITING APPLICATION: *Rewrite the following sentences, making the structure parallel in each*

1. Tan's mother is shown getting rebuffed and she endures rude behavior.

_____

_____

2. The writer hopes for achieving a sense of truth and to reach a receptive audience.

_____

_____

3. Amy Tan is recognized for seeing a world in which various cultures are of equal value and as an astute portrayer of family relationships.

_____

_____

"For the Love of Books" by Rita Dove
"Mother Tongue" by Amy Tan
Vocabulary Builder

Using the Roots *-scrib-* and *-script-*

A. DIRECTIONS: *Knowing that -scrib- and -script- mean "write," use each of the following words in an original sentence that demonstrates the root's meaning.*

1. inscribe _____

2. manuscript _____

Using the Word List

aspirations   benign   daunting   ecstasy   transcribed

B. DIRECTIONS: *For each of the following items, choose the Word List word that best completes the meaning of the sentence. Circle the letter of your choice.*

1. Juanita was in _____ after she received a letter of acceptance from the college that was her first choice.
   A. benign   B. ecstasy   C. daunting   D. transcribed

2. The _____ expression on the man's face was reassuring, so I stopped my car to see if he needed help.
   A. benign   B. ecstasy   C. daunting   D. transcribed

3. During the hearing, every word that the witness spoke was carefully _____ by the court reporter to preserve a permanent, official record of the proceedings.
   A. aspirations   B. benign   C. daunting   D. transcribed

4. Because of my love of animals, I have always had _____ to become a veterinarian.
   A. benign   B. transcribed   C. aspirations   D. daunting

5. Training for the triathlon while studying for finals seemed like too _____ a task, so I reluctantly decided to resign from the track team.
   A. transcribed   B. ecstasy   C. daunting   D. benign

Name _____ Date _____

"Straw Into Gold" by Sandra Cisneros
"For the Love of Books" by Rita Dove
"Mother Tongue" by Amy Tan
Support for Writing

As you prepare to write an e-mail to one of the authors of these three essays, collect information on the essay you like best in the graphic organizer below. Reread the essay before you begin.

e-mail to _____

Ideas, images, characters that I liked in the essay:	Reasons that I liked them:
_____	_____
_____	_____
_____	_____
Ideas, images, characters that concerned me in the essay:	**Reasons for my concern:**
_____	_____
_____	_____
_____	_____

On a separate page, write a draft of your e-mail. Begin by telling the author why you liked her essay. Then, provide more details of your opinion in the following paragraphs. When you revise your e-mail, replace vague words with those that are specific.

Name _____ Date _____

"For the Love of Books" by Rita Dove
"Mother Tongue" by Amy Tan
Enrichment: Career As a Professional Writer

It may surprise you to see that these two nonfiction essays are written by authors known also for their fiction or poetry. In fact, very few writers are able to support themselves by writing and selling only fiction or poetry. With the exception of those authors who enjoy national notoriety and whose books are regularly made into feature films, most professional writers make a living in the world of nonfiction writing.

Staff writers at companies or organizations write company newsletters, public relations literature, usage and training manuals, annual reports, copy for advertisements, and other business-related documents. Reporters and columnists write for daily and weekly newspapers and magazines.

Many writers work full-time for an employer with a prescribed annual salary. Many others work free-lance, or are paid by the job. Nonfiction writing accounts for the bulk of the free-lance writing market, with general-interest and special-interest magazines the primary publishers. Free-lance writers often specialize in a particular field of interest, such as outdoor activities or finance, and submit their writing to magazines that publish those types of articles.

Scriptwriters create manuscripts for movies, television programs, and plays. In this highly competitive field writers often work with a team of people, which might include a producer, a director, and actors.

All of these writing careers demand discipline, dedication, and perseverance. With the exception of staff writers, most writers must submit their writing to a variety of sources before it reaches publication.

DIRECTIONS: *Write your answers to the following questions.*

1. Which of these writing careers most appeals to you? Why?

   _____

   _____

2. Which writing field were you most surprised to discover? Why?

   _____

   _____

3. Why might making a living as a novelist or poet be difficult?

   _____

   _____

   _____

   _____

   _____

   _____

Unit 6 Resources: New Voices, New Frontiers
© Pearson Education, Inc. All rights reserved.
209

"For the Love of Books" by Rita Dove and **"Mother Tongue"** by Amy Tan

Open-Book Test

Short Answer *Write your responses to the questions in this section on the lines provided.*

1. If you were writing an outline of "For the Love of Books," what items would you include under the heading "Things Dove Loves About Books"?

   _____

   _____

   _____

2. In a personal essay, a writer reveals some aspect of his or her personality. What aspect of Dove's personality is revealed in the following passage from "For the Love of Books"? Briefly explain your answer.

   > I even loved to gaze at a closed book and daydream about the possibilities inside—it was like contemplating a genie's lamp.

   _____

   _____

   _____

3. In the second paragraph of "For the Love of Books," Dove reveals a similar reaction to her explorations of both the *Treasury of Best Loved Poems* and *The Complete Works of William Shakespeare*. What was that reaction, and what was it about each book that provoked it? Cite details from the essay to support your answer.

   _____

   _____

   _____

   _____

4. In a reflective essay, the writer uses an informal tone to explore the meaning of an experience or significant event. What was so meaningful to Dove about the scatter-brained boy in the science-fiction story she discusses in the third paragraph of "For the Love of Books"? Why did she identify with him so closely?

   _____

   _____

   _____

5. In "For the Love of Books," what important insight about life does Dove gain from meeting the poet John Ciardi described in the last paragraph?

   _____

   _____

   _____

6. Near the end of the essay "Mother Tongue," Tan acknowledges that in school she had trouble with the kinds of language questions commonly found on standardized tests like the SAT. What qualities of language valued by Tan were missing from these standardized questions, in her view?

_____

_____

_____

7. In "Mother Tongue," Tan reflects that her mother's English caused one kind of reaction in her as a child and adolescent, and another kind of reaction as an adult. How did Tan's perceptions of her mother and her version of English change over time?

_____

_____

_____

8. Near the end of "Mother Tongue," Tan concludes over time that people in the United States who do not speak perfect standard English are treated with less dignity than those with a better command of English. If you were writing an outline of this essay, which incidents would you include as examples of this idea?

_____

_____

_____

9. Throughout "Mother Tongue," Tan discusses the different kinds of English—standard, informal, "broken," and so on—that she has encountered in her personal and professional life. Use the chart below to give three examples of different kinds of English that Tan discusses in her essay. In each case, identify the kind of English it exemplifies—formal or informal, standard or nonstandard—and explain how such language is typically used: in conversation, literature, business, etc.

Example of English	Kind of English	How It Is Used
Example 1:		
Example 2:		
Example 3:		

10. If you scanned the problems on your math test and found them *daunting*, would you expect it to be an easy test? Why or why not? Base you answer on the meaning of *daunting* as it is used in "Mother Tongue."

_____

_____

Essay

Write an extended response to the question of your choice or to the question or questions your teacher assigns you.

11. Both of the essays in this section—"For the Love of Books" and "Mother Tongue" —reflect on the ways in which the authors grew to have a deeper appreciation of the expressive powers of language. Which author's experience spoke more directly to you? Why? Explain your answer in an essay supported by details from the selections.

12. Select one of the essays you have read—"For the Love of Books" or "Mother Tongue." In a brief essay, describe the significance of the personal experience that the writer recounts and explain how she gains increased self-understanding through her reflection on that experience.

13. In both of the essays in this section—"For the Love of Books" and "Mother Tongue"—the authors reflect on personal experiences that fostered personal growth and deeper insights into themselves and other people. In an essay, compare and contrast the insights gained by the authors of these essays. Which author do you think learned the more important lesson about herself and others? Support your answer with details from the essays.

14. **Thinking About the Essential Question: What makes American literature American?** In both of the essays in this section—"For the Love of Books" and "Mother Tongue"—the authors reflect on the influences that helped enhance their love of language and that inspired them to become writers. Are both authors' experiences uniquely American? Why or why not? In a brief essay, compare and contrast the influences recounted.

Oral Response

15. Go back to question 1, 2, or 3 or to the question your teacher assigns you. Take a few minutes to expand your answer and prepare an oral response. Find additional details in "For the Love of Books" or "Mother Tongue" that support your points. If necessary, make notes to guide your oral response.

"For the Love of Books" by Rita Dove and **"Mother Tongue"** by Amy Tan
Selection Test A

MULTIPLE CHOICE

Critical Reading *Identify the letter of the choice that best completes the statement or answers the question.*

____ 1. According to "For the Love of Books," what inspired the author to become a writer?

    A. her parents   C. her early reading

    B. a local librarian   D. her teachers

____ 2. Where did the author feel most alive as a child, according to "For the Love of Books"?

    A. in school   C. at the library

    B. inside a book   D. at a book sale

____ 3. In "For the Love of Books," what did Dove learn about the covers of books?

    A. that all books with hard covers are good books

    B. that a book with a boring cover is always boring

    C. that one should only read books with attractive covers

    D. that a book's cover does not always indicate what the book is really like

____ 4. What does Dove reveal about herself when she says she identified with the village idiot in the science fiction story she read?

    A. that she is not very intelligent

    B. that she was painfully shy and awkward as a child

    C. that she longs to be famous and have a statue made of her

    D. that she thinks her brother is an idiot, too

____ 5. How did the author write the novel she created in fourth grade, according to "For the Love of Books"?

    A. She used characters from Shakespeare.

    B. She used settings from science fiction.

    C. She used her weekly school spelling list.

    D. She used plots from Dante's *Divine Comedy.*

____ 6. One of the topics Dove discusses in "For the Love of Books" is how she did not think of writing as an activity people actually did for a living. Which of the following is a detail that supports that main idea?

    A. She loved the look, feel, and smell of books.

    B. She wrote her first novel in third or fourth grade.

    C. She thought that all writers were long-dead white males.

    D. She read Shakespeare because no-one told her it was too hard.

___ 7. In "For the Love of Books," how did meeting the poet John Ciardi affect the author?

   A. She decided that all writers are men, so she could never be one.

   B. She immediately wrote her first novel and published it soon after.

   C. She realized writers are real people and that she could be one, too.

   D. She was so painfully shy that she thought she decided to keep her writing to herself.

___ 8. How do you know that "For the Love of Books" is a reflective essay?

   A. The author writes about her own thoughts and memories.

   B. The author tries to persuade readers to love books like she does.

   C. The author describes a writer's life and motivations for writing.

   D. The author writes a fictional account of the childhood she wishes she had had.

___ 9. How does the author of "Mother Tongue" alert readers that her essay is a reflective essay?

   A. She writes only in English.

   B. She writes only in Chinese.

   C. She writes about translating languages.

   D. She writes about her own opinions.

___ 10. In "Mother Tongue," what is true of the hospital employees who did not listen to the author's mother's requests for test results?

   A. Because her mother spoke perfect standard English, she was taken seriously.

   B. Because her mother spoke nonstandard English, she was not taken seriously.

   C. Because her mother had a brain tumor, it affected her ability to make herself understood.

   D. Because hospital employees spoke nonstandard English, they understood her mother.

___ 11. Why did Tan have difficulty in English classes growing up?

   A. She only knew Chinese.

   B. She loved math and hated English.

   C. Her mother refused to help her with her homework.

_____ 13. Which detail helps clarify a reader's understanding of Tan's belief that her mother's English almost limited Tan's possibilities in life?

    A. Tan was uncomfortable pretending to be her mother on the phone.

    B. In school, Tan did better in math than in English and thought she was not a good writer.

    C. Tan realizes that she uses several different Englishes for different audiences.

    D. Tan tries to reproduce in writing the way her mother sounds when talking to family members.

_____ 14. Which of these would be a major topic head in an outline of Tan's essay "Mother Tongue"?

    A. Shanghai gangster with same name as Tan's mother

    B. Doctors lost Tan's mother's CAT scan

    C. Tan's dislike of the term "broken English"

    D. Asian Americans' tendency to be good at math

Vocabulary and Grammar

_____ 15. Which answer best replaces *benign* in this sentence: "The tumor was *benign* and therefore not something to worry about"?

    A. not cancerous B. not passionate C. not energetic D. not angry

_____ 16. Which sentence has parallel structure?

    A. Writers write to express themselves.

    B. Writing allows one to inform, persuade, entertain, and inspire others.

    C. Writers are often inspired by reading books, family members, and life experiences.

    D. Some writers start young, while others did not enter the profession until later in life.

Essay

17. In "For the Love of Books," the author reflects on meeting a writer who helped her realize that writers are real people and that she could someday be a "real" writer, too. Write a brief reflective essay of your own about some event in your past that helped you realize something important about yourself.

18. **Thinking About the Essential Question: What makes Ameridan literature American?** In both of the essays in this section—"For the Love of Books" and "Mother Tongue"—the authors reflect on what inspired them to become writers. Are both authors' experiences uniquely American? Why or why not? In a brief essay, compare and contrast the influences the authors mentioned in their essays.

"For the Love of Books" by Rita Dove and **"Mother Tongue"** by Amy Tan
Selection Test B

MULTIPLE CHOICE

Critical Reading *Identify the letter of the choice that best completes the statement or answers the question.*

_____ 1. In "For the Love of Books," what emotion does Dove feel when she holds an unopened book in her hands?
　　A. fear 　　　　　B. anticipation 　　　C. contentment 　　D. disinterest

_____ 2. Why does Dove choose to reflect upon how books look, feel, and smell to her?
　　A. because books inspired her love of reading, writing, and stories
　　B. because she realizes that books are becoming less and less important today
　　C. because she never has time to read anymore now that she is a writer
　　D. because she finds the appearance and smell of old books to be unappealing

_____ 3. What does Dove's family's library in their solarium imply about her family?
　　A. They think having a large collection of books makes them look intelligent and wealthy.
　　B. They feel sorry for their daughter and want her to read more since she has no friends.
　　C. They value reading and learning enough to maintain a growing personal library.
　　D. They do not take good care of their belongings and leave their books to get dusty and old.

_____ 4. By describing her love of the story in which an outcast boy becomes a hero, what point is Dove making in "For the Love of Books"
　　A. Books allow readers to identify with others.
　　B. Even science fiction can stir strong emotions.
　　C. We should be considerate of one another's feelings
　　D. Writers find inspiration in unlikely places.

_____ 5. In "For the Love of Books," Dove describes writing a novel based on her grade-school spelling list. This detail reveals that she
　　A. had a vivid imagination.
　　B. was unhappy and isolated in school.
　　C. decided at an early age to be a writer.
　　D. was a disciplined student.

_____ 6. Which of the following would be a main topic in an outline of Dove's essay "For the Love of Books"?
　　A. Favorite books and stories　　　　　C. Leather bindings
　　B. Analog science fiction magazine　　D. Grade school spelling lists

_____ 7. For the Love of Books" is an appropriate title for Dove's essay because it
　　A. explains why people love to read
　　B. describes how reading gave Dove encouragement and inspired her to pursue writing
　　C. describes the first moment that Dove discovered the power of books.
　　D. lists Dove's best-loved books.

_____ 8. How does Tan's mother's presence in an audience affect Tan's awareness of her speech?
   A. She realizes that she never uses formal, standardized English with her mother.
   B. She realizes that her mother cannot understand her because her mother speaks only Chinese.
   C. She slips into "broken English" out of habit because her mother is there.
   D. She can no longer concentrate on her speech and gives up, apologizing to her audience.

_____ 9. How do you know that Tan's mother understands English better than her spoken English seems to indicate?
   A. Tan's transcribed "family talk" shows that her mother is faking her broken English.
   B. Tan's mother taught her how to write.
   C. Tan's mother can answer word analogies and sentence completion problems.
   D. Tan's mother reads business magazines and novels with ease.

_____ 10. In "Mother Tongue," why does Tan's mother have Tan speak on the phone for her?
   A. because Tan's mother is embarrassed about her broken English
   B. because Tan's mother gets too angry to speak
   C. because Tan's mother can speak only Chinese, so she must rely on Tan's English to communicate
   D. because Tan speaks perfect English and gets better results than her mother, who speaks broken English

_____ 11. In "Mother Tongue," Tan posing as her mother on the telephone reveals that Tan
   A. is dishonest.
   B. is controlling.
   C. feels empathy for her mother.
   D. feels embarrassed by her mother.

_____ 12. Why did Tan become a writer, even though her math skills were better than her English skills in school?
   A. Her mother did not want her to become an engineer.
   B. Her skill with word analogies convinces her that writing is in fact her calling.
   C. She has a rebellious nature and enjoys disproving people's assumptions about her.
   D. She wanted to show her mother that learning English well leads to success in America.

_____ 13. The main idea of "Mother Tongue" is that
   A. immigrants are often misperceived.
   B. Asian American students need to be encouraged in English, as well as in mathematics.
   C. Chinese and English are vastly different languages.
   D. Tan was greatly affected by her mother's use of language.

_____ 14. Which of the following details in "Mother Tongue" supports Tan's message?
   A. When she writes, Tan envisions her mother as her reader.
   B. Her mother reads many English language publications.
   C. Tan received better scores in math than in English.
   D. Tan has become an accomplished writer.

____ **15.** What conclusion does Tan seem to reach through the course of her reflections in "Mother Tongue"?
   A. the broken English is in fact better than standard English
   B. that appropriate use of language depends on one's audience
   C. that her mother must learn to speak English better
   D. that she should have been an engineer instead of a writer

Vocabulary and Grammar *Identify the letter of the choice that best completes the statement or answers the question.*

____ **16.** In which sentence is *empirical* used correctly?
   A. There is empirical evidence proving that many immigrants suffer discrimination because of their broken English.
   B. Her empirical impressions were based on the emotions of resentment and embarrassment that she felt for her mother.
   C. The way she spoke sounded empirical, like a queen speaking to her subjects from her throne.
   D. The empirical style of language she used in her speech was formal standardized English.

____ **17.** What is a *semantic* comparison called?
   A. a clause   C. a reflection
   B. an analogy   D. a quandary

____ **18.** Which sentence has parallel structure?
   A. She loves to read books, stories, and relaxing with poetry.
   B. She never thought she could be a writer.
   C. She wrote stories as a child but was not liking them.
   D. She daydreamed as a child and wrote enchanting novels as an adult.

ESSAY *Write an extended response to the question of your choice or to the question or questions your teacher assigns you.*

19. By describing personal experiences and feelings in a reflective essay, Dove arrives at a deeper understanding of herself. In an essay of your own, explain how the author comes to understand a problem or aspect of herself more deeply through her reflections.

20. In their reflective essays, these two writers describe pivotal experiences in their development as writers. In your opinion, which writer reveals the most about herself in her essay? Write an essay of your own in which you state your opininon and support it with evidence from the original essay.

21. Tan explains that her mother's language had the greatest influence on her understanding of English. Do you agree that family members have the greatest effect on a child's intellectual development? State your opinion in an essay, and support it with evidence from both essays.

22. Thinking About the Essential Question: What makes Ameridan literature American? In both of the essays in this section—"For the Love of Books" and "Mother Tongue"—the authors reflect on the influences that helped to enhance their love of language and that inspired them to become writers. Are both authors' experiences uniquely American? Why or why not? In a brief essay, compare and contrast the influences recounted.

Vocabulary Warm-up Word Lists

Study these words from the selections. Then, complete the activities.

Word List A

accessible [ak SES uh buhl] *adj.* able to be reached or entered
   The mountain lodge was <u>accessible</u> only by a dirt trail.

divert [duh VERT] *v.* to send in a different direction; deflect
   The flooding forced us to <u>divert</u> from the main road.

exhilaration [eg zil uh RAY shun] *n.* a feeling of joy or liveliness
   Accepting the medal, Krista felt <u>exhilaration</u> at her triumph.

fleeting [FLEET ing] *adj.* passing quickly
   For one <u>fleeting</u> moment, Jack thought he had seen her before.

hovered [HUV erd] *v.* lingered or waited nearby
   We <u>hovered</u> over the baby for hours, waiting for her to smile.

outset [OWT set] *n.* beginning; start of something
   Bill warned us at the <u>outset</u> of his talk that he had lost his notes.

pastoral [PAS tuhr uhl] *adj.* having to do with simple country life, especially in literature or art
   The paintings of <u>pastoral</u> scenes contrasted with the big-city setting.

principal [PRIN suh puhl] *adj.* main; most important
   The engineer's <u>principal</u> concern is the safety of the building.

Word List B

cowardice [COW er dis] *n.* lack of courage; fear; weakness of character
   Clara's failure to speak up for her friend was a sign of <u>cowardice</u>.

heyday [HAY day] *n.* period of greatest power or success; prime
   In its <u>heyday</u>, the band played five concerts a week.

inefficient [in e FISH uhnt] *adj.* not making the best use of resources
   Mailing separate boxes is an <u>inefficient</u> way to send those books.

lumbering [LUM ber ing] *v.* moving in a heavy, clumsy way
   Here comes Jayne, <u>lumbering</u> along in her giant parka and boots.

lured [LOORD] *v.* attracted or drawn by something
   The sweet aroma <u>lured</u> us into the bakery.

rangy [RAYN jee] *adj.* tall and thin, with long limbs; lanky
   The <u>rangy</u> Irish setter looked odd next to the stubby Basset hound.

ravine [ruh VEEN] *n.* a narrow valley with steep sides
   We looked over the side of the bridge at the deep <u>ravine</u> below.

shied [SHYD] *v.* moved suddenly, as if startled
   The donkey <u>shied</u> at the sound of the slamming door.

From "The Woman Warrior" by Maxine Hong Kingston and
"The Names" by M. Scott Momaday
Vocabulary Warm-up Exercises

Exercise A *Fill in the blanks, using each word from Word List A only once.*

"We have to [1] _____ the plane away from the airport," Sondra's flight instructor said. "There is an oil spill on the runway." Sondra wasn't nervous. She knew that her instructor [2] _____ nearby, ready to assist her. She looked down at the pleasant [3] _____ landscape and grinned. She still felt the same [4] _____ she'd experienced on her first flight. At the [5] _____ of her training, she may have had [6] _____ moments of fear, but those were gone now. She was grateful for the chance to fly, knowing it was not [7] _____ to most people. She also knew how hard her parents had worked to help pay for her lessons. Her [8] _____ goal was to make them proud of her.

Exercise B *Revise each sentence so that the underlined vocabulary word is used in logical way. Be sure to keep the vocabulary word in your revision.*

1. The piles of trash <u>lured</u> us to have our picnic there.

   _____

2. Maggie's <u>cowardice</u> led her to save the lives of three other soldiers.

   _____

3. The ballet dancer was <u>lumbering</u> gracefully across the stage.

   _____

4. Production at the <u>inefficient</u> factory increased sharply.

   _____

5. The horse <u>shied</u> calmly as it walked back to the barn.

   _____

6. The short, round athlete could best be described as <u>rangy</u>.

   _____

7. When his watch fell to the bottom of the <u>ravine</u>, Will bent over and picked it up.

   _____

8. Now that his <u>heyday</u> had passed, the actor became famous.

   _____

From "The Woman Warrior" by Maxine Hong Kingston and
"The Names" by M. Scott Momaday

Reading Warm-up A

Read the following passage. Then, complete the activities.

The United States is often called a nation of immigrants. In fact, nearly the entire population of this country has ancestors who chose to <u>divert</u> the direction of their lives and create a new life far from home. Some of these immigrants redirected their lives due to wars or other dangers. Others came looking for a better life. The flow of immigrants to the United States has always come in waves. Heavy periods of immigration have usually been followed by a backlash against newcomers.

For many immigrants, the idea of living in America had long <u>hovered</u> in their minds like a floating dream. They saw a golden, <u>pastoral</u> country of green fields and new chances. They saw a land in which opportunity was open and <u>accessible</u> to anyone. This added to the joyful <u>exhilaration</u> that so many must have felt as they sailed past the Statue of Liberty or saw the San Francisco skyline for the first time.

These new arrivals were sometimes inspired by false claims of streets paved with gold, among other lies they had heard about America. Their initial excitement at the <u>outset</u> of life in a new country was sometimes a <u>fleeting</u> emotion, passing as soon as reality set in.

Many newcomers are able to build successful lives in their adopted country. But it is far from simple. Struggling with a new language and new customs are the biggest, <u>principal</u> problems of culture shock. Even so, streams of hopeful people continue to make the journey to the United States.

1. Circle the word that is a synonym for <u>divert</u>. Then underline what the immigrants chose to **divert**.

2. Underline the words that hint at the meaning of <u>hovered</u>. Use *hovered* in a new sentence.

3. Circle the words that give a clue to the meaning of <u>pastoral</u>. Give a word or phrase that means the opposite of *pastoral*.

4. Circle the word that gives a clue to the meaning of <u>accessible</u>. Give an antonym for *accessible*.

5. Underline the word that gives a clue to the meaning of <u>exhilaration</u>. What might create a feeling of *exhilaration*?

6. Give a word that could substitute for <u>outset</u> in this sentence. Then circle the word that gives a clue to *outset*.

7. Underline the phrase that explains the meaning of <u>fleeting</u>. Give a synonym for *fleeting*.

8. Underline the word that gives a clue to the meaning of <u>principal</u>. Use the word *principal* in a new sentence.

From **"The Woman Warrior"** by Maxine Hong Kingston and
"The Names" by M. Scott Momaday
Reading Warm-up B

Read the following passage. Then, complete the activities.

For a brief period of U.S. history, cowboys seemed like the stars of the American West. Ever since their heyday, cowboys were seen as tough, independent individuals, in contrast to the soft folks in the big city. These long, thin riders, and their equally rangy horses, ruled the prairies and plains.

City-dwellers wanted to experience a little of the cowboy life, and the "dude ranch" was born. People were lured to these guest ranches by the promise of a genuine cowboy experience. They were also drawn by the wide-open spaces, the romance of the trail, and by the opportunity to learn to ride a horse. Instead of lumbering and clumping along concrete sidewalks, these city folks would be moving with speed and grace on the back of a horse.

To cowboys, as well as to Native Americans and ranchers, horses had been more than simply vehicles for getting from place to place. These beautiful, intelligent creatures were more like partners in their work. Beginning riders, however, sometimes had a different, less pleasant, experience. Instead of working together with their horses like a smoothly operating machine, the beginners' inefficient style of riding made them very sore the next day. Others, faced with the size and power of the animals, had to confront their own cowardice. Would they have the strength and courage to climb up into the saddle? What if the horse were startled and shied at the edge of a cliff? The rider might be thrown from the horse's back into a deep ravine and that might be dangerous, or worse, humiliating!

Despite these risks, dude ranches remain a popular vacation choice for people who have the resources to afford it, proving that the cowboy is still a vital part of the American imagination.

1. Underline the words in a nearby sentence that give a clue to heyday. Use the word *heyday* in a sentence about a movie star.

2. Circle the words that give a clue to the meaning of rangy. Then give a phrase that means the opposite of *rangy*.

3. Underline the words in a nearby sentence that mean the same as lured. Then state what else might have *lured* people to dude ranches.

4. Circle the word that has the same meaning as lumbering. Then underline a phrase that means the opposite of *lumbering*.

5. Underline the phrase that has the opposite meaning of inefficient. Use the word *inefficient* in a new sentence.

6. Circle the words that mean the opposite of cowardice. What caused the visitors to the dude ranch to face their own *cowardice*?

7. Underline the phrases that give a clue to the meaning of shied. What might cause horses to have *shied*?

8. Underline the words that give a clue to the meaning of ravine. Use *ravine* in a new sentence.

Name _____ Date _____

from The Woman Warrior by Maxine Hong Kingston
from **The Names** by N. Scott Momada
Literary Analysis: Memoirs

Most **memoirs** are similar to autobiographies. They are usually first-person nonfiction narratives describing significant experiences and events in the life of the writer. Maxine Hong Kingston's *The Woman Warrior*, subtitled *Memoirs of a Girlhood Among Ghosts*, has features that are both similar to and different from those of typical memoirs. The excerpt from *The Names* by N. Scott Momaday has a format that is more typical of most memoirs.

DIRECTIONS: *Answer the following questions.*

1. What is the narrative point of view of the excerpt from *The Names*? Is this point of view typically used in memoirs? Explain.

_____

_____

_____

_____

2. What are two significant experiences, moments, or events described in the excerpt from *The Names*? Why are they significant?

_____

_____

_____

_____

3. On whose personal impressions of events does the excerpt from *The Woman Warrior* focus? Describe two passages in the selection that reveal this person's unique perspective.

_____

_____

_____

_____

4. Explain why features of *The Woman Warrior* are different from those of standard memoirs. Why do you think Maxine Hong Kingston chose this unique style for her memoirs? In what way does this style help to convey her central message?

_____

_____

_____

_____

from **The Woman Warrior** by Maxine Hong Kingston
from **The Names** by N. Scott Momada

Reading Strategy: Relate to Your Own Experiences

The writers of these essays describe experience that have great personal significance. You can better understand the writers and their ideas if you look for ways in which the essays relate to your own experiences.

DIRECTIONS: *Write your answers to the following questions.*

1. At age thirteen, Momaday received a horse from his parents. What event can you relate from your own experience?

   _____

   _____

   _____

2. What significance did your experience have?

   _____

   _____

   _____

3. How does recalling your experience help you understand Momaday's?

   _____

   _____

   _____

4. The excerpt from *The Woman Warrior* describes Brave Orchid as having some superstitious beliefs: that she can help to keep an airplane in the air or a ship afloat through sheer will-power. Do you—or does anyone you know—have or practice any superstitions, such as not walking on the cracks of the pavement? Briefly describe any of your own superstitions or those of your friends or family members.

   _____

   _____

   _____

5. In the excerpt from *The Woman Warrior,* Brave Orchid shows impatience with some of the personal habits and tastes of her children, who grown up in the United States. Have your parents or grandparents ever disapproved of any of your tastes in food, music, or other areas? Briefly describe any such "conflict of generations" that you may have experienced.

   _____

   _____

   _____

from **The Woman Warrior** by Maxine Hong Kingston
from **The Names** by N. Scott Momaday
Vocabulary Builder

Using the Root -*aud*-

Thes root comes from the Latin word *audire*, which means "to hear." Most words containing the root -*aud*- are related to sound and hearing.

  audible   audience   audiology   audiovisua

A. DIRECTIONS: *Read each of the following descriptions. On the line provided, write the word containing the root -aud- that is being described.*

1. a kind of presentation that involves both hearing and sight _____

2. a branch of science that deals with hearing _____

3. a group of people gathered to hear a concert, speech, or play _____

4. loud and clear enough to be heard _____

Using the Word List

  gravity   inaudibly   intricate   oblivious   supple

B. DIRECTIONS: *Choose a lettered word pair that best expresses a relationship similar to that expressed in the numbered pair. Circle the letter of your choice.*

1. INTRICATE : SIMPLE ::
   A. cheerfully : gloomily
   B. fortunate : luck
   C. discourage : encourage
   D. courageously : cowardly

2. SUPPLE : FLEXIBLE ::
   A. buyer : regret
   B. problem : solution
   C. strange : alien
   D. softness : texture

3. INAUDIBLY : FAINTLY ::
   A. sincerely : frankly
   B. swift : slow
   C. gradual : movement
   D. lively : animate

4. GRAVITY : PROBLEM ::
   A. friendly : relationship
   B. excitement : surprise
   C. clearly : transparent
   D. complicated : problem

5. OBLIVIOUS : UNAWARE ::
   A. gigantic : impressive
   B. attentive : neglectful
   C. abundant : plentiful
   D. hopelessness : sorrow

from **The Woman Warrior** by Maxine Hong Kingston

from **The Names** by N. Scott Momaday

Grammar and Style: Creating Sentence Variety

A healthy variety of sentence structures can make your writing vital and engaging. Simple sentences contain one independent clause and convey ideas concisely and directly. Compound sentences, which contain two or more independent clauses, and complex sentences, which contain an independent clause and one or more subordinate clauses, can enhance the flow of ideas

A. UNDERSTANDING STYLE: *Write the types of sentence structures used in each of the following quotations. Then explain how each writer's sentence structure affects his or her prose.*

1. When she was about sixty-eight years old, Brave Orchid took a day off to wait at San Francisco International Airport for the plane that was bringing her sister to the United States. She had not seen her sister for thirty years. —Maxine Hong Kingston

   _____

   _____

2. They had said he was in Japan, and then they said he was in the Philippines. But when she sent him her help, she could feel that she was on a ship in Da Nang. — Maxine Hong Kingston

   _____

   _____

3. When the song, which was a song of riding, was finished, I had Pecos pick up the pace. Far down on the road to San Ysidro I overtook my friend Pasqual Fragua. — N. Scott Momaday

   _____

   _____

B. Writing Application: Varying your sentence structure, write a paragraph in which you describe a memorable experience.

   _____

   _____

   _____

   _____

   _____

   _____

   _____

   _____

   _____

Name _____ Date _____

from The Woman Warrior by Maxine Hong Kingston
from **The Names** by N. Scott Momaday
Support for Writing

Memoir on an event that changed your life. Prepare to write a reflective essay. In the diagram below, enter three important events from your past, and describe how they affected you.

Events that Affected or Changed My Life

Event:
_____

Effects it has had on my life:
_____
_____
_____

Event:
_____

Effects it has had on my life:
_____
_____
_____

Event:
_____

Effects it has had on my life:
_____
_____

On a separate page, draft your memoir. Choose one event from your organizer, and explain the insight it provided to you. Describe how the event affects your life today. Add additional information, if necessary, to make your essay clear to your readers.

from The Woman Warrior by Maxine Hong Kingston

from **The Names** by N. Scott Momaday

Enrichment: Memoir Writing

Maxine Hong Kingston based her award-winning memoirs on "talk stories," or anecdotes, from her own life and from her mother's life. N. Scott Momaday's memoir also draws on anecdotes from his youth. Imagine you are a professional writer under contract to write your family memoirs. Think about the yarns, tall tales, humorous stories, or embarrassing moments that you have heard from relatives. How might you tell one of these stories so that it is interesting to someone outside your own family?

DIRECTIONS: *Choose a family story, either humorous or serious, that you would like to include in your memoirs. Then plan how you will turn it into a finished and interesting piece of narrative writing by answering the following questions:*

1. What are the basic events of the story, told in order?

   _____

   _____

   _____

   _____

2. What are key details you would like to emphasize? Will your piece have a particular theme? If so, what will this theme be?

   _____

   _____

   _____

   _____

3. What are the traditional features of a memoir? Will your story be similar to or different from a traditional memoir? Explain.

   _____

   _____

   _____

   _____

4. Why do you think readers will enjoy your story?

   _____

   _____

   _____

   _____

   _____

   _____

from **The Woman Warrior** by Maxine Hong Kingston; *from* **The Names** by N. Scott Momaday
Open-Book Test
Short Answer *Write your responses to the questions in this section on the lines provided.*

1. In the excerpt from *The Woman Warrior,* Brave Orchid refers to many of the people around her as "Ghosts." To whom does she apply this name, and why?

   _____

   _____

2. Most memoirs are written in the first-person point of view. In what voice did Kingston write the excerpt from *The Woman Warrior*? Why do you think she made this choice?

   _____

   _____

   _____

3. The excerpt from *The Woman Warrior* contains many diverse observations and experiences related to a specific scene at an airport. What kinds of experiences in the reader's life might enable him or her to relate more closely to the incidents or characters portrayed in this memoir?

   _____

   _____

4. Most of the excerpt from *The Woman Warrior* centers on the thoughts and feelings and reactions of Brave Orchid. Understanding her character, then, is a key to understanding many of the memoir's themes and concerns: the conflict between cultures, the conflict between generations, the distorting effects on memory by the passage of time. Use the diagram below to identify aspects of the character of Brave Orchid. Use the surrounding boxes to organize her behavior, traits, beliefs, and interactions with other characters.

Brave Orchid

5. The excerpt from *The Woman Warrior* differs from many traditional memoirs. Give at least two reasons why this is the case.

_____

_____

_____

_____

6. Momaday begins the excerpt from *The Names* by discussing the importance of horses to the Kiowa people. Considering that *The Names* is a personal memoir, what is the significance of this opening section?

_____

_____

7. Early on in the excerpt from *The Names*, Momaday writes, "On the back of my horse I had a different view of the world. I could see more of it, how it reached away beyond all the horizons I had ever seen. . . ." Is this expanded view of the world merely physical, or does it have other meanings as well?

_____

_____

_____

8. The excerpt from *The Names* is in large part about Momaday's coming of age through his travels on and his relationship with his horse. What kind of similar experience might allow the reader to identify more closely with Momaday's experiences?

_____

_____

9. The excerpt from *The Names* is a coming-of-age memoir—it recounts a crucial episode in the author's journey toward manhood and an independent sense of self. What, then, is the significance of Momaday's account of his intensive training with the horse to win races after a delayed start?

_____

_____

_____

10. If you were oblivious to most of what your teacher was saying in class, would you be listening to her closely? Why or why not? Base your answer on the meaning of *oblivious* as it is used in the excerpt from *The Woman Warrior*.

_____

_____

Essay

Write an extended response to the question of your choice or to the question or questions our teacher assigns you.

11. Often you can enjoy a story or nonfiction selection by relating all or part of it to your own experience. Which episode of the excerpts from either *The Names* or *The Woman Warrior* echoes one of your own experiences? How does Momaday or Kingston do this—through similarity of circumstances or kind of lesson learned about life, or both? In an essay, identify the episode from the memoir, and explain how it relates to your own experience. Support your answer with specific details from the memoir and your own experience.

12. The two selections in this section—the excerpts from *The Names* and *The Woman Warrior*—are both memoirs, but they use very different techniques. In *The Names*, Momaday sticks to the conventional first-person narrative that focuses on his own thoughts and feelings. In *The Woman Warrior*, Kingston uses an unconventional third-person narrative that focuses on the thoughts and feelings of her mother. Which technique do you think is more effective? Why? Explain your opinion in an essay that cites details from the memoirs.

13. In both of the memoirs in this section—the excerpts from *The Names* and from *The Woman Warrior*—the authors reflect on aspects of their cultural heritage: Kiowa Indian for Momaday, and Chinese for Kingston. In an essay, compare and contrast the attitude the authors show toward their cultural heritage in these memoirs. Is it appreciative? Critical? A mixture of both? Support your answer with details from the memoirs.

14. **Thinking About the Essential Question: What is the relationship between place and literature?** The excerpts from both of the memoirs in this section—*The Woman Warrior* and *The Names*—are deeply rooted in the places of the childhood of both authors: the Great Plains of Momaday's youth and the Chinese subculture in which Kingston grew up. In an essay, explain how this sense of place has shaped the outlook of the author of each selection.

Oral Response

15. Go back to question 1, 2, or 3 or to the question your teacher assigns you. Take a few minutes to expand your answer and prepare an oral response. Find additional details in the excerpts from *The Names* and *The Woman Warrior* that support your points. If necessary, make notes to guide your oral response.

from **The Woman Warrior** by Maxine Hong Kingston and
from **The Names** by N. Scott Momaday
Selection Test A

MULTIPLE CHOICE

Critical Reading *Identify the letter of the choice that best answers the question.*

____ 1. In *The Woman Warrior*, what is the relationship between Brave Orchid and Moon Orchid?
   A. They are mother and daughter.   C. They are sisters.
   B. They are aunt and niece.   D. They are cousins.

____ 2. What is one of the characteristics that makes *The Woman Warrior* a memoir?
   A. It is about people who come to America.
   B. It is about how American children behave.
   C. It is about saving money on lunch.
   D. It is about an important personal event.

____ 3. During which historical period does this portion of *The Woman Warrior* take place?
   A. during the settlement of California
   B. during the Vietnam War
   C. during the last few years
   D. during immigration to Ellis Island

____ 4. What is Brave Orchid's basic feeling toward American culture in *The Woman Warrior*?
   A. acceptance   B. curiosity   C. respect   D. suspicion

____ 5. What is different about *The Woman Warrior*, compared to other memoirs?
   A. It is not written in the first person.
   B. It is fiction rather than nonfiction.
   C. It is about an entire family.
   D. It is not about a personal experience.

____ 6. Which person does the reader learn most about in *The Woman Warrior*?
   A. Brave Orchid's husband   C. Brave Orchid's niece
   B. Brave Orchid's children   D. Brave Orchid

____ 7. To which character's experiences in *The Woman Warrior* would an American teenager most likely relate?
   A. Brave Orchid
   B. Moon Orchid
   C. Brave Orchid's daughter
   D. Brave Orchid's niece

____ 8. Why does Brave Orchid confuse young travelers with her sister in *The Woman Warrior*?

    A. They were both young when they parted.

    B. Her sister is much younger than she is.

    C. Her sister has had plastic surgery.

    D. Brave Orchid has a poor memory.

____ 9. Which of the following experiences would best help a reader relate to Brave Orchid's children in this excerpt from *The Woman Warrior*?

    A. traveling a long distance by airplane

    B. feeling very old when seeing an older relative

    C. packing a lunch and eating it in a public place

    D. having a parent draw embarrassing attention in public

____ 10. In *The Names*, why does the author tell the story of how he learned to mount Pecos on the run?

    A. to show that it is good to challenge oneself

    B. to demonstrate what a great horse Pecos was

    C. to persuade young people to avoid taking risks

    D. to teach others how to do the trick

____ 11. *In The Names*, why does the author feel that having a horse is important?

    A. to be able to travel long distances   C. to be able to race other riders

    B. to be true to his Kiowa nature   D. to be able to rule an animal

____ 12. How might a reader relate to Momaday's experiences with Pecos in *The Names*?

    A. by entering a bicycle race   C. by working with an animal

    B. by making a long trip   D. by traveling to the west

____ 13. In *The Names*, how is the author's experience riding Pecos different from riding the stallion?

    A. The stallion runs faster than Pecos.

    B. The author and Pecos ride as one.

    C. Pecos keeps wanting his head.

    D. The stallion jars the author's bones.

____ 14. How do you know that *The Names* is a memoir?

    A. It is about riding a horse on a long journey.

    B. It is a third-person narrative and is mostly fictional.

    C. It is a first-person narrative that tells a story from the author's life.

    D. It blends the real memories of the author with fictional characters and places.

____ **15.** Why do you think the journey described in *The Names* is such an important time in the author's life?

    A. It is when he runs away from home.

    B. It is when he starts to feel independent.

    C. It is when he realizes that he dislikes animals.

    D. It is when he decides that he will race horses when he grows up.

Vocabulary *Identify the letter of the choice that best answers the question.*

____ **16.** Which word best replaces *gravity* in this sentence: "The child became aware of the *gravity* of the situation when her parents told her not to laugh"?

    A. seriousness

    B. humor

    C. sound

    D. crowd

____ **17.** In which sentence is *permeated* used correctly?

    A. The saddle permeated the horse.

    B. Water permeated down a waterfall.

    C. The scent of pine trees permeated the air.

    D. The horse's permeated rider was able to jump into the saddle.

Essay

Write an extended response to the question of your choice or to the question or questions your teacher assigns you.

18. In *The Woman Warrior*, Brave Orchid's ideas about Moon Orchid cause surprise and discofort for her at the airport. Why? What does this experience say about the value of memories and the mental pictures we carry of the people in our lives? Write a brief essay to address these questions.

19. What is an experience you have had that helps you relate to Momaday's experiences in The Names? In a brief essay, describe your experience and compare it to Momaday's.

20. Thinking About the Essential Question: What is the relationship between place and literature? The excerpts from both of the memoirs in this section—*The Woman Warrior* and *The Names*—are deeply rooted in the places of the childhood of both authors: the Great Plains of Momaday's youth and the Chinese subculture in which Kingston grew up. In an essay, explain how this sense of place has shaped the way the author of each selection sees the world.

from **The Woman Warrior** by Maxine Hong Kingston
and *from* **The Names** by N. Scott Momaday
Selection Test B

MULTIPLE CHOICE

Critical Reading *Identify the letter of the choice that best completes the statement or answers the question.*

_____ 1. This selection from *The Woman Warrior* focuses mainly on the personal impressions of which character?
    A. Brave Orchid
    B. Moon Orchid
    C. Brave Orchid's niece
    D. Brave Orchid's daughter

_____ 2. What is the best description of Brave Orchid's feelings as she waits in the airport?
    A. happy and carefree
    B. bored and indifferent
    C. annoyed and impatient
    D. anxious and uncomfortable

_____ 3. What do Brave Orchid's children do as she waits for the arrival of Moon Orchid?
    A. They sit with their mother.
    B. They talk to soldiers.
    C. They wander around the airport.
    D. They sit at home.

_____ 4. According to Brave Orchid, how were she and other immigrants treated by customs officers at Ellis Island when they arrived in America?
    A. They were given a warm welcome.
    B. They were scrutinized and treated with disdain.
    C. They were virtually ignored.
    D. They were given a great deal of assistance.

_____ 5. In *The Woman Warrior*, why is each sister so shocked by the other's appearance?
    A. They don't remember looking so much alike.
    B. Their aged appearances show how much time has gone by.
    C. They can't believe they didn't recognize each other.
    D. They look like their children.

_____ 6. What is one main reason why this selection from *The Woman Warrior* might be considered different from traditional memoirs?
    A. It is nonfiction.
    B. It is written in the third person and focuses on the personal impressions of someone other than the writer.
    C. It is about a significant personal experience.
    D. It is written in the first person and focuses on the personal impressions of the writer.

_____ 7. What part of this selection from *The Woman Warrior* best illustrates the complications faced by bicultural families?
    A. Brave Orchid's memory of Ellis Island and her own immigration experience
    B. Brave Orchid's concerns about her son in Vietnam
    C. the conflict between Brave Orchid and her children
    D. the meeting between Brave Orchid and Moon Orchid

____ 8. To which experience described in *The Woman Warrior* might an American-born teenager best relate?
A. emigrating to a new country
B. having a mother disapprove of buying food at an airport
C. being embarrassed by a parent drawing attention to herself in a public place
D. feeling old and realizing how quickly time passes

____ 9. The gift of a horse was an important moment in Momaday's life because he
A. longed to travel far from home.
B. viewed the horse as a link to his Kiowa heritage.
C. won many races on the horse.
D. was a skilled horseman.

____ 10. Which words best describe the young Momaday?
A. cautious and intelligent
B. reckless and wild
C. frugal and timid
D. adventurous and determined

____ 11. Which experience might best help a modern teenager relate to Momaday's experiences with Pecos?
A. spending a weekend at a ranch
B. watching a movie about the Southwest
C. restoring a used car
D. reading one of Momaday's books

____ 12. Why does Momaday believe that "it may be that in [Pecos's] last days an image of me like thought shimmered in his brain"?
A. Momaday felt a strong bond with Pecos.
B. Momaday saw Pecos not long before the horse died.
C. Pecos appeared to Momaday in a vision.
D. Pecos resented Momaday for selling him.

____ 13. Which sentence best summarizes the theme of Momaday's essay?
A. Journeys of discovery must be made alone.
B. Life's lessons, though difficult, are worth learning.
C. One must persevere to succeed in life.
D. To know one's true identity, a person must discover his or her heritage.

____ 14. What is one of the characteristics that makes *The Names* a memoir?
A. It is about riding a horse.
B. It is about the Kiowa heritage.
C. It is a fictional story about a journey.
D. It is about important personal events.

____ 15. Why might a reader try to relate his or her own experiences to those Momaday describes in *The Names*?
A. to increase understanding and enjoyment of the story
B. to help decide if the story is fiction or nonfiction
C. to understand the history of unfamiliar cultural traditions
D. to figure out the meaning of new vocabulary terms

____ 16. Why is Momaday's journey with Pecos important enough to him to include in his memoir?
   A. because he won many horse races with Pecos
   B. because it helps him remember his horse after it died
   C. because nothing else of interest happened during his childhood
   D. because it is when he feels he "came of age" and learned to be independent

Vocabulary *Identify the letter of the choice that best completes the statement or answers the question.*

____ 17. Brave Orchid felt the soldiers waiting to go to war should be crying _____ instead of standing there calmly.
   A. inaudibly   C. obviously
   B. cautiously   D. hysterically

____ 18. Momaday's first view of the world from horseback was _____
   A. supple
   B. concocted
   C. flamboyant
   D. revelatory

Essay

Write an extended response to the question of your choice or to the question or questions your teacher assigns you.

19. The subtitle of *The Woman Warrior* is Memoirs of a Girlhood Among Ghosts. On whose impressions and experiences does the selection focus? What are some examples of this character's impressions? What does the reader learn from these impressions? Answer these questions in an essay.

20. In an essay, describe Brave Orchid. What does she value? How does she feel about American culture? What parts of the selection clearly reveal Brave Orchid's concerns and beliefs?

21. The childhood experiences Momaday recalls happened in different places many years ago. How can you relate to his experiences? Choose the experience Momaday describes that you most strongly relate to an experience of your own. In an essay, explain how you connected to the writer's experience and how this experience helped you understand the author's ideas.

22. **Thinking About the Essential Question: What is the relationship between place and literature?** The excerpts from both of the memoirs in this section—*The Woman Warrior* and *The Names*—are deeply rooted in the places of the childhood of both authors: the Great Plains of Momaday's youth and the Chinese subculture in which Kingston grew up. In an essay, explain how this sense of place has shaped the outlook of the author of each selection.

Name _____ Date _____

Narrowing Your Topic: Create a Story Chart

Use this story chart to plan the four stages of your story

Exposition Establish the setting, main characters, and set up the conflict	
Rising Action Describe the events that increase the conflict and tension	
Climax Identify the point of greatest tension	
Resolution Tell how the conflict is or isn't resolved	

Gathering Details: Interview Your Characters

Conduct an interview with each of your main characters, using these question starters:

Where do you live?	
What's a typical day like for you? What would be a perfect day?	
How would you describe yourself?	
What are your big goals?	
What obstacles are standing in your way?	

Unit 6 Resources: New Voices, New Frontiers
238

Name _____   Date _____

Narration: Short Story—Integrating Grammar Skills

Using a character's thoughts and words can help you move your story in an entertaining way. You can use **dialogue** between two characters to establish tension and tell plot events. If you do use dialogue, you will make use of quotation marks. Some writers find it difficult to remember when to place punctuation marks inside quotation marks and when to place them outside quotation marks. The following rules will help you.

Rule	Example
Always place a comma or a period inside the final quotation mark.	One of my favorite short stories by Alice Walker is "Everyday Use."
Always place a semicolon or colon outside the final quotation mark.	First I read "Everyday Use"; then I read some of her other short stories.
Place a question mark or exclamation mark inside the final quotation mark if the end mark is part of the quotation.	Near the beginning of "Everyday Use," Maggie asks, "How do I look, Mama?"
Place a question mark or exclamation mark outside the final quotation mark if the end mark is not part of the quotation.	Have you read Alice Walker's short story "Advancing Luna"?

A. PRACTICE: *Read each of the following passages from "Everyday Use." If the passage is punctuated correctly, write C on the line. If it is punctuated incorrectly, write I on the line. Adjust the punctuation to the incorrect sentences and circle your corrections.*

_____1. "Unnnh", is what it sounds like. Like when you see the wriggling end of a snake just in front of your foot in the road. "Uhnnnh".

_____2. "Wa-su-zo-Tean-o!" she says, coming on in that gliding way the dress makes her move. The short stocky fellow with the hair to his navel is all grinning and he follows up with "Asalamalakim, my mother and sister!"

_____3. "Maggie can't appreciate these quilts"! she said. "She'd probably be backward enough to put them to everyday use."

B. WRITING APPLICATION: *All quotation marks have been removed from the dialogue in the following passage adapted from "Everyday Use." Rewrite the passage, adding quotation marks where necessary. Be sure to follow the rules of punctuation.*

Why don't you take one or two of the others? I asked. These old things was just done by me and Big Dee.

No, said Wangero. I don't want those. They are stitched around the borders by machine.

That'll make them last better, I said.

That's not the point, said Wangero. These are all pieces of dresses Grandma used to wear. She did all this stitching by hand. Imagine! Wangero held the quilts securely in her arms.

Communications Workshop—Unit 6
Comparing Media Coverage of the Same Event

    Choose a single news event that received widespread coverage. Examine how this story was covered by three different types of media. Look for similarities and differences in the way each medium covered the event. Also, look for the ways in which the coverage shaped the audience's understanding of the event.

News event			
Covered by			
Intended audience			
Layout choices			
Sequencing choices			
Language choices			
Strengths /weaknesses of coverage			

Did these different stories affect your understanding of or attitude toward the event in different ways? Explain. _____

_____

_____

Unit 6 Vocabulary Workshop
Cognates

Many English and Spanish words share the same Latin roots. These words are called cognates and they have similar spellings and definitions. If you understand in Spanish that learning cognates is not *arduo*, you easily understand in English that it is not *arduous*. This chart shows some English-Spanish cognates.

English Word	Spanish Word	Meaning
acclamation	aclamación	enthusiastic approval
corroboration	corroboración	support, confirmation
didactic	didáctico	intended to teach
enigma	enigma	riddle, mystery
indifferent	indiferente	uncaring, neutral
itinerary	itinerario	route
potent	potente	powerful
proliferation	proliferación	rapid increase

A. DIRECTIONS: *Use the definition of each italicized cognate to answer each question.*

1. Would a *proliferation* of problems improve a situation or worsen it?

   _____

2. Is a *didactic* poem intended to entertain or to educate?

   _____

3. At a trial, if evidence provides *corroboration* to a witness' story, does the evidence help or hurt the witness?

   _____

4. If your friends are *indifferent* to your problems, would you expect them to help you or ignore you?

   _____

B. DIRECTIONS: *Write a sentence using each of the following cognates.*

1. acclamation _____

2. enigma _____

3. itinerary _____

4. potent _____

Essential Questions Workshop—Unit 6

In their stories, poems, and nonfiction, the writers in Unit Six express ideas that relate to the three Essential Questions framing this book. Review the literature in the unit. Then, for each Essential Question, choose an author and at least one passage from his or her writing that expresses a related idea. Use this chart to complete your work.

Essential Question	Author/Selection	Literary Passage
How does literature shape or reflect society?		
What is the relationship between place and literature?		
What makes American literature American?		

Unit 6: New Voices, New Frontiers
Benchmark Test 12

MULTIPLE CHOICE

Literary Analysis and Reading Skills

Answer the following questions.

1. Which of these is a feature found only in free verse poetry?
   A. a lack of sound devices
   B. the use of symbolism
   C. fixed meter and line length
   D. an irregular pattern of rhyme and meter

Read the poem. Then, answer the questions that follow.

1 The March wind wailed and whistled,
2 flapping and banging
3 the pale blue shutters,
4 and rattling the red, gold, and brown
5 leaves huddled in
6 the gutter.

2. Which line of the poem is end-stopped?
   A. line 1   C. line 4
   B. line 2   D. line 6

3. Which line in the poem is an example of enjambment?
   A. line 1   C. line 3
   B. line 2   D. line 6

4. Which senses are called up in the sensory details of this poem?
   A. sight and sound   C. sight, smell, and touch
   B. sight and smell   D. sight, sound, and smell

5. Which is the most accurate description of the wind as portrayed in the images of this poem?
   A. gentle and murmuring
   B. noisy and aggressive
   C. destructive and hopeless
   D. brisk and refreshing

Name _____ Date _____

Answer the following questions.

6. In literature, what is the term for a brief story about an amusing or interesting event that is told to entertain or make a point?
   A. a novel
   B. an autobiography
   C. an anecdote
   D. an editorial

7. Choose the pair of words or phrases that correctly completes the sentence.

   A parody _____ another piece of writing in order to _____.

   A. borrows ideas from / get credit for them
   B. analyzes / review it
   C. imitates / make fun of it
   D. explains / make it more accessible

8. Choose the pair of words or phrases that correctly completes the sentence.

   A satire _____ something in order to _____.

   A. exaggerates; make it entertaining
   B. mocks; destroy
   C. imitates; improve it
   D. ridicules; criticize it

9. Which topic would be the most obvious choice for a comparison-and-contrast essay?
   A. the historical events leading to the Revolutionary War
   B. an explanation of global warming
   C. the policies of two opposing political candidates
   D. a movie review

10. Which primary source would be the most valuable to a historian who is researching the lives of the wives of World War II American naval officers?
    A. letters from home received by members of the armed forces in the early 1940s
    B. journals kept by German military officers
    C. wartime speeches by President Franklin Delano Roosevelt
    D. classified wartime memoranda from the Department of the Navy

11. Why might an author use idioms when writing dialogue?
    A. Idioms allow the author to show off his or her cleverness.
    B. Idioms help the author show the foolishness of the characters.
    C. Idioms can help an author depict the language of a particular group or area.
    D. Idioms are a way to inject humor into serious dialogue.

12. Which topic is the most obvious choice for a personal, reflective essay?
    A. a biological study of the life of a coyote
    B. your tribute to a sports hero who is entering a hall of fame
    C. your feelings on the day you moved from your childhood home
    D. an essay on how to play the guitar

13. Which sentence would most likely be found in a memoir?
    A. The outcome of the 2000 Presidential election was hotly contested.
    B. The Statue of Liberty was probably the largest birthday present ever sent.
    C. My first day on the job as a community organizer was almost my last.
    D. When she married John Adams, Abigail had no idea how often she would be alone.

Read the selection. Then, answer the questions that follow.

(1) Unlike most land masses, New Zealand has no native mammals. (2) The first mammals arrived long ago, when visitors and settlers arrived from Europe and Asia with their pet cats, dogs, and weasels. (3) Before their arrival, many species of flightless birds, such as the dodo, the moa, the takahe, the kakapo, and the kiwi thrived in New Zealand. (4) Their natural enemies were other birds, such as eagles and hawks, who hunted by sight. (5) Therefore, the flightless birds could protect themselves by standing very still and blending in with their surroundings. (6) However, mammals hunt primarily by scent. (7) Therefore, camouflage was not enough to save the flightless birds. (8) Many, including the dodo and the moa, became extinct. (9) Others, like the takahe and the kakapo, are now seriously endangered.

14. What type of literature is this selection?
    A. an expository essay   C. a reflective essay
    B. a satirical essay   D. an analytical essay

15. Which sentence in the essay explains a cause-effect relationship?
    A. 1   C. 5
    B. 3   D. 9

16. Which sentence is the best paraphrase of sentences 8–9?
    A. Whole species of birds either disappeared, like the dodo and moa, or are on the verge of extinction, like the takahe and the kakapo.
    B. Various species of flightless birds—like the dodo, the moa, the takahe, and the kakapo—died out because they had not learned to adapt to mammals that hunted them by scent.
    C. It was such a shame to lose such interesting birds as the dodo and the moa; we must do all we can to save the takahe and the kakapo while they still exist.
    D. Many, including the dodo and the moa, became extinct; others, like the takahe and the kakapo, are now seriously endangered.

17. Which sentence contains an important detail about the first natural enemies of flightless birds?
    A. sentence 2   C. sentence 5
    B. sentence 4   D. sentence 7

18. If an outline of this essay has I. Animal Life in New Zealand before Visitors and Settlers, what is Roman numeral II?
    A. II. Arrival of Pet Cats
    B. II. Animal Life in New Zealand after Visitors and Settlers
    C. II. Dodos, Moas, Takahes, and Kakapos
    D. II. Flightless Birds

19. To which personal experience would a reader most likely relate to while reading the essay?
    A. an experience of taking care of a pet dog
    B. an experience of touring Europe
    C. an experience of participating in an environmental clean-up day
    D. an experience of studying an endangered species

Vocabulary

Answer the following questions.

20. Based on your understanding of the Latin word *corpus*, choose the best meaning for the English word *corporeal*.
    A. pertaining to the body
    B. high military rank
    C. having to do with a small business
    D. spiritual

21. Use your understanding of the Latin word *corpus* to choose the meaning of the word *corpulent*.
    A. brightly colored
    B. generous
    C. fleshy
    D. not very clean

22. Based on the definition of its Latin root -*script*-, choose the place that you might find a postscript.
    A. in the stage directions of the written version of a dramatic play
    B. at the end of a letter, after the body and signature
    C. in a sidebar of warnings about how to operate a large piece of machinery
    D. as part of the instructions in a computer manual

23. Choose the likeliest meaning for the word *inscribe* based on your understanding of the Latin root -*scrib*-.
    A. to write on a surface
    B. to give a speech praising someone
    C. to cut into pieces
    D. to hide

24. Based on the Latin root -*aud*-, chose the meaning of the phrase *an audible sigh*.
    A. a sigh that shows sad feelings
    B. a sigh showing fear or anxiety
    C. an easily heard sigh
    D. a sigh that hides other emotions

25. Use your knowledge of the Latin root *-aud-* to choose the part of the body in which an audiologist specializes.

    A. the brain   **C.** the mouth

    B. the stomach   **D.** the ear

Grammar

Read the selection. Then, answer the questions that follow.

(1) I stood offstage. (2) I felt nervous. (3) I was prepared for the audition. (4) Still, I felt nervous. (5) I always do. (6) It doesn't matter whether the part is large or small, whether I know the director or not, or whether I am having a good day or a bad one. (7) I always feel nervous before I go onstage. (8) Then I actually step onstage, and I relax.

26. Which edited version of sentences 1–4 varies sentence length the most effectively?

    A. I stood offstage, and I felt nervous. I was prepared for the audition, but I still felt nervous.

    B. I stood offstage and I felt nervous, and, although I was prepared for the audition, I still felt nervous and I always do.

    C. I nervously stood offstage. I was prepared for the audition. I still felt nervous. I always do.

    D. I stood offstage feeling nervous. Although I was prepared for the audition, I still was nervous. I always am.

27. What part of speech gives variety to the beginning of this revision of sentences 1–2?

    As I stood offstage, I felt nervous.

    A. prepositional phrase   **C.** direct object

    B. verb   **D.** pronoun

28. Which sentence in the paragraph uses parallel structure?

    A. sentence 1

    B. sentence 3

    C. sentence 5

    D. sentence 6

Answer the following question.

29. Complete the following sentence, preserving a parallel structure.

    I really love to act, —————

    A. to sing, to dance, and to perform in any way.

    B. singing, dancing, or performing in any way.

    C. to sing, dance, and all aspects of performance.

    D. being a singer and dancer, and to perform in any way.

ESSAY

30. Write an original short story on any subject. Your story should include two or more characters that interact within a definite setting. Describe your setting so that it draws the reader in. Your story should be driven by a conflict (problem) that is either between characters, within a character, or between a character and a situation. Your plot must develop that conflict by building a series of incidents that lead to a climax, or high point, and end in a resolution.

31. Write a personal, reflective essay about a childhood incident that revolved around a misunderstanding. Your essay should be based on a real-life misunderstanding, related in a way that brings it to life for the reader. Your essay should relate the incident and reveal what it taught you about life.

32. Write a short essay presenting instructions about how to do research on a topic of your choosing. Specify a topic that you already know something about—for example, an academic question or a topic from the world of sports or entertainment. Tell your reader how to narrow that topic. Present several useful questions to pursue in doing research on this topic, and tell your readers how to find information about it, from both online and print sources.

Grade 11—Benchmark Test 11
Interpretation Guide

Skill Objective	Test Items	Number Correct	Reading Kit
Literary Analysis			
Plot Devices	1, 2, 9, 12, 13		pp. 184, 185
Character Motivation	3, 4		pp. 50, 51
Contrasting Characters	7		pp. 68, 69
Author's Style	5, 6		pp. 42, 43
Lyric Poetry	10, 11		pp. 150, 151
Theme	14, 15		pp. 260, 261
Reading Skill			
Ask Questions	21		pp. 36, 37
Analyze Author's Beliefs	19		pp. 8, 9
Interpreting	16, 17, 18		pp. 142, 143
Cause and Effect			pp. 48, 49
Vocabulary			
Words from Spanish	22		pp. 342, 343
Latin Prefixes: *doc-, doct*	23, 24		pp. 298, 299
Words and their Relatives: *heritage, brutal,* and *exhaust*	25		pp. 330, 331
Grammar			
Transitions and Transitional Phrases	26, 27		pp. 402, 403
Writing			
Personality Profile	28	Use rubric	pp. 438, 439
Reflective Essay	29	Use rubric	pp. 442, 443
Analytic Essay: Theme	30	Use rubric	pp. 414, 415

Grade 11—Benchmark Test 12
Interpretation Guide

Skill Objective	Test Items	Number Correct	Reading Kit
Literary Analysis			
Free Verse	1, 2, 3		pp. 120, 121
Imagery	4, 5		pp. 136, 137
Anecdote	6		pp. 20, 21
Parody and Pun	7		pp. 172, 173
Dialogue and Stage Directions	11		pp. 78, 79
Memoir	10, 12, 13		pp. 156, 157
Satire	8		pp. 226, 227
Reading Skill			
Essays	14, 15, 16, 18		pp. 94, 95
Identify Important Details	17		pp. 126, 127
Relating to Your Own Experiences	19		pp. 216, 217
Comparing and Contrasting Critical Reviews	9		pp. 64, 65
Vocabulary			
Latin Roots *-grat-*, *-scrib-*, *-script-*, *-aud-*	22, 23, 24, 25		pp. 300, 301
Latin Word Corpus	20, 21		pp. 320, 321
Grammar			
Varying Sentence Structure	26, 27		pp. 410, 411
Using Parallel Structure	28, 29		pp. 408, 409
Writing			
Creative Writing: Short Story	30	Use rubric	pp. 430, 431
Reflective Essay	31	Use rubric	pp. 442, 443
Essay: Research a Topic	32	Use rubric	pp. 446, 447

Unit 6 Resources: New Voice, New Frontiers
250

ANSWERS

Unit 6 Introduction

Names and Terms to Know, p. 2

A. 1. E; 2. A; 3. B; 4. F; 5. C; 6. D; 7. G

B. **Sample Answers**

1. The "Silent Generation" was exhausted from years of upheaval and reacted by trying to live peaceful lives. They were great admirers of President Eisenhower, who had seen them through war in his capacity as a heroic soldier.

2. The Vietnam War represented a time of upheaval, and many Americans responded by becoming more politically conservative. President Richard Nixon, elected in 1968, eventually brought an end to U.S. involvement there.

3. Modernism is a literary movement that was influenced by Freud's study of the unconscious. It placed a high value on the artist and his or her work, seeing fine art as superior to more popular forms of art.

4. Postmodernism is a literary movement that was greatly influenced by studies of media and language, as well as the development of technology. It has a less restrictive view of art and artists than Modernism and believes that all art, including popular art, is worthy of consideration.

Focus Questions, p. 3

Sample Answers

1. When the United States dropped the atomic bomb on Japan, the nation showed the international community its developing power as a world leader. The postwar years were marked by increasing American involvement in international conflicts—the unarmed but intense rivalry with the Soviet Union, known as the Cold War; the assistance to South Korea in 1950; and the eventual involvement in the Vietnam War. All of these actions added to the strengthening of the United States as a world power.

2. After World War II, there was a significant growth in the purchase of televisions and automobiles by the American public. Both of these changes, along with the increased use of the telephone, allowed Americans to be simultaneously more mobile, more independent, and more connected to one another. In addition, the current growth of the Internet has allowed people to connect to each other in completely new ways, revolutionizing the way people work and play.

3. American literature reflects the post-World War II years in being a combination of many different elements, such as fiction and nonfiction (for example, *In Cold Blood* and *Ragtime*); fantasy and reality; and experimentation with form. Authors, essayists, and poets have explored subjects from suburban life to racial identity to personal awareness. Although this period has been turbulent, in literature it has also been marked by creativity that, while original, owes a debt to earlier writers.

from the Author's Desk

Julie Alvarez Introduces "Antojos" p. 7

Suggested Answers

1. It became the first chapter of Alvarez's novel *How the García Girls Lost Their Accents.*

2. As an immigrant who was not a native English speaker, she wanted to start small in the literature of her adoptive country.

3. It made her treat prose as if it were poetry, something beautifully and carefully crafted in which each word is carefully chosen to be as precise as possible.

4. In his biography she read that Wolfe wrote a novel called *You Can't Go Home Again,* an idea she explores in her story.

5. It is based on Julia Alvarez and her experiences of returning home to her native Dominican Republic to visit relatives there.

6. It shows that you can go home again in some ways but not in others.

7. An essay directly addresses an idea, supporting it with facts and examples, while a story like "Antojos" shows characters and events that convey the idea as a life experience.

8. She included it as part of the realistic setting details of her story. It came to be seen as a symbol.

Julia Alvarez

Listening and Viewing, p. 8

Suggested Answers

Segment 1: Meet Julia Alvarez

- She spent her childhood as part of a large, extended family in the Dominican Republican.

- Some classmates were unfriendly and made fun of her accent, but a wonderful teacher taught her to love reading, which helped connect her to the culture.

Segment 2: Julia Alvarez on the Short Story

- It should start with action that gets the reader involved.

- It should end as close to the middle as possible.

Segment 3: Julia Alvarez on the Writing Process

- To be a writer, you must develop the habit of avoiding distractions and writing every day whether you feel like it or not.

- Stories do not work that way; the writer tries different things, and characters sometimes take the writer in unexpected directions. However, the writer must also be willing to edit out material that takes away from the story.

Unit 6 Resources: New Voices, New Frontiers
© Pearson Education, Inc. All rights reserved.
251

Segment 4: Julia Alvarez on the Rewards of Writing

- They do not play a role; she writes because she does not know how to live without writing.

- It helps her to make meaning of life and find the true pattern of life. It also gives her deep pleasure because writing is her calling and her passion.

"Antojos" by Julia Alvarez

Vocabulary Warm-up Exercises, p. 10

A. 1. anniversary
2. descent
3. conversing
4. relishing
5. complexion
6. craved
7. obscuring
8. gratifying

B. Sample Answers

1. F; If someone is appeased, that person is satisfied.
2. F; People who have congregated have come together as a group.
3. T; *Dissuade* means "to convince someone not to do something."
4. F; A wild tiger might be expected to be ferocious.
5. F; A listless person acts without energy.
6. T; *Loath* means "reluctant" or "unwilling."
7. F; A history book would include momentous events.
8. F; Since *wayward* implies "unruliness" or "lack of control," parents might have cause to worry.

Reading Warm-up A, p. 11

Sample Answers

1. second . . . of the day she started . . . for two years; My parents had a special celebration on their twenty-fifth wedding anniversary.
2. (as she stared in the mirror . . . on her face); *Complexion* means "the color and appearance of a person's face."
3. she was pleased; *satisfying*
4. (with delight); *disliking, avoiding*
5. (bits of dialogue); *talking*
6. yearned; *desired*
7. (posed mysteries demanding to be solved); The opposite of *obscuring* is "clarifying."
8. (downstairs); *ascent*

Reading Warm-up B, p. 12

Sample Answers

1. a deep impact; My sixteenth birthday was a momentous day in my life.
2. (want to laze); *energetically*

3. (twists and turns); The opposite of *wayward* is "orderly."
4. economic opportunity seems limited; *reluctant, unwilling*
5. (gathered together); *Congregated* means "gathered together in a group."
6. content with their lot; *obedient*
7. their appetite for a better standard of living; It takes many pounds of meat to appease a hungry tiger's appetite.
8. (hard to convince people to stay); *encourage*

Literary Analysis: Plot Structure, p. 13

Possible Responses

In medias res: "Once her own engine was off, she heard the sound of another motor, approaching, a pained roar as if the engine were falling apart"; the story begins with Yolanda in the middle of her car trip without explaining why she is traveling or where she is traveling to; this technique piques readers' interest by making us wonder who this woman is, why she is traveling, and where she is going.

Flashback: "In the capital, her aunts had plied her with what she most craved after so many years away. 'Any little antojo, you must tell us!'"; the story flashes back to a time before her car trip, when she had first arrived on the island and was visiting her aunts; this flashback tells us that the aunts are wealthy women who can provide her with anything she desires—any *antojo*.

Foreshadowing: "It was a little cluster of houses on either side of the road, a good place to stretch her legs before what she'd heard was a steep and slightly [her aunts had warned her 'very'] dangerous descent to the coast"; the sentence foreshadows difficulties or dangers—real or imagined—that Yolanda will face on her car trip; the passage encourages the reader to anticipate that Yolanda will have some kind of problem on her car trip, perhaps even a dangerous one—it thus anticipates the flat tire and her encounter with the men with the machetes. even though the danger they pose to her is only in her own mind.

Reading Strategy: Make Predictions, p. 14

Possible Responses

1. The "hunger march" shows that there are many poor people in the Dominican Republic, so Yolanda will probably encounter signs of poverty on her trip.
2. This hint about the gulf between rich and poor in the Dominican Republic indicates that Yolanda will probably see signs of his disparity on her trip.
3. Yolanda will take off on some kind of trip or detour involving the satisfaction of her yearning for guavas.
4. Yolanda will encounter some sort of danger—real or imagined—from the desperate poor people on the road as she travels by car.
5. The young boy will have some sort of problem or bad encounter with rich people.
6. Yolanda will have some sort of problem with the car as she makes her detour in search of guavas.

Unit 6 Resources: New Voices, New Frontiers
© Pearson Education, Inc. All rights reserved.
252

Vocabulary Builder, p. 15

A. 1. netting or canvas hung from ropes at both ends and used as a bed; from the Spanish word *hamaca.*

2. public square of marketplace, an open area; shopping center; taken directly from Spanish

3. courtyard or inner, open area of a building; paved area near a house, used for outdoor sitting or eating; taken directly from Spanish

4. powder made from cacao seeds; crushed chocolate; a drink made with milk or hot water and powdered chocolate; from the Spanish word *cacao.*

B. 1. C; 2. D; 3. C; 4. B; 5. C

Grammar and Style: Absolute Phrases, p. 16

A. 1. Her engine turned off
2. none
3. none
4. his head ducking behind his mother

B. Sample Responses

1. The road ahead was rough, its jolts jangling our nerves.
2. They searched through the grove, the best guavas going into the basket.
3. They approached the car, one man asking if there was a problem.
4. One man lay beneath the car, his arms pumping the jack.
5. Jose walked down the road alone, his head bowed sadly.

Enrichment: World Languages, p. 17

Suggested Responses

1. Students might mention that computers, modems, fax machines, and airplanes have made the world seem smaller. The technology of television has been particularly powerful at bringing images of people from other countries into living rooms. Students should support their opinions about whether the world should or should not become smaller.

2. Students might mention clothing, cars, electronic equipment, and food. If a business sets up a factory or office in another country, all people working for that business should learn the language of that country—so that business can be conducted smoothly. Trade with other countries has also increased.

3. Astronauts from a variety of countries can explore together and communicate effectively about their findings. Being able to share and compare information can improve the space program and help make outer space an important world resource.

4. Whenever people get to know each other on a one-on-one basis, prejudices tend to disappear. If people throughout the world were better able to communicate, they might not feel so different from one another. People would be able to learn about different customs and ideas.

5. In responding, students might refer to their responses to the other questions. They might say that language

gives people the power to communicate, study, and explore a variety of options. Encourage students to back up their statements with examples.

Open-Book Test, p. 18

Short Answer

1. *In medias* res means "in the middle of things." The story begins in medias res because at the beginning, Yolanda is driving through the hills, but the reader is not told how or why she has come to be there.
   Difficulty: *Average*   **Objective:** *Literary Analysis*

2. The roar of the engine foreshadows the approach of a bus full of men on their way to a march in the capital.
   Difficulty: *Easy*   **Objective:** *Literary Analysis*

3. The key piece of background knowledge is that, for many years, the Dominican Republic was a dictatorship.
   Difficulty: *Challenging*   **Objective:** *Reading*

4. The phrase that begins the flashback is "In the capital. . . ."
   Difficulty: *Easy*   **Objective:** *Literary Analysis*

5. Students should note that guavas represent something that is unique to Yolanda's homeland; they are sweet; Yolanda can't get them easily; she obviously remembers picking them when she was younger; they are something she craves. The guavas symbolize something essential that she needs that is missing in her life in the United States—connectedness with nature, a simpler way of life.
   Difficulty: *Average*   **Objective:** *Interpretation*

6. Because she has been away from the Dominican Republic for so long, Yolanda has forgotten much of the Spanish that she once knew. Her lack of understanding relates to the theme of her conflict between her longing for her homeland and the opportunities of life in the United States.
   Difficulty: *Challenging*   **Objective:** *Interpretation*

7. Something will go wrong on the trip to the guava grove.
   Difficulty: *Challenging*   **Objective:** *Literary Analysis*

8. Knowing that there is widespread poverty and hunger in the Dominican Republic, readers can predict that Yolanda will react with fear when she sees the two men with machetes because she thinks they might be poor and desperate and want to rob her.
   Difficulty: *Easy*   **Objective:** *Reading*

9. Jose's inability to get help shows that there is a great gap and mistrust between the rich and the poor of the country.
   Difficulty: *Average*   **Objective:** *Interpretation*

10. No, you would not have any problem in convincing your friend to do what you want, because *docile* means "easy to direct or manage; obedient."
    Difficulty: *Average*   **Objective:** *Vocabulary*

Essay

11. Students might note that Yolanda's family is obviously well-off. The people Yolanda meets are dressed in old clothing, and they are used to making a living from serving rich people and doing their errands. Yolanda fears that people are going to take advantage of her, but she learns that poor people can be very kind and helpful.

    Difficulty: *Easy* **Objective:** *Essay*

12. Students' essays should suggest that Yolanda learns that not all strangers are dangerous. The stranger who offer to change her tire refuses her money. Jose accepts her money, but is hurt by the fact that people did not believe him and he cannot enjoy earning the money.

    Difficulty: *Average* **Objective:** *Essay*

13. Students might note that antojos—unfulfilled desires or cravings—are the main reason that Yolanda takes her trip and discovers the people of her country (which leads her to understand her heritage better). Guavas are her antojos because they give her an authentic taste of her homeland and her native culture, they lead her into contact with the poor people who make up the majority of her native land, and those encounters—with Jose and the men with the machetes—increase her appreciation of the poor people of her country.

    Difficulty: *Challenging* **Objective:** *Essay*

14. Some students might suggest that because of the powerful unconscious emotional forces and attachments at work in childhood, the places of childhood are bound to have a more lasting and stronger impact in shaping one's character. Others might argue that as an adult, one can appreciate one's surroundings more, so the places of adulthood might be more meaningful in shaping one's character.

    Difficulty: *Average* **Objective:** *Essay*

Oral Response

15. Oral responses should be clear, well organized, and well supported by appropriate examples from the selection.

    Difficulty: *Average* **Objective:** *Oral Response*

Selection Test A, p. 21

Critical Reading

1. ANS: C   DIF: Easy   OBJ: Comprehension
2. ANS: B   DIF: Easy   OBJ: Literary Analysis
3. ANS: A   DIF: Easy   OBJ: Comprehension
4. ANS: B   DIF: Easy   OBJ: Reading Strategy
5. ANS: B   DIF: Easy   OBJ: Literary Analysis
6. ANS: B   DIF: Easy   OBJ: Reading Strategy
7. ANS: B   DIF: Easy   OBJ: Interpretation
8. ANS: D   DIF: Easy   OBJ: Interpretation
9. ANS: D   DIF: Easy   OBJ: Reading Strategy
10. ANS: A   DIF: Easy   OBJ: Reading Strategy

11. ANS: A   DIF: Easy   OBJ: Comprehension
12. ANS: B   DIF: Easy   OBJ: Interpretation

Vocabulary and Grammar

13. ANS: B   DIF: Easy   OBJ: Vocabulary
14. ANS: D   DIF: Easy   OBJ: Grammar

Essay

15. Students' essays should suggest that Yolanda learns that not all strangers are dangerous. The strangers who offer to change her tire refuse her money. Jose accepts her money but is hurt by the fact that people did not believe him and cannot enjoy earning the money.

    Difficulty: *Easy*

    Objective: *Essay*

16. Students should note that Yolanda's family is obviously well-off. The people Yolanda meets are dressed in old clothing, and they are used to making a living from doing rich people's errands. Yolanda acts as if people are going to take advantage of her, but she learns that poor people can be very kind.

    Difficulty: *Easy*

    Objective: *Essay*

17. In her youth in the Dominican Republic, she was surrounded by family who told her what to do. She spoke Spanish. She lived a sheltered life. In the United States as an adult, Yolanda has her own job and the freedom to do what she wants. She speaks English, and she is independent. She is not near her family and sometimes feels isolated.

    Difficulty: *Average*

    Objective: *Essay*

Selection Test B, p. 24

Critical Reading

1. ANS: B   DIF: Easy   OBJ: Comprehension
2. ANS: A   DIF: Easy   OBJ: Comprehension
3. ANS: B   DIF: Average   OBJ: Literary Analysis
4. ANS: B   DIF: Average   OBJ: Literary Analysis
5. ANS: C   DIF: Average   OBJ: Reading Strategy
6. ANS: D   DIF: Average   OBJ: Reading Strategy
7. ANS: A   DIF: Average   OBJ: Interpretation
8. ANS: C   DIF: Challenging   OBJ: Interpretation
9. ANS: C   DIF: Challenging   OBJ: Reading Strategy
10. ANS: B   DIF: Average   OBJ: Comprehension
11. ANS: B   DIF: Average   OBJ: Interpretation
12. ANS: B   DIF: Challenging   OBJ: Interpretation
13. ANS: C   DIF: Challenging   OBJ: Interpretation
14. ANS: A   DIF: Easy   OBJ: Comprehension

Vocabulary and Grammar

15. ANS: A   DIF: Average   OBJ: Vocabulary
16. ANS: B   DIF: Average   OBJ: Vocabulary

Essay

17. Students should understand that the flashback scene plays an important role in this story. In the scene, Yolanda talks with her family, telling them that she wants to go for a drive to get guavas. They respond by telling her that she should not drive through the countryside by herself. This scene gives readers the following information: that Yolanda comes from a wealthy, sheltered family; that she has been living in the United States; and that her family wishes she were home. Also, the family's reaction to the fact that she wants to take a drive through the countryside indicates that the country is experiencing political problems that make parts of it unsafe. This scene also reveals that Yolanda is slightly different from her family, in that she is outgoing and unwilling to give up her independence out of fear.

Difficulty: *Easy*

Objective: *Essay*

18. The title "Antojos" relates both to Yolanda's craving for guavas and to her craving to reconnect herself to the country of her birth. The word is first introduced in the story's flashback scene, when Yolanda is having a conversation with her aunts. Happy to have her home after she has been in the United States for many years, her aunts tell Yolanda they want to indulge "any little *antojo*" she might have. She reveals to them that she has been away so long, she no longer remembers what the word means. This shows Yolanda's separation from her country and her language. Yolanda then decides what her *antojo* is—fresh guavas. To find the fruit, she is forced to go on a trip out into the countryside. Once there, she meets people and sees parts of her country that help her to realize her true *antojo*—getting back in touch with her homeland, which has been wounded by war.

Difficulty: *Average*

Objective: *Essay*

19. Explain how the background information about the country's political unrest contributes to Yolanda's initial reaction to the men with the machetes in "Antojos." Why does she respond the way she does? What does she think might happen? What is your prediction based on her reaction, and is your prediction correct? Is Yolanda's prediction about her own situation correct? Write a brief essay to discuss your ideas.

The background information suggests that it can be dangerous to be out on your own, because people are in the mood to act in aggressive ways. Yolanda knows that some people are ready to act outside the law, so she is suspicious of the men. She thinks they might resent her because she appears wealthier than they. She predicts that they might even harm her, and readers might think

so, too. Yolanda's prediction is wrong. The men are nothing but helpful and wrong hard to fix her car.

Difficulty: *Challenging*

Objective: *Essay*

20. Some students might suggest that because of the powerful unconscious emotional forces and attachments at work in childhood, the places of childhood are bound to have a more lasting and stronger impact in shaping one's character. Others might argue that as an adult, one can appreciate one's surroundings more, so the places of adulthood might be more meaningful in shaping one's character.

Difficulty: *Average*

Objective: *Essay*

"Everyday Use" by Alice Walker

Vocabulary Warm-up Exercises, p. 28

A. 1. collards
2. scalding
3. deliberately
4. lavender
5. centerpiece
6. orchid
7. temptation
8. embrace

B. Sample Answers
1. F; Since *dingy* has unattractive connotations, there would not be purchasers for such an outfit.
2. F; By definition, *doctrines* are beliefs or principles.
3. F; *Flannel* would be more appropriate for a chilly or cold day.
4. F; Since *furtive* behavior connotes secrecy or deceit, it would not usually be worthy of trust.
5. T; By definition, *ignorant* means "uninformed."
6. F; People acting *mercilessly* would not display compassion; instead, they would be ruthless.
7. F; *Oppress* means "to keep down by cruel or unjust use of power or authority."
8. T; Since *witty* means "clever" or "humorous," such remarks might easily provoke smiles or laughter.

Reading Warm-up A, p. 29

Sample Answers

1. make it her own; As a convert to Buddhism, Nan felt content with the philosophy she had decided to *embrace*.
2. (consciously); I *unintentionally* dialed the wrong number.
3. fabric borders around her paintings . . . story quilts . . . thus became like a . . . to display narrative images; on a table
4. (striking, bright colors); I might feel calm, refreshed, or cheerful.

5. (beautiful flowers); An orchid has an unusual shape.

6. yield to the . . . to sentimentalize . . . avoids such a trap; inadvisable

7. (an elderly cook, chopping . . . and then tossing them); Since she grew up in the deep South, my mother was extremely fond of *collards*.

8. (Into a pot . . . to boil); *Scalding* means "burning hot."

Reading Warm-up B, p. 30

Sample Answers

1. smart one . . . amused and impressed; The comedian's *witty* one-liners had the audience rolling in their seats with laughter.

2. (quiet . . . not wanting anyone to notice her); *open, candid, honest*

3. had always dressed neatly, but now she wore . . . she had bought in a second-hand store . . .; The bathroom walls were sparkling *clean*.

4. soft cotton . . . like a carpenter or woodsman; cold weather

5. (did things to bother their mother); The little girl treated her cat *kindly*.

6. the small town where they lived . . . narrow-minded; *unaware, uneducated, uninformed*

7. (people questioned the ideas . . . they had been brought up to believe in)

8. (constant bickering . . . crying in her bedroom); *keep down*

Literary Analysis: Characterization, p. 31

Sample Answers

Possible responses might include the following: Standard English: "Sometimes I dream a dream in which Dee and I are suddenly brought together on a TV program of this sort. Out of a dark and soft-seated limousine I am ushered into a bright room filled with many people." What it reveals about narrator's character: She is an imaginative woman and longs to be reconciled with her daughter Dee.

Dialect: " 'Why don't you take one or two of the others?' I asked. 'These old things was just done by me and Big Dee from some tops your grandma pieced before she died.'" What it reveals about narrator's character: She is a skilled craftsperson with a deep feeling for her family and its traditions.

Reading Strategy: Contrast Characters, p. 32

Sample Responses

1. His mouth is twisted into a frown; his teeth like dirty jagged stones.

2. She gently sliced an apple on the smooth, clean counter.

3. She marched into the living room, her hands waving in the air.

4. She gently lifted the lid and peeked inside to see if the quilts were there.

5. She gazed silently at the simmering stew.

Vocabulary Builder, p. 33

A. 1. doctorate; 2. documented; 3. docent; 4. doctrinaire

B. 1. C; 2. B; 3. D; 4. B

Grammar and Style: Transitional Expressions, p. 34

A. Sample Response

1. between the eyes [spatial relationship]

2. before we raised the money [time relationship]

3. as she walks closer [time relationship]

4. down the road [spatial relationship]

5. where hands pushing the dasher up and down [spatial relationship]

6. like those lavender ones [comparison]

B. Sample Response

Paragraphs must use transitions and transitional phrases.

Enrichment: Art, p. 36

Sample Responses

1. Mother, Father, sister Mia, Grandma Freeman, myself

2. Mother—blue and yellow; Father—brown and green; Mia—orange; Grandma Freeman—pink and white; myself—green, white, black. I'll use bright blue thread to unite the squares because it's my favorite.

3. Mother—daisies and blue sky for her garden; Father—a giant oak tree for his strength; Mia—big sun with rays for her laughter and sunny disposition; Grandma—pink and white for her pretty tea roses; myself—a green book open to pages with print for my love of reading.

4. I'll include the year, a poem by Robert Frost, an outline of our dog Molly, and a small piece of flannel from each of our winter pajamas.

5. Students' quilt patterns should reflect and incorporate details expressed in their answers.

Open-Book Test, p. 37

Short Answer

1. Dee's mother is a large, strong hardworking woman who can perform work that is usually associated with a man—slaughtering and cleaning a hog, slaughtering a calf and preparing the meat, and so on.
   Difficulty: *Easy*   Objective: *Literary Analysis*

2. Maggie is insecure, lacking self-confidence because of her burn scars; Dee is stylish and attractive and Maggie envies her luck and confidence.
   Difficulty: *Easy*   Objective: *Reading*

3. Dee's mother has this fantasy because she does not feel close to Dee, and she imagines that such a televised reunion would draw them closer together.
   Difficulty: *Average*   Objective: *Interpretation*

4. Dee is interested in taking some of the family's "everyday" items, such as quilts, to display in her own home as "quaint" reminders of the folk culture in which she grew up. At one point. Dee says to her mother, "Mama, can I have these old quilts?"

   Difficulty: *Easy*   **Objective:** *Interpretation*

5. According to Dee's mother, Dee reads to her and Maggie in order to show off her superior education.

   Difficulty: *Challenging*   **Objective:** *Interpretation*

6. The language of the first and last paragraphs shows that Maggie and her mother can take deep satisfaction from simple pleasures of nature—looking up into an elm tree, enjoying the evening air—whereas Dee seems to require lots of "cultured," artificial possessions to make her think she is happy.

   Difficulty: *Challenging*   **Objective:** *Literary Analysis*

7. Contrasts include Dee's beauty and Maggie's scarred, disfigured skin; Dee's self-confidence and Maggie's insecurity; Dee's superior education and Maggie's lack of schooling; Dee's sophisticated outlook and Maggie's simplicity and innocence. In summary, Dee is fashionable, attractive, worldly, and superficial, whereas Maggie is uneducated, unattractive, but simple and sincere.

   Difficulty: *Average*   **Objective:** *Reading*

8. Students might suggest that Maggie would use the quilts in an everyday manner, as useful household items. Dee would hang them as cultural "artifacts" or as objects that represent her family's culture as someone who has moved far away from it and therefore has no real use for such objects.

   Difficulty: *Average*   **Objective:** *Reading*

9. Maggie is a modest person who has gracefully accepted the hardships that life has dealt to her but who feels no jealousy or resentment at the achievements of others.

   Difficulty: *Challenging*   **Objective:** *Literary Analysis*

10. No, other people would not be likely to notice the glance because *furtive* means "sneaky."

    Difficulty: *Average*   **Objective:** *Vocabulary*

Essay

11. "Everyday Use" describes many aspects of life on the farm to which Dee returns. For Maggie and her mother, many of the objects that Dee would like to have — the butter churn or the quilts —are just basic parts of a pattern of everyday life, things that they use to support their simple way of life in the country. To Dee, who has been educated, these objects are not objects of everyday use, but rather symbols of the family's quaint cultural heritage. The different attitudes toward these objects shows their different approaches to life: Maggie and her mother just live their simple lives, whereas Dee feels the need to "reflect" on that simple life as part of a culture from which she has moved away.

    Difficulty: *Easy*   **Objective:** *Essay*

12. Students might note that Dee sees various objects around her—the butter churn, the quilts—merely as symbols of a lost, quaint way of life, whereas that life is still very present and real to Maggie and her mother, who still use those objects in their everyday lives. They might note, therefore, that for Maggie these objects are not symbols but real things to be put to real use. Students might note, therefore, that it is Maggie who is really closer to her family's heritage than Dee because Maggie really lives in that heritage, whereas Dee merely "appreciates" it from an educated distance.

    Difficulty: *Average*   **Objective:** *Essay*

13. Students might note that Dee's family has not oppressed her because her mother took great pains to assure that she got a good education that would allow her to advance beyond their simple circumstances in life. They will probably feel that Dee's mother has been loving and supportive and helpful to Dee.

    Difficulty: *Challenging*   **Objective:** *Essay*

14. Students might note that "Everyday Use" both reflects truths about aspects of American society and comments on how people relate to their cultural heritage through the portrayal of Dee. The story reflects the homespun wisdom and honesty of country folk like Maggie and her Mother, as well as the sophisticated, "educated" tastes of college graduates like Dee. But the story's portrayal of Dee's shallow attitudes toward collecting objects from her cultural past—and her distance from their real meaning — stresses the authenticity of Maggie and her mother over the snobbery of Dee.

    Difficulty: *Average*   **Objective:** *Essay*

Oral Response

15. Oral responses should be clear, well-organized, and well supported by appropriate examples from the selections.

    Difficulty: *Average*   **Objective:** *Oral Response*

Short Answer

16. "Everyday Use" describes many aspects of life on the farm to which Dee returns. For Maggie and her mother, many of the objects that Dee would like to have—the butter churn or the quilts—are just basic parts of a pattern of everyday life, things they use to support their simple way of life in the country. To Dee, who has been educated, these objects are not objects of everyday use but are rather symbols of the family's quaint cultural heritage. Their differing attitudes toward these objects shows their different approaches to life: Maggie and her mother just live their simple lives, whereas Dee feels the need to "reflect" on that simple life as part of a culture from which she has moved away.

Selection Test A, p. 40

Critical Reading

1. ANS: C   DIF: Easy   OBJ: Comprehension
2. ANS: B   DIF: Easy   OBJ: Literary Analysis
3. ANS: D   DIF: Easy   OBJ: Comprehension
4. ANS: C   DIF: Easy   OBJ: Literary Analysis
5. ANS: B   DIF: Easy   OBJ: Interpretation
6. ANS: B   DIF: Easy   OBJ: Literary Analysis
7. ANS: D   DIF: Easy   OBJ: Comprehension
8. ANS: B   DIF: Easy   OBJ: Reading Strategy
9. ANS: B   DIF: Easy   OBJ: Interpretation
10. ANS: C   DIF: Easy   OBJ: Comprehension

Vocabulary and Grammar

11. ANS: B   DIF: Easy   OBJ: Vocabulary
12. ANS: D   DIF: Easy   OBJ: Grammar
13. ANS: A   DIF: Easy   OBJ: Vocabulary
14. ANS: D   DIF: Easy   OBJ: Grammar
15. ANS: C   DIF: Easy   OBJ: Grammar

Essay

16. Students' essays should suggest that Dee wants the quilts to hang on her wall. Mama and Maggie, on the other hand, have been involved in the making and using of the quilts. They also value the memory of family members who are connected to the quilts.

    Difficulty: *Easy*

    Objective: *Essay*

17. Students' essays should reflect that Mama describes these standards: light skin rather than dark skin; thin rather than fat, well-dressed rather than dressed as a farmer. However, she is the opposite of the standards she lists. They are found in her daughter Dee, who is the character with the least amount of inner beauty.

    Difficulty: *Easy*

    Objective: *Essay*

Selection Test B, p. 43

Critical Reading

1. ANS: A   DIF: Average   OBJ: Comprehension
2. ANS: D   DIF: Easy   OBJ: Comprehension
3. ANS: D   DIF: Average   OBJ: Interpretation
4. ANS: B   DIF: Average   OBJ: Literary Analysis
5. ANS: C   DIF: Average   OBJ: Interpretation
6. ANS: C   DIF: Average   OBJ: Interpretation
7. ANS: B   DIF: Challenging   OBJ: Interpretation
8. ANS: C   DIF: Challenging   OBJ: Interpretation
9. ANS: C   DIF: Challenging   OBJ: Literary Analysis
10. ANS: D   DIF: Challenging   OBJ: Reading Strategy
11. ANS: B   DIF: Average   OBJ: Reading Strategy
12. ANS: A   DIF: Challenging   OBJ: Reading Strategy
13. ANS: C   DIF: Easy   OBJ: Literary Analysis
14. ANS: D   DIF: Easy   OBJ: Comprehension

Vocabulary and Grammar

15. ANS: D   DIF: Average   OBJ: Vocabulary
16. ANS: A   DIF: Average   OBJ: Vocabulary
17. ANS: D   DIF: Average   OBJ: Grammar
18. ANS: C   DIF: Average   OBJ: Grammar

Essay

19. Students should note that the narrator is a strong, practical, hard-working woman. Students should support this analysis with details such as her "rough, man-working hands" and her ability to "kill and clean a hog as mercilessly as a man." The narrator is uneducated but intelligent and capable of insights such as, "in 1927 colored asked fewer questions than they do now." Dee is brash, spoiled, ashamed of her family's poverty, and insensitive toward her mother and sister. She wears "a dress so loud" it hurts the narrator's eyes. Supportive details of Dee's brashness include her uninformed reasons for changing her name; she thinks Dee is the name of her oppressors, when in fact, Dee was the name of her Aunt Dicie, Grandma Dee, and other relatives. In contrast with her large mother and thin sister, Dee has a "fuller figure" as well as a light complexion and "nicer hair." Dee has received an education, which opened her to reading, just as it closed her from her family: "She washed us in a river of make-believe, burned us with a lot of knowledge we didn't necessarily need to know. Pressed us to her with the serious way she read, to shove us away at just the moment, like dimwits, we seemed about to understand." Dee's insensitivity is also illustrated in the way she "rifles" through her mother's belongings looking for the quilts. Maggie, thin and scarred from a fire, walks with her "chin on chest, eyes on ground, feet in shuffle." She is not the beauty Dee is, and she has not had the benefit of education. Yet she is very insightful: "Mama, when did Dee ever *have* any friends?" Maggie does not expect anything and is, therefore, astounded ("Maggie just sat there on my bed with her mouth open") when the narrator takes the quilts out of Dee's arms and gives them to Maggie.

    Difficulty: *Easy*

    Objective: *Essay*

20. Most students will state that Dee's interest in her heritage seems motivated by her educated name change, which, ironically, through her uninformed knowledge of her own heritage, means she is throwing away a name handed down to her from her Aunt Dicie and Grandma Dee. Furthermore, at the sight of specific objects, such as the butter dish ("That's it! I knew there was something I wanted to ask you if I could have"), Dee is

motivated to possess objects that symbolize her heritage—the butter dish, the churn top, the dasher, and Grandma Dee's quilts. In contrast, Maggie lives and works with these objects. To Maggie they are not symbols but real things, made by real people and put to real use. For Dee's professed interest in her heritage, she has removed herself from her family's life, does not know details pertaining to her heritage (her name, who whittled or made what), and does not know the crafts of her heritage. It is Maggie, however, who knows how to quilt, who knows who made what, and who lives a daily life in acceptance of that heritage.

Difficulty: *Challenging*

Objective: *Essay*

21. Dee tries too hard. She makes a lot of fuss about her family's possessions to show that she appreciates her heritage and family history. However, she is superficial. She is so busy showing that she is sensitive and superior that she fails to value her family. She does not seem capable of "just enjoying" anything. Maggie, on the other hand, pays attention and captures the details of her family. She can sit still long enough to become part of her heritage by learning to quilt. She understands her family history and does not use it just to show off.

Difficulty: *Challenging*

Objective: *Essay*

"Everything Stuck to Him" by Raymond Carver

Vocabulary Warm-up Exercises, p. 47

A. 1. striking
2. jiggled
3. marveled
4. refills
5. overcast
6. waterfowl
7. dozed
8. survivor

B. Sample Answers

1. F; *Minor* means of lesser importance, and a house burning down would be a major disaster.
2. T; *Involves* means includes, so you would be participating in the project.
3. F; *Letterhead* is stationery with a name and address at the top of the page.
4. F; Washing machines and dryers are appliances; *utilities* are services like electricity, water, sewer, and gas.
5. F; *Maintain* means to keep in good condition, so you would not ignore a garden you *maintain*.
6. T; A person's *correspondence* includes the letters he or she has written to others.
7. F; *Ambitions* are desires to succeed enormously; a person with ambitions will have large goals.

8. T; *Attractive* means that the person's appearance or personality pleases you in some way.

Reading Warm-up A, p. 48

Sample Answers

1. gray and dreary; An *overcast* sky is covered with clouds that can range in color from light gray to very dark gray, almost black; the light coming through these clouds looks muted and dull.
2. (admired); A synonym for *marveled* is *amazed, gaped, stared,* or *goggled.*
3. he got through that hard time just fine; My grandmother had cancer so she underwent some tough treatments and is now doing fine.
4. their glasses with lemonade; After a trip to the grocery store, Peter *refills* the refrigerator with food.
5. (wood ducks); Swans and geese are other types of *waterfowl.*
6. (fascinating, extraordinary); Another synonym for *striking* is *astonishing, stunning, wondrous,* or *startling.*
7. He has just started dreaming; just enough to wake him; *Dozed* means drifted off into a light sleep temporarily.
8. (jerks it just enough); She *jiggled* the drawer in her dresser to loosen it so it would open again.

Reading Warm-up B, p. 49

Sample Answers

1. admirable goal; One of my *ambitions* is to start my own lawn care business.
2. (choice); A synonym for *attractive* is *beautiful, pleasing, tempting,* or *interesting.*
3. keeping it in good condition; I help *maintain* my family's home by doing the vacuuming.
4. (less important); An antonym for *minor* is *major, significant,* or *important.*
5. because a renter's chores do not usually include fixing the roof, furnace, or a major appliance; Teaching *involves* many things, including learning a subject, communicating knowledge clearly, reading, writing, evaluating, listening, and inspiring.
6. (electricity, gas, and water service); Where I live, we use these *utilities*: gas, water, sewer, electricity and phone services.
7. letters and forms; My *correspondence* includes emails, text messages, and cards that I write on and mail to others.
8. with the landlord's name, address, and other contact information at the top of the pages; The letter of admission that I received from my college arrived on *letterhead* with the name, address and emblem of the institution printed at the top of the page.

Literary Analysis: Author's Style, p. 50

Sample Answer

Possible responses: No quotation marks in dialogue—adds to bare-bones feel of the story, and allows dialogue to blend in with the action; no names given to father and daughter—encourages the reader to focus on their inner thoughts and feelings rather than external details of their lives; The husband and wife are called "boy" and "girl"—the names "boy" and "girl" emphasize the youth of the husband and wife and encourage the reader to regard them as standing in for all young couples of this type; No physical descriptions of characters—encourages readers to focus on inner thoughts and feelings rather than external features; Simple, direct language—encourages reader to focus on details of story and character instead of abstract ideas.

Reading Strategy: Ask Questions, p. 51

Sample Responses

1. The two characters are the father and his daughter. The main clue is that he says, "I could tell you about something that happened when you were a baby."

2. The omniscient narrator (the author) narrates the outer story. The father narrates the inner story.

3. This admission of interest in girl's sisters shows that boy has a roving eye that might create problems for their marriage in the future.

4. "Boy" and "girl" are no longer together. "Girl" is not there in Milan, and there is no mention of her in the present—only in the story from twenty years earlier.

5. On a surface level, the title refers to the breakfast that sticks to his long johns after he spills the meal in his lap. On a deeper level, it might refer to the way the emotions of that period of his life seem to stick as to him so many years later as he retells the "inner" story.

Vocabulary Builder, p. 52

A. 1. No, he was often not free of exam pressures on his birthday, because *coincide* means "to occupy the same place in space or in time."

2. No, Juanita does not lack goals if she is known for her ambitions, because *ambitions* means "desires to achieve particular ends."

3. Yes, people would be likely to notice the decor of the hotel lobby, because *striking* means "attracting attention through unusual or conspicuous qualities."

4. No, he would not have slept soundly through the night, because *fitfully* means "erratically or intermittently."

B. 1. D; 2. B; 3. B;

Enrichment: Art, p. 54

TK

Open-Book Test, p. 55

Short Answer

1. Students might note that the characters speak in short sentences and that there is very little description of either the characters or their physical surroundings. There is also very little punctuation—no quotation marks. All of these features could be considered "minimalist."

   Difficulty: *Average* **Objective:** *Literary Analysis*

2. The first two people to speak in the story are an adult daughter and her father. The first detail that helps the reader to clarify this relationship is the daughter request, "Tell me what is was like when I was a kid."

   Difficulty: *Average* **Objective:** *Reading*

3. The reader can get a sense that the husband and wife are poor from the fact that they lived in a small apartment beneath a dentists's office and cleaned his office in exchange for rent and utilities. This detail shows that they could not afford their own home and did not even have enough money for rent.

   Difficulty: *Easy* **Objective:** *Reading*

4. The narrator refers to the husband and wife as "the boy" and "the girl," which contributes to the simple, minimalist style of the story.

   Difficulty: *Easy* **Objective:** *Literary Analysis*

5. The author does not describe the physical appearance of the boy, the girl, or their daughter. This aspect of the story shows that the author wants to create a minimalist style. His focus in on the characters' inner thoughts and feelings rather than their external appearance.

   Difficulty: *Challenging* **Objective:** *Literary Analysis*

6. The swearing seemed like an especially terrible thing because it may have shown that the boy had limited patience and love for his daughter. He was showing a selfish side of his personality. The wife was upset because she may have sensed that his swearing showed a lack of devotion to the family.

   Difficulty: *Challenging* **Objective:** *Interpretation*

7. The girl's attitude softens after the boy decides to give in to her wishes and not go hunting with Carl. Her attitude softens because she believes that the boy has chosen to make his family a priority, not his friend and his hunting.

   Difficulty: *Average* **Objective:** *Literary Analysis*

8. Students might note that the memory of his early happy years with the girl have stuck with the narrator. Even though he is no longer with the girl, he cannot leave behind thoughts and feelings about those days.

   Difficulty: *Challenging* **Objective:** *Interpretation*

9. The mother is not present as the father tells his daughter the story, so it is evident that the father and the mother—the boy and girl—are no longer together.

   Difficulty: *Easy* **Objective:** *Interpretation*

10. No, you would likely not feel rested, because *fitfully* means "erratically or irregularly."

Difficulty: *Average* **Objective:** *Vocabulary*

Essay

11. Students' essays should provide clear, vivid, and detailed physical descriptions of the characters in a way that the story does not. Some students might suggest that such descriptions would detract from the story's emphasis on the characters' thoughts and feelings. Others might suggest that the descriptions would bring the reader in closer touch with the characters.

Difficulty: *Easy* **Objective:** *Essay*

12. Most students will note that as the older version of the boy tells this story of his early marriage to his now-grown daughter, his wife is absent, so the marriage has obviously ended. Students should offer reasons that they think the marriage did not work. Some may point to the boy's early tendency to be distracted by activities outside his family, such as hunting. Others will point to the girl's readiness to issue an ultimatum over what some might consider a small matter, thus foreshadowing more conflicts and arguments.

Difficulty: *Average* **Objective:** *Essay*

13. Students might note that the biggest change that is evident in the story is that the wife is absent from the present-day setting of the tale, indicating that the marriage has not worked out. They might also note that boy's retelling of this early part of his marriage is full of fondness and love, and that he is not fully sure why things changed so drastically between him and his wife. They might also note that there are hints of why things changed: the boy's tendency to pursue interests outside the marriage, and the girl's tendency to draw a line in the sand as a way of settling arguments. Students might note that such tendencies might have driven the couple apart over the years.

Difficulty: *Challenging* **Objective:** *Essay*

14. Students might point to several characteristics that give this story its distinctively American character: the grand dreams and ambitions of boy and girl; their willingness to work hard to get ahead; the spare tone and style of the narrative. These characteristics get right to the point and right to the heart of the characters in a way that is often typical of modern American writing.

Difficulty: *Average* **Objective:** *Essay*

Oral Response

15. Oral responses should be clear, well organized, and well supported by appropriate examples from the selections.

Difficulty: *Average* **Objective:** *Oral Response*

Selection Test A, p. 58

Critical Reading

1. **ANS:** A   **DIF:** Easy   **OBJ:** Comprehension
2. **ANS:** B   **DIF:** Easy   **OBJ:** Literary Analysis

3. **ANS:** C   **DIF:** Easy   **OBJ:** Comprehension
4. **ANS:** D   **DIF:** Easy   **OBJ:** Literary Analysis
5. **ANS:** B   **DIF:** Easy   **OBJ:** Reading Strategy
6. **ANS:** A   **DIF:** Easy   **OBJ:** Reading Strategy
7. **ANS:** A   **DIF:** Easy   **OBJ:** Interpretation
8. **ANS:** D   **DIF:** Easy   **OBJ:** Interpretation
9. **ANS:** B   **DIF:** Easy   **OBJ:** Interpretation
10. **ANS:** C   **DIF:** Easy   **OBJ:** Interpretation
11. **ANS:** A   **DIF:** Easy   **OBJ:** Comprehension
12. **ANS:** A   **DIF:** Easy   **OBJ:** Literary Analysis
13. **ANS:** A   **DIF:** Easy   **OBJ:** Literary Analysis

Vocabulary

14. **ANS:** A   **DIF:** Easy   **OBJ:** Vocabulary
15. **ANS:** A   **DIF:** Easy   **OBJ:** Vocabulary

Essay

16. The two frames in "Everything Stuck to Him" are the story told by the narrator and the story he tells about the boy, the girl, and the baby. The characters in the first story are the narrator and the young woman, who is his daughter. She is visiting him and asks to hear a story about her childhood, which he tells her. The characters in the story within the story are a young couple and their infant daughter. The story is about a time when the baby was crying and the boy wanted to go hunting. The boy in the story is the narrator, and the baby is the young woman.

17. The relationship between the narrator and the young woman, his daughter, in "Everything Stuck to Him," is distant. They do not have a close relationship. She wants to become closer to him, but he does not seem to want to talk to her. She encourages him to share stories with her, but he is reluctant to do so. He remains rather cold while she tries to be warm and accepting.

Difficulty: *Easy*

Objective: *Essay*

18. Students might point to several characteristics that give this story its American character: the grand dreams and ambitions of boy and girl; their willingness to work hard to get ahead; the spare tone and style of the narrative, which quickly get to the core of the story and the characters. This direct style is often found in modern American writing.

Difficulty: *Average*

Objective: *Essay*

Selection Test B, p. 61

Critical Reading

1. **ANS:** A   **DIF:** Challenging   **OBJ:** Interpretation
2. **ANS:** B   **DIF:** Average   **OBJ:** Interpretation
3. **ANS:** D   **DIF:** Challenging   **OBJ:** Literary Analysis

4. ANS: B	DIF: Average	OBJ: Reading Strategy
5. ANS: D	DIF: Average	OBJ: Literary Analysis
6. ANS: C	DIF: Easy	OBJ: Comprehension
7. ANS: C	DIF: Average	OBJ: Literary Analysis
8. ANS: A	DIF: Average	OBJ: Interpretation
9. ANS: C	DIF: Average	OBJ: Reading Strategy
10. ANS: A	DIF: Easy	OBJ: Comprehension
11. ANS: A	DIF: Challenging	OBJ: Interpretation
12. ANS: B	DIF: Average	OBJ: Comprehension
13. ANS: D	DIF: Average	OBJ: Literary Analysis
14. ANS: C	DIF: Challenging	OBJ: Reading Strategy
15. ANS: A	DIF: Easy	OBJ: Comprehension

Vocabulary

16. ANS: A	DIF: Average	OBJ: Vocabulary
17. ANS: B	DIF: Average	OBJ: Vocabulary
18. ANS: D	DIF: Average	OBJ: Vocabulary

Essay

19. The two frames in "Everything Stuck to Him" are the story told by the narrator and the story he tells about the boy, the girl, and the baby. The characters in the first story are the narrator and the young woman, who is his daughter. She is visiting him and asks to hear a story about her childhood, which he tells her. The characters in the story within the story are a young couple and their infant daughter. The story is about a time when the baby was crying and the boy wanted to go hunting. The boy in the story is the narrator, and the baby is the young woman.

Difficulty: *Easy*

Objective: *Essay*

20. The relationship between the narrator and the young woman, his daughter, in "Everything Stuck to Him," is distant. They do not have a close relationship. She wants to become closer to him, but he does not seem to want to talk to her. She encourages him to share stories with her, but he is reluctant to do so. He remains rather cold while she tries to be warm and accepting. She is probably eager because she wants to become closer to him and learn more about her past. He is probably distant because he does not want to think about the past. He might be embarrassed by his lack of warmth toward his daughter.

Difficulty: *Average*

Objective: *Essay*

21. One characteristic of Carver's style is the short dialouge. Characters do not say much and much of the dialogue between the boy and girl is described by the narrator. Another characteristic is the use of few words. There are no long descriptions. Every word counts. A third characteristic is that he focuses on the relationship between the characters instead of excessive use of

language. The atmosphere created by these characteristics rather bleak and distant. The reader's feelings, like the text, streamlined and even hardened.

Difficulty: *Challenging*

Objective: *Essay*

22. Students might point to several characteristics that give this story its distinctively American character: the grand dreams and ambitions of boy and girl; their willingness to work hard to get ahead; the spare tone and style of the narrative, which get right to the point and right to the heart of the characters in a way that is often typical of modern American writing.

Difficulty: *Average*

Objective: *Essay*

"Traveling Through The Dark"
by William Stafford,

"The Secret" by Denise Levertov, and "The Gift" by Li-Young Lee

Vocabulary Warm-up Exercises, p. 65

A. 1. recent
2. canyon
3. aimed
4. glare
5. swerve
6. heap
7. stumbled
8. sliver

B. Sample Answers
1. False. When you are *assuming* something, you are thinking or guessing that it's so, but you're not sure.
2. False. When a person has *hesitated*, he has waited a moment.
3. True. *Lowered* thermostats have been turned down, so they conserve energy.
4. True. *Recited* means the same thing as *told*.
5. False. The *wilderness* is land that has few signs of human habitation.
6. False. An *assassin* is a person who kills others, so has little respect for life.
7. True. Drying in the sun makes things stiff, so the towel may have *stiffened*.
8. True. A *shard* is a piece of something, so can be a clue to earlier civilizations.

Reading Warm-up A, p. 66

Sample Answers
1. veer; *Go straight ahead* means the opposite of *swerve*.
2. sometime in the past; *Recent* means not too long ago or lately.
3. (over the edge to the valley); The Grand *Canyon* is possibly the world's most famous *canyon*.

4. (bit of wood); A *sliver* is usually removed with a pair of tweezers.

5. (pile); A *heap* is something that is just piled up loosely, so it is usually messy.

6. (staggered); The toddler spun around in a circle, then *stumbled* dizzily across the playground.

7. directed straight; A weapon might be *aimed* towards a target.

8. light, bright; The *glare* of the sun off the windshield was almost blinding.

Reading Warm-up B, p. 67

Sample Answers

1. unspoiled landscape far removed from people; In the *wilderness* you would expect to find birds and other animals.

2. (story to relate); A synonym for *recited* is *related*.

3. (supposed); it would be about a random bee she had seen

4. for a moment or that short pause; Because I *hesitated*, I missed the chance to ask my question.

5. fragments; A *shard* is a broken-off piece of something.

6. been turned down; *Elevated* is an antonym for *lowered*.

7. (rigid); *Stiffened* means became hard or stiff.

8. killer, murderer; The *assassin* waited on the rooftop until his victim came into view.

Literary Analysis: Epiphany, p. 68

Sample Answer

1. This is not a true epiphany; although the speaker does make a discovery, it has not yet provoked any larger insight into himself or life.

2. This is a true epiphany; the speaker reaches the major insight that preserving the safety of the people in the oncoming cars in more important than trying to preserve the life of the fawn inside the lifeless doe.

3. This is a true epiphany—there can be no insight or truth more important or profound than discovering the secret of life.

4. Students might suggest that this is a true epiphany as well, for the speaker finds inspiration in the girls' passion and idealism about discovering the secret of life; the speaker acknowledges, thanks to the girls' example, that there may be such a secret after all.

5. This is not a true epiphany—it describes a moment that led to an epiphany for the speaker, but it is only a description of an event, not a description of a profound or sudden insight.

6. This is a true epiphany. The passage describes how the father's care in removing the metal shard inspired the boy to understand the importance of love and compassion, prompting him to return his father's love with a kiss.

Reading Strategy: Interpret Poetry, p. 69

Sample Responses

1. Students might note that the speaker of these lines is the poet herself. She is commenting on the enthusiastic reaction to her poems by two young girls that she has never met in person. The lines show that the poem is about how the poet gets as much inspiration from her readers' reactions to her ideas as from the ideas themselves. It even shows that the readers' reactions can help the poet to find meanings in her poems that she didn't even know were there.

2. Students might note that the title "Traveling Through the Dark" has a double meaning. In the literal sense, it refers to the speaker driving at nighttime on a lonely country road. On a deeper level, it refers to an emotional and ethical darkness—the speaker's inability to find a clear answer to the dilemma of whether to toss aside the carcass of the doe even though there is a living fawn in it. His decision to toss the carcass does not dispel the element of ambiguity and doubt that lingers over this agonizing decision.

3. Students might suggest the gift in "The Gift" is the gift of love that the father gives to his son in the example of the care and compassion he shows in removing a metal splinter from his hand when he was a terrified little boy, thinking he would die. The image of "silver tear" relates to the emotion the boy feels at his father's tenderness, and the "tiny flame" is a kind of enduring warmth that the father has ignited in his soul, a warmth that he carries over to his wife when he performs a similar procedure on her with the same love and compassion.

Building Vocabulary, p. 70

A. 1. exhaustible; 2. exhausted; 3. exhaustively

B. 1. C; 2. B; 3. D

Enrichment: Science, p. 72

Sample Responses

1. spinning pinwheel; trip to fair at age four; first time on amusement ride, loved thrill, felt exhilarated

2. song "Turkey in the Straw" played by ice cream truck; brings back anticipation of ice cream truck coming down the street in summertime

3. pumpkin pie baking; Thanksgiving; happy memories of family gatherings at grandparents' house

4. spicy curry; first daring food experience; proud of myself for trying something new

5. sheepskin blanket; childhood safety blanket; evokes feelings of security and comfort

Open-Book Test, p. 73

Short Answer

1. The encounter between the driver and the dead deer can be interpreted as an example of the conflict between expanding human civilization—in this case, cars and roads—and nature, as represented by the deer.

   Difficulty: *Challenging*   **Objective:** *Interpretation*

2. The speaker hesitates before rolling the dead doe into the canyon, which is the normal procedure to prevent cars from swerving or running into the carcass; but in this case he hesitates because he thinks about saving the unborn and still-living doe.

   Difficulty: *Average*   **Objective:** *Interpretation*

3. "Us all" represents all people—the collective conscience of humanity facing a choice between saving the doe or not. The insight the speaker finally arrives at is that the safety of approaching motorists is more important than saving the life of the fawn, but the poem's title—traveling through the dark—shows that the speaker is groping in moral and mental darkness for the right answer and is not sure if he is right.

   Difficulty: *Challenging*   **Objective:** *Literary Analysis*

4. The epiphany is two girls discovering the secret of life in "a sudden line of poetry."

   Difficulty: *Easy*   **Objective:** *Literary Analysis*

5. These images tell the reader that finding the secret of life is a lifelong process, not a one-time event.

   Difficulty: *Average*   **Objective:** *Interpretation*

6. The two girls are young, enthusiastic, and optimistic about the existence of a secret of life that they can discover and rediscover throughout life. The older and more cynical narrator is not even sure there is such a secret but loves the girls for—and is inspired by—their inspiring optimism and faith.

   Difficulty: *Challenging*   **Objective:** *Interpretation*

7. The narrator came to understand that the metal splinter was not life-threatening after all, as he had initially thought it was.

   Difficulty: *Average*   **Objective:** *Literary Analysis*

8. The narrator received the gift of love and compassion. The gift still bears fruit later in his life in the way that inspires him to a similar tenderness and sensitivity in removing a splinter from his wife's finger.

   Difficulty: *Easy*   **Objective:** *Interpretation*

9. Suggested response: "Traveling Through the Dark": Key Recurring Image—The dead deer lying in the road carrying a foal; Major Insight or Theme—Clash of human civilization and nature. "The Secret": Key Recurring Image—Two girls discovering and rediscovering the secret of life; Major Insight or Theme—Discovering the secret of life is a lifelong act of faith and optimism. "The Gift": Key Recurring Image: Removing a metal splinter from a hand; Major Insight or Theme—The gift of love is most apparent in small moments of life that help us to conquer pain and/or fear.

   Difficulty: *Average*   **Objective:** *Literary Analysis*

10. You could assume that the vase has been smashed or broken, because shard means "a sharp fragment."

    Difficulty: *Average*   **Objective:** *Vocabulary*

Essay

11. Some students will argue that the narrator makes the right decision—that clearing away the carcass of the doe as soon as possible is necessary to protect his own safety (from oncoming cars) and the safety of the cars who might be traveling on that dark, narrow road. Others will argue that saving a life—even an unborn animal's life—was the immediate reality and should have taken precedence over other possible scenarios.

    Difficulty: *Easy*   **Objective:** *Essay*

12. Students should note the following key theme from each poem: "Traveling Through the Dark"—the conflict between humans and nature; "The Secret"—the search for meaning in life; and "The Gift"—the importance of being able to give and receive love as a way of helping people through the rough times of life. Students should express a clear opinion about which theme spoke to them most strongly, and should give clear reasons for their preference.

    Difficulty: *Average*   **Objective:** *Essay*

13. Students might note that "The Secret" is a poem that deals mainly with the love of ideas. Initially the two anonymous girls are in love with a line of poetry that they think puts them in touch with the secret of life. Then the narrator expresses love for these girls, but it is not a personal love, because she does not know them—it is a love for their innocence and their enthusiasm for finding the truth of life, an enthusiasm that inspires the older narrator, who no longer feels that same degree of idealism. Students might note that, by contrast, the love discussed in "The Gift" is of a far more personal nature: the love shown by a father for his child in easing the pain and fears that accompany the removal of a splinter, the love the child shows his father in return, and the love the son passes on from that example in treating his own wife's painful splinter years later. Students might note that the poem is about the power of love to enlarge one's sense of compassion and to help people through painful or difficult times.

    Difficulty: *Challenging*   **Objective:** *Essay*

14. Most students will suggest that in "Traveling Through the Dark" the influence of the social on the personal is most evident—it is because of the inroads that humans have made on nature that deer are routinely run over on rural highways of the kind depicted in this poem. Others might argue that because the family is such an important social force, the ways in which family love are transmitted make "The Gift" a significant example of the influence of the social on the personal. Some students might note that "The Secret" focuses on an enthusiasm for poetry and finding the secret of life, which is the

most individual—and least social—of the insights portrayed in these three poems.

Difficulty: *Average*   **Objective:** *Essay*

Oral Response

15. Oral responses should be clear, well organized, and well supported by appropriate examples from the selections

    Difficulty: *Average*   **Objective:** *Oral Response*

Selection Test A, p. 76

Critical Reading

1. ANS: C	DIF: Easy	OBJ: Interpretation
2. ANS: D	DIF: Easy	OBJ: Comprehension
3. ANS: A	DIF: Easy	OBJ: Interpretation
4. ANS: C	DIF: Easy	OBJ: Reading Strategy
5. ANS: B	DIF: Easy	OBJ: Literary Analysis
6. ANS: A	DIF: Easy	OBJ: Reading Strategy
7. ANS: B	DIF: Easy	OBJ: Comprehension
8. ANS: B	DIF: Easy	OBJ: Interpretation
9. ANS: A	DIF: Easy	OBJ: Literary Analysis
10. ANS: B	DIF: Easy	OBJ: Comprehension
11. ANS: D	DIF: Easy	OBJ: Interpretation
12. ANS: C	DIF: Easy	OBJ: Reading Strategy
13. ANS: D	DIF: Easy	OBJ: Literary Analysis

Vocabulary

14. ANS: A	DIF: Easy	OBJ: Vocabulary
15. ANS: B	DIF: Easy	OBJ: Vocabulary

Essay

16. In "Traveling Through the Dark," the speaker is thinking for himself, the dead mother deer, and the unborn fawn. The speaker must make the best decision for everyone. He must decide if he wants to deliver the fawn from its dead mother. The fawn would be born but would be vulnerable and unsafe next to the road. It might even die in the end anyway. He must also decide if he has the nerve to deliver the fawn or if he has the courage to kill it by disposing of the mother. He decides to push the mother into the river.

    Difficulty: *Easy*

    Objective: *Essay*

17. The title of "The Secret" refers to poetry. It can also refer to discovering thah poetry can have many meanings. A final meaning of the title might be the secret of life the two girls think they have found. The title of "The Gift" could refer to the metal splinter that was in the boy's hand. The title can also refer to the gift of tenderness the father gives the boy when he gently removes the splinter. The titles refer to similar things, because they

can both refer to ideas or both refer to things (poetry and the splinter).

Difficulty: *Easy*

Objective: *Essay*

18. Writing About the Essential Question

TK

Difficulty: *Average*

Objective: *Essay*

Selection Test B, p. 79

Critical Reading

1. ANS: D	DIF: Average	OBJ: Comprehension
2. ANS: A	DIF: Challenging	OBJ: Reading Strategy
3. ANS: A	DIF: Average	OBJ: Interpretation
4. ANS: B	DIF: Challenging	OBJ: Literary Analysis
5. ANS: A	DIF: Easy	OBJ: Comprehension
6. ANS: C	DIF: Average	OBJ: Interpretation
7. ANS: D	DIF: Average	OBJ: Comprehension
8. ANS: A	DIF: Easy	OBJ: Reading Strategy
9. ANS: C	DIF: Challenging	OBJ: Reading Strategy
10. ANS: B	DIF: Average	OBJ: Interpretation
11. ANS: A	DIF: Average	OBJ: Literary Analysis
12. ANS: B	DIF: Average	OBJ: Comprehension
13. ANS: C	DIF: Easy	OBJ: Comprehension
14. ANS: A	DIF: Average	OBJ: Interpretation
15. ANS: B	DIF: Challenging	OBJ: Reading Strategy
16. ANS: C	DIF: Average	OBJ: Interpretation
17. ANS: A	DIF: Challenging	OBJ: Literary Analysis
18. ANS: A	DIF: Average	OBJ: Interpretation

Vocabulary

19. ANS: C	DIF: Esay	OBJ: Vocabulary
20. ANS: B	DIF: Average	OBJ: Vocabulary

Essay

21. The title of "The Secret" refers to poetry. It can also refer to discovering that poetry can have many meanings. A final meaning of the title might be the secret of life the two girls think they have found. The title of "The Gift" could refer to the metal splinter that was in the boy's hand. The title can also refer to the gift of tenderness the father gives the boy when he gently removes the splinter. The titles refer to similar things, because they can both refer to ideas or both refer to things.

    Difficulty: *Easy*

    Objective: *Essay*

22. The title, "Traveling Through the Dark," describes what the deer was doing and what the speaker was doing. The deer was walking beside or in the road at night; the speaker and the driver who hit the deer were driving their cars at night. The deer probably would not have been hit during the day, because it is easier to see deer in daylight. The title also symbolizes the mental journey the speaker must make as he thinks about what to do with the deer's body and the unborn fawn. That journey is symbolically dark because the speaker is deciding between life or death for the fawn.

Difficulty: *Average*
Objective: *Essay*

23. The epiphany in "Traveling Through the Dark" is that the speaker realizes he will choose death over life for the fawn. His encounter with a dead deer helps him understand that nature is filled with death. The epiphany in "The Secret" is about embracing the mysteries of life. The narrator does not know the secret of life but two girls help her understand that others think they do, and that is a valuable insight. The epiphany in "The Gift" is that something that starts out painful can result in a true understanding of tenderness and humanity. The speaker learns this lesson from his father. The epiphany in "Traveling Through the Dark" brings a more somber mood. The epiphanies in "The Secret" and "The Gift" bring happiness.

Difficulty: *Challenging*
Objective: *Essay*

24.

TK

Difficulty: *Average*
Objective: *Essay*

Selections by Espada, Komunyakaa, Nye

Vocabulary Warm-up Exercises, p. 83

A. 1. terrain
2. bamboo
3. sluggish
4. branches
5. songbirds
6. hummingbird
7. grackles
8. oozing

B. Sample Answers
1. T. Animals with *spines* are called vertebrates.
2. T. An *upturned* pot would catch water.
3. F. If she learned the vocabulary words *completely* she would have done well on the test.
4. F. If he worked in a factory, he would have had to use a *punchclock*.
5. T. Many toys are *manufactured* in China and imported into the U.S.

6. F. A person who does not work hard at anything is not likely to achieve *perfection*.
7. T. If a ride *revolved* rapidly, it could have made some people motion sick.
8. F. If someone is *refreshed* after a shower, they feel good.

Reading Warm-up A, p. 84

Sample Answers
1. the land where they live; The *terrain* where I live is hilly.
2. (tall, slender); chopsticks, furniture, fences
3. trickling; *seeping, soaking, flowing slowly*
4. boughs; A lot of *branches* blew off the tree during the storm.
5. (birds, large and noisy); *crow, blackbird*
6. melodious; It is great to hear *songbirds* when you walk in the forest.
7. tiny yet brilliant; No, I have never seen a *hummingbird*.
8. slow; *lively, energetic*

Reading Warm-up B, p. 85

Sample Answers
1. running the whole operation, from start to finish; *totally*
2. (skills of artisans); I feel *refreshed* after a shower.
3. practiced hard to achieve a level, attain excellence; It is not possible to achieve *perfection*.
4. goods in larger and larger workshops and then factories; cars, toasters...
5. (rotated); *merry-go-round*
6. exposed; *overturned, turned over*
7. injuries; Yes, injuries to *spines* would be painful.
8. a machine that recorded when they arrived and when they left; No, I don't know anyone who has to use a *punchclock*.

Literary Analysis: Voice, p. 86

Sample Responses
"Camouflaging the Chimera": This poem about guerilla warfare in Vietnam expresses a tone of intense, watchful waiting, at first through the use of concrete details ("We hugged bamboo & leaned / against a breeze against the river"); but it also builds to a tone of desperation and anguish by scattering surreal images among the matter-of-fact ones ("slow-dragging with the ghosts," "we waited till the moon touched metal," "black silk wrestling iron through grass," "a world revolved / under each man's eyelid").

"Streets": The tone of this poem is dreamlike and meditative, with the poet stretching words through figures of speech to try to grapple with the mystery of death ("the streets he lived on / grow a little shorter," "the sky which sews and sews, tirelessly sewing, / drops her purple hem." The voice is gentle and mystical, gazing both ways from the border between life and death ("They dream thickly, / dream double, they wake from a dream / into another one. . . .)

Reading Strategy: Analyze Author's Implicit Beliefs, p. 87

Sample Responses

Possible responses: **"Who Burns for the Perfection of Paper"**—Author's beliefs: behind many manufactured products is a process of factory labor that is harsh and demeaning to the humans who make them. Details: "the glue would sting, / hands oozing / till both palms burned / at the punchclock"; "a pair of hands / upturned and burning." **"Camouflaging the Chimera"**—Author's beliefs: war takes an almost inhuman toll of anxiety and fear on soldiers of both sides. Details: "something almost broke inside us. . ."; "we held our breath, ready to spring the L-shaped / ambush . . ." **"Streets"**: The death of a human being diminishes the world around him/her; in death we cross over from one kind of dream into another. Details: "A man leaves the world / and the streets he lived on / grow a little shorter"; "They dream thickly, / dream, double, they wake from a dream / into another one. . . ."

Building Vocabulary, p. 88

A. 1. terrain
   2. crevices
   3. refuge
   4. terrain
   5. refuge
   6. crevices

B. 1. in the air
   2. yes
   1. yes
C. 1. c; 2. a; 3. c

Enrichment: Vietnam Veterans, p. 90

Sample Answer

Students should use the suggested questions only as a guide. They should be encouraged to think up their own prepared questions and to pursue questions that arise in the course of the interview.

Open-Book Test, p. 91

Short Answer

1. The message is that behind the products we enjoy there is often a process of labor than can be both painful for the workers who make the products.
   Difficulty: *Average* **Objective:** *Literary Analysis*

2. The poet implicitly believes that many paper products are the result of labor that is both painful and demeaning to the people who have to perform it to survive.
   Difficulty: *Average* **Objective:** *Reading*

3. The title implies that the final perfected product is considered more important than the real human beings who suffer to make it.
   Difficulty: *Easy* **Objective:** *Interpretation*

4. In this passage Komunyakaa's voice creates an atmosphere of tension and suspense, of watchful waiting, as the soldiers prepare for their encounter with the VC.
   Difficulty: *Challenging* **Objective:** *Literary Analysis*

5. Students might note that it would be hard to identify any particular feelings that the author has about the Vietnam War in particular because there is nothing in the poem's language or feelings that relates uniquely to the political circumstances of the Vietnam War. Rather, he seems to be conveying his belief that war in general turns the soldier into an alert, struggling animal among other animals—almost reduces him to being part of nature.
   Difficulty: *Challenging* **Objective:** *Reading*

6. The speaker does not seem to hate the VC; rather, the VC seems to be like a part of nature that the soldier has to contend with, just as they must struggle with nature: "VC struggled / with the hillside, like black silk / wrestling iron through grass."
   Difficulty: *Easy* **Objective:** *Reading*

7. These lines show the aspect of the poet's voice that is sensitive to and celebrates the movements and rhythms of nature.
   Difficulty: *Easy* **Objective:** *Literary Analysis*

8. The poet seems to believe that life itself is a kind of dream, because people "wake from a dream / into another one," and that they seem to make their own reality.
   Difficulty: *Challenging* **Objective:** *Reading*

9. Words that describe voice from "Who Burns . . . "crevices of the skin" "sting of hidden cuts." Words that describe voice from "Camouflaging . . . " - "station of shadows" "The river ran through our bones." Words that describe voice from "Street" - "waking refreshed" "lost and remembered."
   Difficulty: *Average* **Objective:** *Interpretation*

10. The weather would have suddenly turned stormy, because *refuge* means "shelter or protection from danger."
    Difficulty: *Average* **Objective:** *Vocabulary*

Essay

11. Students should clearly state which of the three poems spoke to them most strongly. They should explain why the poem spoke to them the most strongly, citing details from the poem of their choice to support their answer.
    Difficulty: *Easy* **Objective:** *Essay*

12. Students might note that in "Who Burns for the Perfection of Paper," the poet's voice is at first very straightforward, almost journalistic, as the poet reports the details of his daily job at the paper factory. Later in the poem, using that same journalistic tone, a voice of anger emerges as the poet describes the injury and pain that resulted from his work. Students should note that

in "Camouflaging . . . ," Komunyakaa's language is more intense and concentrated, more figurative, to enable him to convey a voice of anxiety and fear about the impending fight with the enemy: Nye's language in "Streets" is the most dreamlike as she tries to give voice to the mysteries of death and absence.

Difficulty: *Average*   **Objective:** *Essay*

13. Students might note that in "Who Burns . . . " the author's beliefs about factory labor are evident in the title, which implies that people suffer to make a perfect paper product, so that the product is considered more important than the exploited human being who hurts and suffers to make it. The poem reinforces these points with pointed references to the physical pain of the laborer. Students might suggest that in "Camouflaging . . . ," Komunyakaa does not seem to for or against the Vietnam War in particular—rather, he seems to present the belief that war takes an almost inhuman toll of anxiety and fear on soldiers of both sides.

Difficulty: *Challenging*   **Objective:** *Essay*

14. Students might suggest that all three poems both reflect social realities and seek to shape the reader's response to those realities. "Who Burns . . . " is a harsh portrayal of the pain and exhuastion of factory labor, but in reflecting this reality it seeks to rouse the reader's sense of compassion over this injustice; "Camouflaging . . . ," in portraying the dehumanizing effects of war--reducing men to the level of nature—not only depicts the realities of war but tries to awaken the reader's sensitivity to the savagery of warfare; and "Streets" both portrays human attitudes toward death and seeks to mold them by contrasting the ways in which people confront this ultimate reality of life.

Difficulty: *Average*   **Objective:** *Essay*

Oral Response

15. Oral responses should be clear, well organized, and well supported by appropriate examples from the selections.

Difficulty: *Average*   **Objective:** *Oral Response*

Selection Test A, p. 94

Critical Reading

1. ANS: B	DIF: Easy	OBJ: Comprehension
2. ANS: B	DIF: Easy	OBJ: Interpretation
3. ANS: A	DIF: Easy	OBJ: Literary Analysis
4. ANS: B	DIF: Easy	OBJ: Reading Strategy
5. ANS: D	DIF: Easy	OBJ: Interpretation
6. ANS: B	DIF: Easy	OBJ: Interpretation
7. ANS: A	DIF: Easy	OBJ: Literary Analysis
8. ANS: B	DIF: Easy	OBJ: Interpretation
9. ANS: A	DIF: Easy	OBJ: Literary Analysis
10. ANS: B	DIF: Easy	OBJ: Comprehension
11. ANS: B	DIF: Easy	OBJ: Reading Strategy
12. ANS: B	DIF: Easy	OBJ: Comprehension
13. ANS: A	DIF: Easy	OBJ: Interpretation

Vocabulary

14. ANS: C	DIF: Easy	OBJ: Vocabulary
15. ANS: A	DIF: Easy	OBJ: Vocabulary

Essay

16. Students' essay should reflect that the law student understands what the laborers are going through to produce the legal pads he is using today. The speaker remembers the pain of the paper cuts and the sting of the glue on the cuts. He also implies that he is lucky to be doing what he is doing instead of working at harsh labor in a paper factory making legal pads for others.

Difficulty: *Easy*

Objective: *Essay*

17. Students' essays should suggest that when the moon reflected on metal they knew they were looking at a weapon, since there is no metal object found in the natural environment. At that point, the soldiers knew they would soon be attacking the enemy.

Difficulty: *Easy*

Objective: *Essay*

18. In "Who Burns for the Perfection of Paper," the social issue is the exploitation of labor. The poet thinks that laborers are used to support the better, easier jobs of those in higher social classes or those with education. In "Camouflaging the Chimera," the social issue is the harshness of war. The poet thinks that war is dehumanizing and reduces living people to the level of unthinking elements of nature. In "Streets," the social issue is death. The poet thinks that people handle the death of a person in many different ways, sometimes alone and sometimes as a group.

Difficulty: *Average*

Objective: *Essay*

Selection Test B, p. 97

Critical Reading

1. ANS: A	DIF: Average	OBJ: Interpretation
2. ANS: B	DIF: Easy	OBJ: Comprehension
3. ANS: D	DIF: Challenging	OBJ: Literary Analysis
4. ANS: C	DIF: Average	OBJ: Interpretation
5. ANS: A	DIF: Average	OBJ: Reading Strategy
6. ANS: D	DIF: Average	OBJ: Interpretation
7. ANS: A	DIF: Average	OBJ: Literary Analysis
8. ANS: B	DIF: Average	OBJ: Comprehension
9. ANS: A	DIF: Challenging	OBJ: Reading Strategy
10. ANS: C	DIF: Challenging	OBJ: Interpretation
11. ANS: B	DIF: Average	OBJ: Interpretation
12. ANS: D	DIF: Average	OBJ: Reading Strategy
13. ANS: B	DIF: Average	OBJ: Literary Analysis
14. ANS: D	DIF: Challenging	OBJ: Literary Analysis
15. ANS: A	DIF: Challenging	OBJ: Reading Strategy

Vocabulary

16. ANS: A   DIF: Average   OBJ: Vocabulary
17. ANS: A   DIF: Average   OBJ: Vocabulary
18. ANS: A   DIF: Easy   OBJ: Vocabulary

Essay

19. Students' essay should reflect that the law student understands what the laborers are going through to produce the legal pads he is using today. The speaker remembers the pain of the paper cuts and the sting of the glue on the cuts. He also implies that he is lucky to be doing what he is doing instead of working at harsh labor in a paper factory making legal pads for others.
    Difficulty: *Easy*
    Objective: *Essay*

20. Students' essays should suggest that when the moon reflected on metal they knew they were looking at a weapon, since there is no metal object found in the natural environment. At that point, the soldiers knew they would soon be attacking the enemy. The soldiers worked hard to become one with the natural world. They wanted to look like the natural surroundings, so they used branches, mud, and grass to disguise themselves.
    Difficulty: *Easy*
    Objective: *Essay*

21. Students' responses will generally say that the world changes. Some might note that the people who "sleep completely" accept death and continue with their normal lives. Most students will note that streets are shorter and a window is dark, which shows that a person has a place in the city that changes upon his or her death. People often react to death by getting together. Some people continue to dream about the person who died. The birds and the sun continue on even in the face of death.
    Difficulty: *Challenging*
    Objective: *Essay*

22. Students might suggest that all three poems both reflect social realities and seek to shape the reader's response to those realities. "Who Burns . . ." is a harsh portrayal of the pain and exhaustion of factory labor, but in reflecting this reality it seeks to rouse the reader's sense of compassion over this injustice; "Camouflaging . . . ," in portraying the dehumanizing effects of war—reducing men to the level of nature—not only depicts the realities of war but tries to awaken the reader's sensitivity to the savagery of warfare; and "Streets" both portrays human attitudes toward death and seeks to mold them by contrasting the ways in which people confront this ultimate reality of life.
    Difficulty: *Average*
    Objective: *Essay*

"Halley's Comet" by Stanley Kunitz

Vocabulary Warm-up Exercises, p. 101

A. 1. flannel
2. steal
3. coarse
4. scolded

B. Sample Answers

1. scarcely   Synonym: hardly

We *hardly* had time to finish cleaning up before the guests arrived.

2. sprawled   Synonym: slouched

They spent the entire day *slouched* on the couch watching television.

3. proclaiming   Synonym: declaring

After *declaring* victory, the senator said some kind words about her opponent.

4. repent   Synonym: regret

When time had passed, I grew to *regret* my harsh words.

Reading Warm-up A, p. 102

Sample Answers

1. (creep); This definition of *steal* means to sneak or move without being noticed.
2. soft, pajamas; *Flannel* can also be used to make warm shirts or can be used as a lining for wool pants.
3. (disciplinary action); An antonym for *scolded* is *praised*.
4. rough surface; An old towel could also feel *coarse*.

Reading Warm-up B, p. 103

Sample Answers

1. declare their views; As soon as she finished *proclaiming* that she was right, someone proved her wrong.
2. (atonement for past sins); make them eligible for salvation
3. hardly; An antonym for *scarcely* is *frequently*.
4. lying on a blanket; The only way to be *sprawling* while standing up would be if a person were leaning against something. Usually, to be *sprawling*, the arms and/or legs would have to be in awkward or sloppy positions.

Literary Analysis: Free Verse, p. 104

Sample Response

Examples of each kind of ending might include the following: End-stopped lines: "there'd be no school tomorrow. / A red-bearded preacher . . ."—emphasizes break between idea of no school and presence of the preacher; "with my mother and sisters; / but I felt excited too . . ."—emphasizes contrast between his anxiety and his excitement; Enjambed Lines: "wrote its name in chalk / across the board and told use / it was roaring . . ."—emphasizes continuity of process of writing on the board and speaking at the same time; "They never heard me steal / into the stairwell hall and climb / the ladder to the fresh night air"; emphasizes the secretiveness of "stealing" into the stairwell and the continuous action of climbing the ladder.

Reading Strategy: Identify Changes in Tense and Tone, p. 105

Sample Response

Possible response: Type of Change: Change in tense and tone. Where It Occurs: "So mother scolded me / and sent me early to my room. / The whole family's asleep /except for me"; Possible Meaning: past tense in first two lines, present tense in last two lines emphasizes shift in recounting mealtime events to the speaker's current urgent excitement that keeps him awake. Type of Change: Change in tense and tone. Where It Occurs: between end of first stanza and beginning of second stanza. Possible meaning: emphasizes break between memory of past events and the more immediate and pressing sense of the boy praying to / addressing his dead father in the hopes that the end of the world will reunite them.

Building Vocabulary, p. 106

A. 1. No, he was not saying it in a whisper, because *proclaiming* means "declaring proudly or openly."

2. Yes, he was passing judgment on the sinners, because *repent* means "feel sorry" or "feel regret," so he was implying that their sins were wrong and required them to make amends or seek forgiveness.

3. No, the narrator did not tell his mother and sister, because *steal* means "sneak"; he went to the roof without wanting them to know about it.

B. 1. B; 2. C; 3. A

Enrichment: Astronomy, p. 108

Sample Answers

1. mathematics, science, physics, chemistry

2. Astronomers now use sophisticated electronic equipment to record their observations rather than relying on optical devices alone.

3. An astronomer needs to interpret and explain his or her observations for others scientists and nonscientists.

4. Astronomy connects us to the larger universe by finding ever newer and better ways of seeing what is going on in space and by using this and other data to expand our knowledge of it.

Open-Book Test, p. 109

Short Answer

1. The narrator is frightened—the comet's "frightful" speed and the idea that it might "[smash] into the earth" give evidence of his reaction.

   Difficulty: *Easy*   **Objective:** *Interpretation*

2. The entire first stanza is written in the past tense.

   Difficulty: *Easy*   **Objective:** *Reading*

3. The word that is emphasized is "God." Putting this word at the end of the line emphasizes the idea that the coming of Halley's Comet stirs religious ideas about the meaning of life and death in the mind of the narrator.

   Difficulty: *Challenging*   **Objective:** *Literary Analysis*

4. By ending line 16 with the word "shouted," the poet emphasizes the loud and dramatic delivery of the quoted words, "Repent, ye sinners!"

   Difficulty: *Easy*   **Objective:** *Literary Analysis*

5. The narrator feels a combination of unhappiness ("I felt sad to think / that it was probably / the last meal I'd share / with my mother and sisters . . .") and alert anticipation at the arrival of this great event ("but I felt excited too / and scarcely touched my plate.").

   Difficulty: *Average*   **Objective:** *Interpretation*

6. The narrator wishes to underscore two meaning of steal: "to move secretly" and "to take without permission," since he is taking time to stay up and look at the night sky in a way that he knows his mother would not allow if she knew about it.

   Difficulty: *Challenging*   **Objective:** *Literary Analysis*

7. The change in tense is from past to present tense. The change in tone is an increased sense of urgency as the narrator directs a deeply felt prayer about Halley's Comet. It is a prayer that taps into his deepest fears and hopes about the coming of the comet.

   Difficulty: *Average*   **Objective:** *Reading*

8. Students might suggest that the narrator is addressing either his dead father or God or both.

   Difficulty: *Challenging*   **Objective:** *Interpretation*

9. Examples of each kind of ending might include the following: Enjambed Lines: "wrote its name in chalk / across the board and told us / it was roaring . . ."; "it was probably / the last meal I'd share / with my mother and sisters . . ." End-stopped lines: "there'd be no school tomorrow. / A red-bearded preacher . . ."; "with my mother and sisters; but I felt excited too . . ."; "at the foot of Green street— / that's where we live, you know, on the top floor."

   Difficulty: *Average*   **Objective:** *Literary Analysis*

10. Yes, you would probably feel guilt about having done it because *repent* means "feel sorry for what one has done."

    Difficulty: *Average*   **Objective:** *Vocabulary*

Essay

11. Students might note that in some respects the young boy's understanding of the approach of Halley's Comet is accurate. He realizes that it is an object in outer space traveling at tremendous speed that is approaching the planet earth. They might also note that in other respects his understanding is inaccurate or exaggerated: he takes his teacher's remark that the comet could go off course and hit the earth as a virtual certainty, and his encounter with the preacher in the park loads the impending event with tremendous

emotional and religious meanings that it would not otherwise have for him.

Difficulty: *Easy* **Objective:** *Essay*

12. Students might suggest that from the very beginning of "Halley's Comet," the poet discusses the arrival of the comet in terms that emphasize its emotional as well as its scientific meaning: "roaring down the stormtracks / of the Milky Way" evokes an event of almost mythic significance, as does the idea—the likelihood, in the young boy's mind—that it might smash into the earth. Students should note that the idea of the end of the world soon takes on religious meaning, especially after the boy's encounter with the wild-eyed preacher in the park. Students might note that the boy's prayer to his dead father (and/or God) in the last stanza clinches the religious sense of the poem—that the end of the world will permit the living on earth to be reunited with those who have passed on to some mysterious life beyond.

Difficulty: *Average* **Objective:** *Essay*

13. Students might note that the poem is full of hints of death from the very beginning: "if it wandered off its course / and smashed into the earth / there'd be no school tomorrow." Thus does the teacher's passing joke become magnified into a prediction of the end of the world, reinforced by the strange and menacing preaching of the wild man in the park. Students might note that the boy is sad that he might not share another meal with his family, but that he is also strangely excited, staying up into the night to witness the great event he expects, and uttering a prayer to his dead father in the expectation—hope—that he will soon be reunited with him. For the young boy, the imagined impending crash of the comet is an invitation to wonder about crossing over from life to death—perhaps, indeed, to another life that stirs deep feelings in the young boy about the mysterious possibilities of life and death.

Difficulty: *Challenging* **Objective:** *Essay*

14. Students might note that the first significant place the narrator mentions is his first-grade schoolroom, where he learns of the approach of Halley's Comet. They might further note the mention of the public square near the playground's edge where the eccentric man does his preaching. Finally, they should note the mention of the household he shares with his mother and sisters, from which his father is notably absent. These various places—school, public square, home—are all obviously critical in shaping the emotional makeup of the young boy and, therefore, of the adult who recalls this episode, thus confirming the essential importance of place in forming the worldview and thematic concerns of the poet.

Difficulty: *Average* **Objective:** *Essay*

Oral Response

15. Oral responses should be clear, well organized, and well supported by appropriate examples from the selections.

Difficulty: *Average* **Objective:** *Oral Response*

Selection Test A, p. 112

Critical Reading

1. ANS: B	DIF: Easy	OBJ: Literary Analysis
2. ANS: C	DIF: Easy	OBJ: Comprehension
3. ANS: C	DIF: Easy	OBJ: Interpretation
4. ANS: B	DIF: Easy	OBJ: Comprehension
5. ANS: D	DIF: Easy	OBJ: Literary Analysis
6. ANS: C	DIF: Easy	OBJ: Interpretation
7. ANS: D	DIF: Easy	OBJ: Interpretation
8. ANS: A	DIF: Easy	OBJ: Reading
9. ANS: B	DIF: Easy	OBJ: Literary Analysis
10. ANS: A	DIF: Easy	OBJ: Comprehension
11. ANS: C	DIF: Easy	OBJ: Interpretation
12. ANS: C	DIF: Easy	OBJ: Interpretation

Vocabulary

13. ANS: A	DIF: Easy	OBJ: Vocabulary
14. ANS: B	DIF: Easy	OBJ: Vocabulary
15. ANS: B	DIF: Easy	OBJ: Vocabulary

Essay

16. Students may mention such lines as 16–17 and 32-33 as examples of end-stopped lines and lines 1–8 and 18–21 as examples of enjambed lines. Responses should offer a reasonable interpretation of why each type of line was employed in the context.

Difficulty: *Easy*

Objective: *Essay*

17. Responses should mention that the speaker is presented as a naive but sensitive young person. Knowledge of Halley's comet or of the potential end of the word lies outside his experience. At the same time, however, his poignant attachment to his family and his longing for his absent father are profound emotions that move the reader to empathize with him.

Difficulty: *Easy*

Objective: *Essay*

18. Responses should mention that the final scene stands out largely because of the speaker's solitude and his direct address to the "Father"—either his biological parent, or God the Father, or both. The final scene also contains an element of resignation, or even of welcome, about the end of the world—in contrast to the apprehensions and anxiety recorded in the previous three scenes.

Difficulty: *Average*

Objective: *Essay*

Selection Test B, p. 115

Critical Reading

1. ANS: B	DIF: Easy	OBJ: Literary Analysis
2. ANS: A	DIF: Easy	OBJ: Comprehension

3. ANS: D   DIF: Challenging   OBJ: Interpretation
4. ANS: D   DIF: Average   OBJ: Comprehension
5. ANS: B   DIF: Challenging   OBJ: Literary Analysis
6. ANS: C   DIF: Average   OBJ: Interpretation
7. ANS: B   DIF: Average   OBJ: Comprehension
8. ANS: A   DIF: Average   OBJ: Interpretation
9. ANS: B   DIF: Easy   OBJ: Reading
10. ANS: A   DIF: Average   OBJ: Literary Analysis
11. ANS: A   DIF: Average   OBJ: Comprehension
12. ANS: B   DIF: Challenging   OBJ: Interpretation
13. ANS: A   DIF: Average   OBJ: Reading
14. ANS: D   DIF: Average   OBJ: Interpretation

Vocabulary

15. ANS: B   DIF: Easy   OBJ: Vocabulary
16. ANS: A   DIF: Average   OBJ: Vocabulary
17. ANS: C   DIF: Challenging   OBJ: Vocabulary

Essay

18. As examples of end-stopped lines that create a conversational mood or produce a storytelling atmosphere, students may single out such examples as lines 16–17 and 32–33. As examples of enjambed lines, students may focus on lines 1–8 and 18–21.
    Difficulty: *Easy*
    Objective: *Essay*

19. Students may mention that the classroom scene establishes the situation—the approach of Halley's comet—and lays the groundwork for the speaker's fears. The second scene intensifies the speaker's anxiety and introduces the concepts of God, sin, punishment, and repentance. The third scene pivots on a delicate balance between the boy's apprehension and his suspenseful excitement. In the fourth scene, the tone becomes more poignant, as the boy reaches out to his absent father and perhaps also to God. Each scene contributes to the rounded, complex portrayal of the boy's personality and emotions.
    Difficulty: *Average*
    Objective: *Essay*

20. Students may mention that the frst three scenes in the poem exhibit a tone that mingles apprehension with curiosity and excitement. In the final section, the speaker's tone shifts to one of poignant longing, especially as he directly addresses his absent "Father." The plaintive close of the poem suggests that the end of the world might, in fact, be a comforting event for the speaker, in that he would become reunited with his father.
    Difficulty: *Challenging*
    Objective: *Essay*

21. Students might note that the first significant place the narrator mentions is his first-grade schoolroom, when he first learns about what seem to him to be the frightening details of the approach of Halley's Comet. They might further note the mention of the public square near the playground's edge where the eccentric man does his preaching. Finally, they should note the mention of the household he shares with his mother and sisters, from which his father is notably absent. These various places—school, public square, home—are all obviously critical in shaping the emotional makeup of the young boy and, therefore, of the adult who recalls this episode, thus confirming the essential importance of place in forming the worldview and thematic emotions of the poet.
    Difficulty: *Average*
    Objective: *Essay*

"Ars Poetica" by Judith Ortiz Cofer

Vocabulary Warm-up Exercises, p. 119

A.
1. aisles
2. gaze
3. votive
4. patroness
5. portrait
6. plump
7. maternal
8. magnetized

B. Sample Answers
1. The *stale* bread is good for feeding to the birds.
2. The customers pulled their chairs up to the *formica* counter.
3. It took her a long time to learn to deal with her *disillusions* when people let her down.
4. Mary rang up their purchases on the old *register* in the general store.
5. That cabin held so many *memories* of family vacations.
6. James recited poetry so *lyrically* that people love to listen to him.
7. Randolph spent hours *perfecting* his golf swing.

Reading Warm-up A, p. 120

Sample Answers
1. pictured; Yes, I have seen a portrait of my grandmother.
2. (Virgin Mary and Christ Child, devotion); *paternal*
3. paintings of the Madonna and Child; *passageways, walkways*
4. candles; The man made a *votive* offering.
5. (the portraits); *stare, look at length*
6. protector; *patron*
7. rounded; thin, slim, bony
8. refrigerator art; *made like a magnet so that metal things are attracted to it*

Reading Warm-up B, p. 121

Sample Answers

1. of their childhoods, recalling; *recollections*
2. (pink counter); The area around the sink was made of *formica*.
3. ancient manual cash; The burglars broke into the *register* and stole the money.
4. selling their goods; The United States trades with China, Japan, Great Britain, more.
5. (disappointments); the foods that his parents remembered
6. speak longingly; *good food, love*
7. strange, old and tough; *fresh*
8. improving; I am working on *perfecting* my writing skills.

Literary Analysis: Imagery, p. 122

Sample Response

Students might cite some of the following: dried codfish, green plantains (smell, sight, touch)—foods associated with native countries; Bustelo coffee (smell, sight)—brand associated with Latin subculture; Patroness of Exiles (sight)—contributes to sense of deli as sacred gathering ground for Latinos; plain wide face, ample bosom (sight)—evokes image of deli owner as maternal figure who brings community together; plain ham and cheese (sight, smell, touch, taste)—an item that is familiar and comforting to Latinos immigrants from diverse lands; fragile old man lost in the folds of his winter coat (sight, touch)—reinforces idea of Latinos as lost in alien culture of North America.

Reading: Analyzing Sensory Details, p. 123

Sample Response

Students' responses might include the following sensory details from the poem: "heady mix of smells from the open bins / of dried codfish, the green plantains . . .," "selling canned memories," "a pound of Bustelo coffee," "her plain wide face, her ample bosom / resting on her plump arms . . .," "the stale candy of everyone's childhood . . . ," "plain ham and cheese," "the fragile old man lost in the folds / of his winter coat." What the details have in common: they evoke the sensory experience of the customers' homelands, a kind of home away from home for the Latinos in exile in a North American city. Overall feeling or idea expressed by details: the importance of feeling a sense of home or belonging, especially when the surrounding culture is different from one's familiar traditions and values.

Building Vocabulary, p. 124

A. 1. False; a heady mix of smells would be intoxicating and therefore very noticeable.
2. False; if you had ample supplies, you would have enough, so there would be no need to go out shopping.
3. True; experiencing a number of disillusions means you would be exposed to truths about life and therefore have fewer false notions.

4. True; if you had mastered all the material for the test, there would be no need to divine, or guess, the answers, because you would know them.

B. 1. D; 2. A; 3. B; 4. B

Enrichment: Geography, p. 126

Sample Answers

1. Cuba
2. Haiti and the Dominican Republic
3. the Gulf of Mexico
4. Venezuela
5. San Juan
6. Mexico and Cuba

Open-Book Test, p. 127

Short Answer

1. Students might cite some of the following: dried codfish, green plantains (smell, sight, touch)—foods associated with native countries; Bustelo coffee (smell, sight)—brand associated with Latin subculture; Patroness of Exiles (sight))—contributes to sense of deli as sacred gathering ground for Latinos; plain wide face, ample bosom (sight))—evokes image of deli owner as maternal figure who brings community together; plain ham and cheese (sight, smell, touch, taste)—an item that is familiar and comforting to Latinos immigrants from diverse lands; fragile old man lost in the folds of his winter coat (sight, touch))—reinforces idea of Latinos as lost in alien culture of North America

   Difficulty: *Average*   **Objective:** *Literary Analysis*

2. The sensory detail of the formica counter helps to establish the deli as an informal, homey atmosphere where locals can gather in comfort.

   Difficulty: *Average*   **Objective:** *Reading*

3. The plastic Mother and Child portray the deli as a kind of sacred environment where Latinos of various cultures come to share their common interests and dreams. The "ancient register" reminds the reader that this holy place is really just a place of business that somehow gives the local people a sense of belonging.

   Difficulty: *Challenging*   **Objective:** *Literary Analysis*

4. The "Patroness of Exiles;" is the deli owner. In the poem she is a kind of symbolic high priestess whose deli provides the local immigrants with a place where they feel a temporary sense of home and belonging.

   Difficulty: *Easy*   **Objective:** *Interpretation*

5. These details paint a picture of a plain woman of no particular age who, because of her lack of distinctive features, can be all things to all the people who patronize her store.

   Difficulty: *Easy*   **Objective:** *Reading*

6. The main activity of the customers of the deli is talking and daydreaming. This detail tells the reader that the

deli is more significant as a local social gathering place than as a place of business.

Difficulty: *Easy* **Objective:** *Interpretation*

7. The image tells the reader that her features are plain and wide enough to be those of any family member of the customers, so her appearance enhances the customers' sense of family, of belonging, when they shop there.

Difficulty: *Average* **Objective:** *Literary Analysis*

8. Students might note that the phrase suggests that most of the customers have unrealized ambitions ("dreams") and unfulfilled expectations and regrets ("disilllusions") in their adopted homeland of North America.

Difficulty: *Challenging* **Objective:** *Interpretation*

9. The fact that the customers continue to shop at the deli even though some items are more expensive there tells the reader that they regard the deli as more of a social or cultural center than as a place of business.

Difficulty: *Average* **Objective:** *Interpretation*

10. Yes, you would expect to have enough to last for the entire trip, because ample means "sufficient."

Difficulty: *Average* **Objective:** *Vocabulary*

Essay

11. Students should be clear about the nature of the place they are describing and should explain why it serves a function similar to the one served by the deli in the poem. They should support their answer with rich, specific descriptive details.

Difficulty: *Easy* **Objective:** *Essay*

12. Students might note that in calling the woman "the Patroness of the Exiles," the poet calls attention to the fact that most of the customers—perhaps even the woman herself—are people who have been uprooted from their homelands to come to North American to make a new life. Many of these people feel a constant sense of homesickness for their native lands, so the deli—with its stream of Spanish-language conversation and familiar foods and aromas—becomes a kind of oasis of familiarity and "home" amid the unfamiliar rhythms, language, and culture of North America. The woman's warm, receptive personality and appearance—"her look of maternal interest"—helps to endear her to the customers and create an atmosphere in which a sense of family or home is more important than the business that is transacted there.

Difficulty: *Average* **Objective:** *Essay*

13. Most students might note that many of the customers seem to have a deep sense of loss or nostalgia about the lands they have left: the Puerto Ricans who complain about the price of coffee, the Cubans who dream of marching home in "glorious return:" to Havana, the others who simply wander the aisles of the store savoring the smells and even the names of products that remind them of their native lands: "reading the

labels of packages aloud, as if / they were the names of lost lovers . . ." These images, plus the customers' talk of their "dreams and their disillusions" suggest that life in North America has not fulfilled their dreams and home still seems more like their homelands—an atmosphere that is evoked by the aromas, sights, and language of the deli.

Difficulty: *Challenging* **Objective:** *Essay*

14. Students might suggest that the poem balances a sense of place so that both kinds of places are portrayed in a very vivid and memorable way. The deli itself, with its pungent array of sights and aromas, presided over by the maternal owner, is a memorable and deeply felt place in itself. But, students might note, the deli achieves this sense of place only by recalling the homelands of the patrons.

Difficulty: *Average* **Objective:** *Essay*

Oral Response

15. Oral responses should be clear, well organized, and well supported by appropriate examples from the selection.

Difficulty: *Average* **Objective:** *Oral Response*

Selection Test A, p. 130

Critical Reading

1. ANS: B	DIF: Easy	OBJ: Comprehension
2. ANS: C	DIF: Easy	OBJ: Literary Analysis
3. ANS: C	DIF: Easy	OBJ: Interpretation
4. ANS: B	DIF: Easy	OBJ: Interpretation
5. ANS: D	DIF: Easy	OBJ: Interpretation
6. ANS: B	DIF: Easy	OBJ: Comprehension
7. ANS: D	DIF: Easy	OBJ: Comprehension
8. ANS: A	DIF: Easy	OBJ: Reading
9. ANS: A	DIF: Easy	OBJ: Comprehension
10. ANS: B	DIF: Easy	OBJ: Interpretation
11. ANS: B	DIF: Easy	OBJ: Interpretation
12. ANS: A	DIF: Easy	OBJ: Interpretation

Vocabulary

13. ANS: A	DIF: Easy	OBJ: Vocabulary
14. ANS: B	DIF: Easy	OBJ: Vocabulary
15. ANS: C	DIF: Easy	OBJ: Vocabulary

Essay

16. Students may mention such images as the following: "heady mix of smells from the open bins of dried cod-fish" (smell), "green plantains hanging in stalks" (sight), "listening to the Puerto Ricans complain" (hearing), "perfecting their speech of a 'glorious return'" (hearing),

or "the stale candy of everyone's childhood" (taste). Students should identify the poem's overall message as compassion for the immigrants' longing for the culture of their roots. Essays should explain how each image relates to this theme.

Difficulty: *Easy*
Objective: *Essay*

17. Students may mention that the customers all find in the deli comforting reminders of their past and their native culture. Although the deli provides consolation for their emotional "hunger," however, the prices there are somewhat higher than what the customers might pay if they shopped elsewhere. The customers have different disillusions and hopes for the future: for example, the Mexicans look forward to making money in their new home, while the Cubans dream of a "glorious return" to Havana.

Difficulty: *Easy*
Objective: *Essay*

18. Responses should recognize that the setting is a key element in the poem, and that this is the most likely reason for Ortiz Cofer's choice of title. The "hunger" of the deli customers for the sights, sounds, and tastes of their native lands causes them to shop at the deli, even though cheaper items are available elsewhere. The mood of longing is established by the poet's descriptions of the deli owner, the items, and the customers. The setting is closely linked to the overall message, which concerns the immigrants' emotional conflicts about old and new surroundings.

Difficulty: *Average*
Objective: *Essay*

Selection Test B, p. 133

Critical Reading

1. ANS: B	DIF: Average	OBJ: Comprehension
2. ANS: D	DIF: Easy	OBJ: Literary Analysis
3. ANS: B	DIF: Easy	OBJ: Comprehension
4. ANS: B	DIF: Challenging	OBJ: Interpretation
5. ANS: C	DIF: Easy	OBJ: Comprehension
6. ANS: A	DIF: Challenging	OBJ: Interpretation
7. ANS: C	DIF: Average	OBJ: Reading
8. ANS: C	DIF: Easy	OBJ: Interpretation
9. ANS: A	DIF: Average	OBJ: Literary Analysis
10. ANS: C	DIF: Average	OBJ: Interpretation
11. ANS: B	DIF: Average	OBJ: Interpretation
12. ANS: D	DIF: Challenging	OBJ: Interpretation
13. ANS: C	DIF: Average	OBJ: Interpretation
14. ANS: C	DIF: Challenging	OBJ: Reading

Vocabulary

15. ANS: C	DIF: Average	OBJ: Vocabulary
16. ANS: A	DIF: Easy	OBJ: Vocabulary

17. ANS: C	DIF: Challenging	OBJ: Vocabulary
18. ANS: A	DIF: Average	OBJ: Vocabulary

Essay

19. Students may mention images such as the following: "presiding over the formica counter" (sight), "heady mix of smells from the open bins of dried codfish" (smell), "perfecting their speech" (hearing), "the stale candy of everyone's childhood" (taste), and "wrapping it in wax paper" (touch). Students should explain the impression created by each image.

Difficulty: *Easy*
Objective: *Essay*

20. Students may mention that Cofer chose to describe the deli because its sights, sounds, smells, and tastes serve to symbolize an entire culture: the Hispanic background of the Puerto Rican, Cuban, and Mexican customers. The customers, in turn, are a key element in interpreting the poem's theme or overall message, which relates to a compassionate understanding of the position of immigrants who are forced to live in two cultures. The deli serves as a symbol for the nostalgic longing of the immigrants for their roots. Cofer's own experience as a bicultural writer may also be included as a reason for her choice of subject matter and theme.

Difficulty: *Average*
Objective: *Essay*

21. Students may mention that both the subtitle and the figurative language Cofer uses for the lists of deli items suggest that a poem, in Cofer's view, may take the ordinary stuff of everyday experience—grocery shopping, lists of items—and transform this material into a rich, complex reflection on roots, cultural heritage, and a state of mind. Poetry, therefore, serves to connect people with their past, as well as to reinforce the need for understanding and compassion between people in the present.

Difficulty: *Challenging*
Objective: *Essay*

22. Students might suggest that the poem balances a sense of place so that both kinds of places are portrayed in a very vivid and memorable way. The deli itself, with its pungent array of sights and aromas, presided over by the maternal owner, is a memorable and deeply felt place in itself. But, students might note, the deli achieves this sense of place only by recalling the homelands of the patrons.

Difficulty: *Average*
Objective: *Essay*

Benchmark Test 11, p. 136

MULTIPLE CHOICE

1. ANS: D
2. ANS: C

3. ANS: B
4. ANS: A
5. ANS: B
6. ANS: B
7. ANS: C
8. ANS: C
9. ANS: B
10. ANS: A
11. ANS: B
12. ANS: A
13. ANS: C
14. ANS: A
15. ANS: C
16. ANS: D
17. ANS: A
18. ANS: D
19. ANS: B
20. ANS: C
21. ANS: C
22. ANS: B
23. ANS: C
24. ANS: B
25. ANS: B
26. ANS: C
27. ANS: A

ESSAY

28. Students' stories should be imaginative, using rich sensory details and frightening plots. The characters should be based on those in an existing work of fiction, movie, or television show. The stories may use exaggeration for humorous effects.

29. For each song or poem, students' essays should tell whether the title directly or indirectly points to the meaning, and how. Essays should then compare the two songs or poems, indicating which title more effectively communicates the meaning.

30. Students' essays should identify the work and state its theme. Essays should discuss the view of life (for example, optimistic or pessimistic) that is inherent in the theme, and explain how the theme of the work can be applied to real life.

"Onomatopoeia" by William Safire

Vocabulary Warm-up Exercises, p. 143

A. 1. superpowers
2. eloquence
3. rhetorical
4. imitative
5. paralyzing
6. icebreaker

7. theories
8. upend

B. **Sample Answers**

1. She received several ribbons *denoting* that she was a wonderful gymnast.
2. He was such a *dictator* that everyone hated working with him.
3. People who are *columnists* have excellent writing skills and like to share their opinions.
4. Mothers are always *watchful* when their young children are playing in the park.
5. The letters to Santa Claus *originated* from small children throughout the world.
6. She had an *obsession* with the television star and watched every show he was on.
7. *Lexicographers* spend much of their time reading and studying words.
8. Sports *mavens* know what they are talking about when they discuss games.

Reading Warm-up A, p. 144

Sample Answers

1. persuasiveness; My uncle is a minister and he speaks with *eloquence*.
2. similar; *original*
3. (language skills); *politician, teacher, minister*
4. warring empires; *United States, China, Soviet Union*
5. (the advancing nuclear age); *hypotheses*
6. disturb; *upset, bother greatly*
7. gun; The drug had a *paralyzing* effect.
8. ice breaker; An *icebreaker* might be used in frozen waters near Alaska or in the Arctic.

Reading Warm-up B, p. 145

Sample Answers

1. people who compile dictionaries; I never knew that people who write dictionaries were called *lexicographers*.
2. (a lot of time researching and thinking about words); *fascination, passion*
3. spelling, pronunciation, meaning, and examples of usage of words in a given language; *designating, specifying, naming*
4. experts; *amateurs*
5. (making tyrannical rules); As far as the play was concerned, the director was the *dictator*.
6. writings in the nation's top newspapers; *newspapers, magazines, online*
7. in 1999; *began, started*
8. perusal; *alert, careful*

Literary Analysis: Expository Essay, p. 146

Sample Responses

A. Students' responses might include the following: "six copy editors will get zapped"—formal English: six copy editors will be dismissed from their jobs; "started us all yak-king toward language"—started us all progressing toward spoken language; "Edgar Allan Poe one-upped him"—Edgar Allan Poe outdid him; "in the crunch"—in a quandary or difficult situation; "has blasted its way into the dictionaries"—"has become listed formally in the dictionaries."

B. Students essays should be brief, using at least two idiomatic words or phrases to establish an informal and/or humorous tone.

Reading Strategy: Identify Changes in Tense and Tone, p. 147

Sample Responses

A. Possible responses: 1. Some people hold the *bow-wow theory*, according to which language originated from people imitating sounds from nature and animals. 2. People create new words by imitating sounds that people hear only in their imagination. 3. That use filled a need for a new usage and expanded the vocabulary.

B. Sample response: Onomatopoeia means "words that imitate a sound." Some people think that spoken language originated in this way—people imitating sounds of animals or nature. Onomatopoeia can imitate imaginary as well as real sounds—*zap* in an example.

Building Vocabulary, p. 148

Possible Responses

A. 1. No, she is asking for a word that is similar in meaning to *stubborn*, because *synonymous* means "alike in meaning or significance."

2. Yes, Safire is discussing the origin of the word *onomatopoeia*, because one can derive—or trace the meaning of—*onomatopoeia* from the earlier Greek word.

3. No, the theory is not well grounded in facts because *speculation* means "taking to be true on the basis of insufficient evidence."

4. Yes, he is talking about the way the word came into being, because *coinage* in this context means "something made up or invented."

B. 1. D; 2. A; 3. A; 4. C

Enrichment: p. 150

Sample Answer

allegory: allos (other) and agora (marketplace or gathering place), a symbolic representation; barbarian (babblers), lacking refinement, learning, or artistic culture; nemesis (Greek goddess of vengeance), a formidable rival or opponent or one who inflicts vengeance; narcissist (Narcissus, handsome boy in Greek mythology who fell in love with his own reflection), person who thinks too much of himself or herself; hector (Trojan warrior in the Iliad; killed by Achilles), to bully; mentor (in Greek mythology, wise friend who advised Odysseus), wise advisor or teacher.

Open-Book Test, p. 151

Short Answer

1. Among examples are yakking and *murmur*. Accept any word that is listed in the dictionary and that approximates a sound.

   Difficulty: *Easy*   **Objective:** *Interpretation*

2. "Onomatopoeia," is an expository essay, which explains a topic.

   Difficulty: *Easy*   **Objective:** *Literary Analysis*

3. An onomatopoeia is a word that sounds like what it means, such as *zap*.

   Difficulty: *Easy*   **Objective:** *Reading*

4. It is an example of onomatopoeia in which the word sounds like an imaginary noise.

   Difficulty: *Easy*   **Objective:** *Interpretation*

5. He is using the technique of comparison—he is comparing the meaning of *onomatopoetic* to that of words with a similar meaning such as *imitative* and *echoic*.

   Difficulty: *Average*   **Objective:** *Literary Analysis*

6. Students' charts should include main points, reasons, facts, and examples that support them.

   Difficulty: *Average*   **Objective:** *Literary Analysis*

7. The pooh-pooh theory holds that spoken language originated in interjections like *ow!*

   Difficulty: *Average*   **Objective:** *Reading*

8. *thunders, crackles*

   Difficulty: *Challenging*   **Objective:** *Interpretation*

9. In this paragraph zap is used to mean "wipe out" or "erase" or "mute" to avoid having to listen to or watch commercials on television.

   Difficulty: *Average*   **Objective:** *Reading*

10. No, you would not have a good grasp of the subject matter, because *speculation* means "theorizing on the basis of insufficient evidence."

    Difficulty: *Average*   **Objective:** *Vocabulary*

Essay

11. Students should note that an expository essay is one in which the author explains a topic. They might note that in "Onomatopoeia" Safire explains the origin and meaning of onomatopoeia through the use of facts, examples, and quotations that support his explanations.

    Difficulty: *Easy*   **Objective:** *Essay*

12. Students' expository essays should clearly identify a main topic that they seek to explain. In addition to using the standard expository techniques of logic,

examples, and facts, students should use at least three examples of onomatopoeia.

Difficulty: *Average*   **Objective:** *Essay*

13. Students should briefly state each theory in their own words. Then, they should state which theory they find to be more persuasive, offering clear reasoning and relevant examples in support of their opinions.

Difficulty: *Challenging*   **Objective:** *Essay*

14. Some students might suggest that Safire's discussion of onomatopoeia initially focuses on the more universal, rather than specifically American, aspects of this usage. He cites the Greek origins of the word and a 1577 definition of the word by an Englishman. Later, however, he discusses at some length an American form of onomatopoeia—*zap*—in a way that leaves the reader with the impression that some of the more creative uses of this technique are unique to American culture.

Difficulty: *Average*   **Objective:** *Essay*

Oral Response

15. Oral responses should be clear, well organized, and well supported by appropriate examples from the selections.

Difficulty: *Average*   **Objective:** *Oral Response*

Selection Test A, p. 154

Critical Reading

1. ANS: D	DIF: Easy	OBJ: Literary Analysis
2. ANS: C	DIF: Easy	OBJ: Comprehension
3. ANS: C	DIF: Easy	OBJ: Interpretation
4. ANS: C	DIF: Easy	OBJ: Comprehension
5. ANS: A	DIF: Easy	OBJ: Comprehension
6. ANS: D	DIF: Easy	OBJ: Literary Analysis
7. ANS: B	DIF: Easy	OBJ: Interpretation
8. ANS: A	DIF: Easy	OBJ: Reading
9. ANS: B	DIF: Easy	OBJ: Comprehension
10. ANS: D	DIF: Easy	OBJ: Interpretation
11. ANS: A	DIF: Easy	OBJ: Interpretation
12. ANS: C	DIF: Easy	OBJ: Literary Analysis
13. ANS: B	DIF: Easy	OBJ: Interpretation
14. ANS: A	DIF: Easy	OBJ: Interpretation
15. ANS: C	DIF: Easy	OBJ: Interpretation

Vocabulary

16. ANS: A	DIF: Easy	OBJ: Vocabulary
17. ANS: D	DIF: Easy	OBJ: Vocabulary

Essay

18. Responses should explain that the main purpose of expository writing is to convey facts or information about a topic. Essays should then cite details from the selection that support its classification as expository: for example, Safire's definition of *onomatopoeia*, his historical discussion, and various examples of onomatopoetic words from noted writers.

Difficulty: *Easy*

Objective: *Essay*

19. Responses should define an idiom as an informal or colloquial expression that means something different from its literal meaning. Possible examples of idioms that students may cite include the following: "started us all yakking toward language," "in the mind's ear," "slammed the vocabulary right in the kisser," "took me a while," and "take it from me." Responses should recognize that the idioms give the writing a breezy, informal tone.

Difficulty: *Easy*

Objective: *Essay*

20. Some students may suggest that Safire's discussion begins by focusing on the more universal, rather than specifically American, aspects of onomatopoeia. For example, he discusses the Greek origins of the word, as well as the definition and usage of it by an English writer in 1577. Later, however, Safire discusses at some length the example of zap, which is an American example of onomatopoeia. He gives the reader the impression that some of the more creative uses of the device are unique to American culture. In addition, he quotes or alludes to three American writers: Edgar Allan Poe, Gertrude Stein, and Ellen Goodman.

Difficulty: *Average*

Objective: *Essay*

Selection Test B, p. 157

Critical Reading

1. ANS: B	DIF: Easy	OBJ: Comprehension
2. ANS: C	DIF: Average	OBJ: Interpretation
3. ANS: D	DIF: Average	OBJ: Comprehension
4. ANS: A	DIF: Average	OBJ: Comprehension
5. ANS: A	DIF: Average	OBJ: Reading
6. ANS: B	DIF: Easy	OBJ: Comprehension
7. ANS: D	DIF: Challenging	OBJ: Literary Analysis
8. ANS: C	DIF: Challenging	OBJ: Literary Analysis
9. ANS: B	DIF: Average	OBJ: Interpretation
10. ANS: A	DIF: Average	OBJ: Literary Analysis

11. ANS: D   DIF: Easy   OBJ: Interpretation
12. ANS: C   DIF: Challenging   OBJ: Interpretation
13. ANS: C   DIF: Easy   OBJ: Interpretation
14. ANS: C   DIF: Average   OBJ: Interpretation
15. ANS: B   DIF: Easy   OBJ: Interpretation
16. ANS: C   DIF: Easy   OBJ: Interpretation
17. ANS: A   DIF: Average   OBJ: Interpretation

Vocabulary

18. ANS: A   DIF: Average   OBJ: Vocabulary
19. ANS: B   DIF: Average   OBJ: Vocabulary

Essay

20. Responses should begin by defining an expository essay as a brief discussion intended to convey facts or information about a subject. Essays should then cite details from the selection that support its classification as expository: for example, Safire's definition of *onomatopoeia*, the historical discussion of the ways in which the word has been used, and various examples of onomatopoetic words from noted writers.

    Difficulty: *Easy*

    Objective: *Essay*

21. Responses should focus on Safire's deft use of idioms to convey his points and to entertain. Possible examples of idioms include the following: "started us all yakking toward language," "in the mind's ear," "slammed the vocabulary right in the kisser," "ache for color words," "took me a while," and "take it from me."

    Difficulty: *Average*

    Objective: *Essay*

22. Responses may mention Safire's historical information about the use of the word *onomatopoeia*, his discussion of different theories of language, his citations from well-known authors such as Edgar Allan Poe and Gertrude Stein, his use of humorous parenthetical material, his use of breezy idioms, and his self-deprecating tone in such statements as "I did not know what the point was when I started." Overall, students should recognize that Safire wears his learning lightly.

    Difficulty: *Challenging*

    Objective: *Essay*

23. Some students might suggest that Safire's discussion of onomatopoeia initially focuses on the more universal, rather than specificasly American, aspects of this usage: he cites the Greek origins of the word and a 1577 definition of the word by an Englishman. Later, how-ever, he discusses at more length an American form of onomatopoeia—*zap*—in a way that leaves the reader with the impression that some of the more creative uses of this technique are unique to American culture.

Difficulty: *Average*

Objective: *Essay*

"Coyote v. Acme" by Ian Frazier

Vocabulary Warm-up Exercises, p. 161

A. 1. detriment
2. detonation
3. veered
4. combustion
5. silhouette
6. disintegration
7. nonexistent
8. liability

B. Sample Answers

1. F; If you *compressed* a pile, you made it smaller.
2. T; If a person is *eligible*, that means he or she is qualified and can cast a ballot.
3. F; A *premature* baby has been born too early.
4. T; *Subsequently* means that it happened after.
5. F; *Implications* are things that are indicated, implied, or suggested, but not necessarily certain.
6. F; *Affixed* means attached, so the label is still on the jar.
7. T; *Encumbered* means burdened, so a meeting burdened by speakers has too many.
8. F; *Virtual* means essentially or almost the same as, but it does not mean *exactly* the same.

Reading Warm-up A, p. 162

Sample Answers

1. (responsibility); The company would not want to have to pay his medical bills or be the subject of a lawsuit if Uncle Oscar were injured while testing the company's toys.
2. disadvantage; A synonym for *detriment* is *damage*, *impairment*, or *hurt*.
3. (Nothing would happen to him); An antonym for *nonexistent* is *real* or *actual*.
4. (exploded); The *detonation* shook the windows of his house.
5. he must have dived onto the grass; The opposite of *veered* is *stayed straight* or *went directly*.

5. he must have dived onto the grass; The opposite of *veered* is *stayed straight* or *went directly*.

6. (outline); We admired the black *silhouette* of the tree limbs against the moonlit sky.

7. a chemical reaction; Most car engines use *combustion* to burn gas and propel cars forward.

8. the car had broken into a thousand pieces; *Disintegration* means to break or fall apart into many tiny pieces that cannot be put back together in their old form.

Reading Warm-up B, p. 163

Sample Answers

1. (too early); The radio station made a *premature* announcement of the election's winner.

2. of making the choice to pursue a career in law; One of the *implications* is that a law degree can be useful for employment in many professions.

3. (burden); Antonyms for *encumbered* include *eased* or *lightened*.

4. (shortened); Antonyms for *compressed* include *expanded*, *prolonged*, or *elongated*.

5. the letters J.D. to his or her name; Synonyms for *affixed* include *glued*, *fastened*, or *pasted*.

6. after obtaining a law degree; *Subsequently* means 'following immediately or soon afterwards in time.'

7. (qualify); I hope to become *eligible* for college by obtaining a high school diploma and completing any other necessary requirements.

8. passport; The race was a *virtual* tie, since the top two finishers crossed the line only a few thousands of a second apart.

Literary Analysis: Parody, p. 164

Sample Responses

1. It is ridiculous that an animal—even a cartoon-character animal—would be launching a lawsuit. It is also ridiculous and amusing to think that a coyote, who roams in the wild, would be considered a legal "resident" of one or more states. It is also amusing that the brief refers to an animal as "Mr. Coyote."

2. It is both ridiculous and exaggerated to think of a predator's natural hunting activities as "making a living." It is also a form of humorous exaggeration to think of a wild predator as "self-employed."

3. Part of the ridiculous and exaggerated element here is the overblown legal language—"sudden and precipitate force"; the absurd exaggeration of Coyote's forelimbs stretching to fifty feet adds to the humor.

4. The ridiculous, exaggerated extent of the injuries here has a comical effect because such a disastrous combination of injuries would be unimaginable in real life.

5. This exaggerated list of damages is amusing because it parodies the wildly inflated dollar claims that are typical of many lawsuits; it is also amusing in the exaggerated details of kinds of damages claimed, including "days lost from professional occupation," as though a coyote's

stalking and hunting of a bird can be considered a "professional occupation."

Reading Strategy: Cause and Effect, p. 165

Sample Responses

Example	Key Word or Phrase	Cause(s)	Effect(s)
1. "Mr. Coyote is self-employed and thus not eligible for Workmen's compensation."	thus	Coyote is self-employed.	He is not eligible for workmen's compensation.
2. "Mr. Coyote vigorously attempted to follow this maneuver but was unable to, due to poorly designed steering system on the Rocket Sled and a faulty or nonexistent braking system."	due to	poorly designed steering system, faulty or nonexistent braking system	Coyote was unable to follow the specified maneuver.
3. "The force of this impact then caused the springs to rebound, whereupon Mr. Coyote was thrust skyward."	caused	force of impact	Springs rebounded, Coyote was thrust skyward.
4. The sequence of collisions resulted in systemic physical damage to Mr. Coyote, viz., flattening of the cranium, sideways displacement of the tongue...	resulted in	sequence of collisions	Physical damage to Coyote, including flattening of the cranium and sideways displacement of the tongue.

Vocabulary Builder, p. 166

Possible Responses

A. 1. c; 2. A; 3. A;

B. 1. B; 2. D; 3. C; 4. D 5. A; 6. C

Enrichment: p. 168

Sample Answers

1. Students might suggest that Ramsay was trying to come to terms with his feelings of shock and grief by seeking out the tokens of other people's feelings and reactions to the tragic events of 9-11.

2. New Yorkers had become far more compassionate and considerate than usual, as exemplified in the sanitation workers' concern to protect the impromptu memorials from the rain and put them back out the next day.

3. It tell about events in intimate, familiar language, expresses spontaneous thoughts and feelings, and provides moving details, all of which ar often absent from news reports.

4. Harvey's account shows that in emergencies people can tap wells of energy, stamina, and dedication that would not be available to them under normal circumstances.

5. The written e-mail can allow the author to provide much more detail and more thoughtful reflection on events than one would typically find in a spontaneous oral account like "Urban Renewal."

Open-Book Test, p. 169

Short Answer

1. This selection parodies a legal brief--in particular a lawsuit that initiates a complaint against another party—in this case, the Acme Company.

   Difficulty: *Easy*   **Objective:** *Literary Analysis*

2. The cause of Coyote's problems, according to the opening paragraph, is the "actions and/or gross negligence" of the Acme Company.

   Difficulty: *Easy*   **Objective:** *Reading*

3. Coyote's profession is described as that of "predator" and he is further described as self-employed in this "profession."

   Difficulty: *Easy*   **Objective:** *Literary Analysis*

4. First column details; :the sled caused Coyote to "stretch [his] forelimbs to a length of fifty feet; he disappeared over the horizon at such a high speed that he left a jet trail behind him; stretched his forelimbs to a length of fifty feet. Second column elements: hyperbole; exaggeration, exaggeration

   Difficulty: *Average*   **Objective:** *Literary Analysis*

5. The satirical effect in this paragraph is heightened by the pretentious, high-flown legal language used to describe the absurd and physically impossible mishaps that Coyote suffers in a manner typical of cartoons.

   Difficulty: *Challenging*   **Objective:** *Literary Analysis*

6. Wile E. Coyote hopes to overcome his disadvantage in speed by using Acme Products. His repeated use of them despite all the inevitable disasters shows that he does not learn from his mistakes.

   Difficulty: *Average*   **Objective:** *Interpretation*

7. These exhibits support the lawyer's argument that it is the defective nature of Acme Products that has caused Wile E. Coyote such severe injuries.

   Difficulty: *Average*   **Objective:** *Reading*

8. The characteristic of satire used in the statement about Coyote's social life is understatement. It is an example of understatement because a limitation of Coyote's social life would be the mildest of problems he would suffer as the results of such a terrible condition.

   Difficulty: *Challenging*   **Objective:** *Literary Analysis*

9. The last paragraph of "Coyote v. Acme" parodies the tendency of contemporary lawsuits to seek ridiculously large dollar amounts in damages.

   Difficulty: *Challenging*   **Objective:** *Literary Analysis*

10. Yes, the countries would be right next to each other because *contiguous* means "bordering; adjacent."

    Difficulty: *Average*   **Objective:** *Vocabulary*

Essay

11. Students' legal briefs should be supported by specific facts and examples and clear reasoning. Students can adopt a serious or satirical tone in their essays.

    Difficulty: *Easy*   **Objective:** *Essay*

12. Students might construct a counterargument along several basic lines: that Wile E. Coyote has ignored the operating instructions that come with the various products (students should cite details from these instructions); that Wile E. Coyote has used the products for purposes for which they were never intended; that his injuries, according to Acme's doctors, were not as severe or extensive as he claims, that he is just trying to enrich himself with a baseless lawsuit. Students essays should be as specific and "fact"- and logic-based as the document to which they are responding, preferably in point-by-point manner.

    Difficulty: *Average*   **Objective:** *Essay*

13. Students might suggest that Coyote v. Acme takes satirical aim at several topics and issues in the real world: the increasing tendency of people to launch lawsuits as a way of settling disputes or complaints; the ridiculously overblown and complicated language used by lawyers in their briefs; the public suspicion that big companies often try to sell them shoddy or poorly made products; the tendency of lawyers or consumers to attempt to use the legal system as a means of achieving quick riches. Students should support their answers with facts and clear reasoning.

    Difficulty: *Challenging*   **Objective:** *Essay*

14. Students might suggest that "Coyote v. Acme" reflects an over-readiness of Americans to sue one another—and large corporations—as a means of settling complaints or grievances or as a way of trying to go for easy money. Others might suggest that this critique implies that Americans should be less inclined to resort to lawsuits and so seeks to shape society as well.

Difficulty: *Average* **Objective:** *Essay*

Oral Response

15. Oral responses should be clear, well organized, and well supported by appropriate examples from the selection.

Difficulty: *Average* **Objective:** *Oral Response*

Selection Test A, p. 172

Critical Reading

1. ANS: A	DIF: Easy	OBJ: Literary Analysis
2. ANS: C	DIF: Easy	OBJ: Reading
3. ANS: B	DIF: Easy	OBJ: Comprehension
4. ANS: D	DIF: Easy	OBJ: Interpretation
5. ANS: A	DIF: Easy	OBJ: Interpretation
6. ANS: B	DIF: Easy	OBJ: Reading
7. ANS: A	DIF: Easy	OBJ: Interpretation
8. ANS: B	DIF: Easy	OBJ: Comprehension
9. ANS: C	DIF: Easy	OBJ: Literary Analysis
10. ANS: B	DIF: Easy	OBJ: Comprehension
11. ANS: B	DIF: Easy	OBJ: Interpretation
12. ANS: C	DIF: Easy	OBJ: Interpretation
13. ANS: A	DIF: Easy	OBJ: Literary Analysis
14. ANS: B	DIF: Easy	OBJ: Interpretation

Vocabulary

| 15. ANS: C | DIF: Easy | OBJ: Vocabulary |
| 16. ANS: A | DIF: Easy | OBJ: Vocabulary |

Essay

17. Students' essays should analyze what is humorous or unreasonable about one of the demands. For example, it is amusing that Coyote is injured by products he plans to use to injure someone else.

Difficulty: *Easy*

Objective: *Essay*

18. Responses will vary, depending on the passage chosen. For example, in the paragraph beginning, "Mr. Coyote states that on December 13th he received . . . ", students may mention the absurd exaggeration of Coyote's forelimbs being stretched fifty feet and of the "diminishing jet trail." They may also note such formal "legalese" as the phrases "precipitate force," "vigorously attempted to follow this maneuver," "a faulty or nonexistent braking system." and "shortly thereafter."

Difficulty: *Easy*

Objective: *Essay*

19. Students may suggest that "Coyote v. Acme" reflects an over-readiness of Americans to sue one another—and large corporations—as a means of settling complaints or grievances or as a way to go for easy money. Students may also suggest that Frazier's critique implies that Americans should be less inclined to resort to lawsuits and so seeks to shape society in a more constructive direction.

Difficulty: *Average*

Objective: *Essay*

Selection Test B, p. 175

Critical Reading

1. ANS: B	DIF: Easy	OBJ: Literary Analysis
2. ANS: C	DIF: Average	OBJ: Reading
3. ANS: A	DIF: Average	OBJ: Comprehension
4. ANS: C	DIF: Challenging	OBJ: Interpretation
5. ANS: B	DIF: Average	OBJ: Reading
6. ANS: A	DIF: Average	OBJ: Interpretation
7. ANS: D	DIF: Average	OBJ: Reading
8. ANS: B	DIF: Easy	OBJ: Comprehension
9. ANS: A	DIF: Challenging	OBJ: Literary Analysis
10. ANS: C	DIF: Easy	OBJ: Interpretation
11. ANS: B	DIF: Easy	OBJ: Comprehension
12. ANS: B	DIF: Easy	OBJ: Interpretation
13. ANS: B	DIF: Easy	OBJ: Interpretation
14. ANS: A	DIF: Average	OBJ: Interpretation

Vocabulary

15. ANS: B	DIF: Challenging	OBJ: Vocabulary
16. ANS: B	DIF: Average	OBJ: Vocabulary
17. ANS: A	DIF: Easy	OBJ: Vocabulary
18. ANS: C	DIF: Average	OBJ: Vocabulary

Essay

19. Students' essays should analyze what is humorous about one of the demands. For example, it is amusing that Coyote is injured by products he plans to use in order to injure someone else in his "profession" as predator.

Difficulty: *Easy*

Objective: *Essay*

20. Responses may mention the following examples of exaggeration: Coyote's 85 product purchases, his forelimbs stretched to a length of 50 feet, the hole in the billboard caused by Coyote's entire body, the list of disfigurements caused by the "Little Giant" firecracker, and the demand for $38,750,000 in damages. Essays should explain how exaggeration contributes to the satirical humor in each case.

Difficulty: *Average*

Objective: *Essay*

21. Students should note that Wile E. Coyote is a popular icon, one that readers will readily identify. As Frazier details Mr. Coyote's complaints against Acme, the reader recognizes the incidents described and juxposes them with the lawsuit's formal language. This absurd juxtaposition constitutes the core of Franzier's satire. Students should recognize that Frazier's essay is a critique of persons who deny individual responsibility, preferring to blame their misjudgments or character flaws on others.

Difficulty: *Challenging*

Objective: *Essay*

22. Students might suggest that "Coyote v. Acme" reflects an over-readiness of Americans to use one another—and large corporations—as a means of settling complaints or grievances or as a way to go for easy money. Others might suggest that this critique implies that Americans should be less inclined to resort to lawsuits and so seeks to shape society as well.

Difficulty: *Average*

Objective: *Essay*

"Urban Renewal" by Sean Ramsay

"Playing for the Fighting Sixty-Ninth" by William Harvey

Primary Sources: Oral History and E-mail, p. 178

1. Students might suggest that Ramsay was trying to come to terms with his feelings of shock and grief by seeking out the tokens of other people's feelings and reactions to the tragic events of 9-11.

2. New Yorkers had become far more compassionate and considerate than usual, as exemplified in the sanitation workers' concern to protect the impromptu memorials from the rain and put them back out the next day.

3. It tell about events in intimate, familiar language, expresses spontaneous thoughts and feelings, and provides moving details, all of which ar often absent from news reports.

4. Harvey's account shows that in emergencies people can tap wells of energy, stamina, and dedication that would not be available to them under normal circumstances.

5. The written e-mail can allow the author to provide much more detail and more thoughtful reflection on events than one would typically find in a spontaneous oral account like "Urban Renewal."

Vocabulary Builder p. 179

A. 1. A; 2. C; 3. D; 4. B 5. D; 6. C; 7. B; 8. D 9. A; 10. C

Selection Test, p. 180

Critical Reading

1. ANS: C	DIF: Easy	OBJ: Comprehension
2. ANS: D	DIF: Average	OBJ: Interpretation
3. ANS: C	DIF: Easy	OBJ: Literary Analysis
4. ANS: C	DIF: Average	OBJ: Literary Analysis
5. ANS: D	DIF: Average	OBJ: ReadingStrategy
6. ANS: B	DIF: Easy	OBJ: ReadingStrategy
7. ANS: C	DIF: Average	OBJ: Comprehension
8. ANS: A	DIF: Average	OBJ: Interpretation
9. ANS: A	DIF: Easy	OBJ: Literary Analysis
10. ANS: A	DIF: Average	OBJ: Literary Analysis
11. ANS: B	DIF: Average	OBJ: ReadingStrategy

"One Day, Now Broken in Two" by Anna Quindlen

Vocabulary Warm-up Exercises, p. 183

A.
1. embodiment
2. motivation
3. pessimists
4. reflexively
5. optimists
6. personified
7. realists
8. psyche

B. Sample Answers

1. F; A *coincidence* happens by accident, so if you make a prior arrangement to meet somebody, it is not a *coincidence.*

2. T; Money passed from one generation to the next is a *legacy.*

3. F; *Transformations* are changes.

4. F; If a man is *obsessed* with golf, that means he is preoccupied by it, so he would want to play the game again.

5. T; *Indelible* means permanent, so if you never forget that person, he or she has left an *indelible* impression.

6. F; *Monotonous* means unchanging or unvarying, so a trip that constantly offers new things is not *monotonous.*

7. T; A person in a *trance* would be in a distracted, dreamy state, making conversation difficult.

8. T; *Muting* means softening, quieting or subduing, so the argument would be harder to hear.

Reading Warm-up A, p. 184

Sample Answers

1. The water in that glass; Christine is the *embodiment* of goodness.

2. (hopeful); *Optimists* are people who expect that good, positive outcomes are possible .

3. (habitually); I reach *reflexively* into my backpack for my notebook at the start of each class.

4. pessimists have a tendency to think that bad things may happen, or will certainly happen; Sure, the sun is shining now, but it's bound to become gray and overcast sometime soon.

5. (symbol); The jewelry box on my dresser has *personified* happiness for me because it was a gift from my sister, and it is beautiful to look at.

6. (soul); Another synonym for *psyche* is *self*, *spirit*, or *mind*.

7. to take action to improve our lives and the lives of others; My goal of breaking a school record in swimming gives me *motivation* to practice hard.

8. Realists are practical and focused on what actually seems possible; My parents are *realists* who expect me to do my best but they know that my best is sometimes average compared to others.

Reading Warm-up B, p. 185

Sample Answers

1. She could not erase the memory of her teacher; An antonym for *indelible* is *temporary* or *erasable*.

2. (daze); The opposite of being in a *trance* is being extremely alert, focused, and attentive the to the world around you.

3. the sound of the set had been softened by the loud noise of the students; She might have appreciated that the noise was *muting* the television so that she could have a few moments to learn the news without alarming the young children in her classroom.

4. (changing their grief to healing); *Transformations* are changes that people or things undergo, so that they change from one state, or form, to another.

5. the following year, Isabel and Lizzie had left each other phone messages on September 11, each asking if the other one wanted to do the lemonade stand again; My friend and I were thinking of each other at the same time on a Saturday morning and she called me up just as I was about the phone her.

6. (boring and unchanging); An *antonym* for monotonous is *fascinating* or *varied*.

7. (preoccupied); I was *obsessed* by a television show for a while, and had to watch every episode whenever it was on.

8. this personal tradition of community service; Another *legacy* of 9-11 is that there is much greater security on airplanes and in airports than there used to be. Also, many important monuments have been built to commemorate the victims of 9-11.

Literary Analysis: Comparison and Contrast Essay, p. 186

Sample Response

Possible responses: Personal Feelings—secure, confident / insecure, wary; Daily Routines—as usual / as usual, with added attention to family and personal ties; Travel—normal / gradually returning to normal; What Kind of People Are We—mostly proud of our achievements and culture / doubting the worth of some aspects of our achievements and culture; What Kind of World Do We Live In—ordered, comprehensible / frightening, confusing."

Reading Strategy: Relate a Literary Work to Primary Source Documents, p. 187

Possible Responses

Primary Source	Where It to Find It	Advantage of Source
Newspaper article	Library microfilm, Internet	University and government archives, Internet
Video footage	Internet, TV stations	Gives immediate audiovisual impact of events
Personal eyewitness accounts	Internet, personal interviews, newspaper and magazine interviews and reporting, essays, articles	Tells what it was like to be in the middle of the events
Government communications and activities	Government archives	Explains how government officials and first responders reacted to and handled events
Reports of scientists and engineers who inspected and analyzed the evidence at the scene	University and government archives, Internet	Helps to understand the physical chain of cause-and-effect of the events of 9-11.

Vocabulary Builder, p. 188

Possible Responses

A. 1. mundane
2. revelations
3. savagery
4. prosperity
5. induce

B. 1. B; 2. A; 3. C; 4. A 5. D;

Enrichment:Heroes, p. 190

Sample Answers

A. Students should name three heroic qualities and give examples of people who display them. Examples might include the following: Courage—firefighters, police officers, movie action heroes; Extraordinary abilities: Olympic athletes, circus performers, very successful business leaders, skilled surgeons; Setting a good example—parents, teachers, literary or movie heroes.

B. Students' answers should show that they understand the qualities of heroism and how those qualities apply to today's culture.

Open-Book Test, p. 191

Short Answer

1. The primary-source is his driver's license, which shows the policemen that his birthday falls on September 11.
   Difficulty: *Easy* **Objective:** *Reading*

2. Quindlen is contrasting how American's viewed themselves before and after 9-11.
   Difficulty: *Average* **Objective:** *Literary Analysis*

3. Some Americans might think that such a question would amount to making an excuse—or giving a valid reason for—the actions of the 9-11 terrorists.
   Difficulty: *Challenging* **Objective:** *Interpretation*

4. Quindlen is implying that Americans might have become too preoccupied with owning and consuming things, perhaps at the expense of other values in life.
   Difficulty: *Average* **Objective:** *Literary Analysis*

5. Quindlen calls the third category of Americans the realists, and Quindlen endorses their views.
   Difficulty: *Easy* **Objective:** *Literary Analysis*

6. Quindlen is calling attention to the tendency among post-9–11 Americans to be both more concerned about their loved ones yet still caught up in the pre-9–11 mentality of wanting life to be easy and convenient.
   Difficulty: *Challenging* **Objective:** *Literary Analysis*

7. Quindlen relies mostly on reporting her own personal experiences or those of family members like her son.
   Difficulty: *Easy* **Objective:** *Reading*

8. Passages supporting "mundane": "babies to be fed, dogs to be walked, jobs to be done," "complained about the long lines at the airport and obsessed about the stock market"; monstrous: "the plane, the flames, the plane, the fire, the falling bodies, the falling buildings," "unimaginable cruelty and savagery," "the willingness to slam headlong into one great technological achievement while piloting another."
   Difficulty: *Average* **Objective:** *Literary Analysis*

9. The events experienced by Quindlen on September 10, 2001, were all sad and terrible, and her purpose in recounting them is to show that, as bad as those events were, they were still not as bad as the events of September 11th.
   Difficulty: *Average* **Objective:** *Interpretation*

10. Yes, the stock market would likely be doing well, because prosperity means "economic well-being."
    Difficulty: *Average* **Objective:** *Vocabulary*

Essay

11. Students' essays should clearly and specifically describe how the events of 9—11 affected their lives and the lives

of those around them. Students should support their answers with specific examples to illustrate their points.
   Difficulty: *Easy* **Objective:** *Essay*

12. Students should note that Quindlen summarizes the three kinds of viewpoints as follows: the optimists say that we are better people than we were before 9–11, the pessimists say that we live in a world of terrible cruelty and savagery, and the realists believe that the truth is a combination of these two views. Students should express their own views about which of the three viewpoints most fully captures the reality of the 9–11 world. Their answers should use clear reasoning and relevant examples from Quindlen's essay and from recent and contemporary national and world events.
   Difficulty: *Average* **Objective:** *Essay*

13. Most students will argue that the events of 9–11 have had a permanent effect on the way Americans view themselves and the world around them. They might note that Americans probably now view the world—especially their own country—as a less safe and secure place than they did before the events of 9-11. They might also feel that Americans might be less sure of who their friends and enemies are in a world where terrorists, not governments, can strike major blows against large countries. Other students might argue that warfare and terrorism have always been part of the human condition and that, in the long run, the events of 9–11 will blur into the long history of human violence and warfare but will not stand out as a unique or distinctive event.
   Difficulty: *Challenging* **Objective:** *Essay*

14. Students might suggest that Quindlen is seeking to reflect the impact of the events of 9–11 on American society rather than attempting to suggest how Americans should react. There are really no recommendations or advice offered in the essay; the language and tone are more concerned to recount and explain how the events of that day have changed Americans' perceptions and behavior: making them more serious, more anxious, yet still caught up in the small details of everyday life.
   Difficulty: *Average* **Objective:** *Essay*

Oral Response

15. Oral responses should be clear, well organized, and well supported by appropriate examples from the selections.
    Difficulty: *Average* **Objective:** *Oral Response*

Selection Test A, p. 194

MULTIPLE CHOICE

1. ANS: B   DIF: Easy   OBJ: Comprehension
2. ANS: A   DIF: Easy   OBJ: Interpretation
3. ANS: C   DIF: Average   OBJ: Comprehension
4. ANS: A   DIF: Average   OBJ: Comprehension

5. ANS: C	DIF: Average	OBJ: Interpretation
6. ANS: D	DIF: Average	OBJ: Comprehension
7. ANS: C	DIF: Easy	OBJ: Interpretation
8. ANS: A	DIF: Average	OBJ: Literary Focus
9. ANS: B	DIF: Average	OBJ: Interpretation
10. ANS: B	DIF: Easy	OBJ: Literary Analysis
11. ANS: B	DIF: Easy	OBJ: Comprehension
12. ANS: D	DIF: Easy	OBJ: Comprehension
13. ANS: A	DIF: Average	OBJ: Comprehension

Vocabulary

14. ANS: C	DIF: Easy	OBJ: Vocabulary
15. ANS: B	DIF: Average	OBJ: Vocabulary
16. ANS: D	DIF: Easy	OBJ: Comprehension

Essay

17. Students may refer to any of the following:

optimists v. pessimists

motivation v. mitigation

loss of innocence v. loss of life

prosperity v. probity

hugging kids v. long airport lines

stock market v. soul-searching

looking forward v. flashing back

mundane v. monstrous

18. Students may point to the following ideas in their essays:

The optimists, seeing people give blood to the 9-11 casualties, donate money for relief, and volunteer their time, saw human nature at its best; they had reason to suppose that the world is a place of goodness and caring. They are right—these things did happen.

The pessimists, seeing the horrors and devastation wrought by the terrorists, concluded that the world itself is a place of "unimaginable cruelty and savagery." They, too, are right—nothing can erase the reality of the terrorism visited on America that day.

Some students may take the argument further, pointing out that both extremes are also wrong, because reality is neither good nor evil in itself, but a messy mixture of the two. Like Quindlen's cracked/repaired bowl, it is whole and entire but not perfect or pure.

Selection Test B, p. 197

MULTIPLE CHOICE

1. ANS: B	DIF: Average	OBJ: Literary Analysis
2. ANS: A	DIF: Average	OBJ: Interpretation
3. ANS: A	DIF: Average	OBJ: Literary Analysis
4. ANS: C	DIF: Average	OBJ: Comprehension
5. ANS: B	DIF: Challenging	OBJ: Literary Analysis

6. ANS: D	DIF: Average	OBJ: Comprehension
7. ANS: A	DIF: Average	OBJ: Literary Analysis
8. ANS: C	DIF: Average	OBJ: Interpretation
9. ANS: C	DIF: Average	OBJ: Interpretation
10. ANS: A	DIF: Challenging	OBJ: Literary Focus
11. ANS: B	DIF: Challenging	OBJ: Interpretation

Vocabulary

12. ANS: D	DIF: Average	OBJ: Vocabulary
13. ANS: D	DIF: Average	OBJ: Vocabulary

Essay

14. Students may identify the theme as the idea that the 9–11 terrorists attacks brought on a fundamental split in America's worldview, with our native sense of optimism now counteracted by a backward-looking pessimism. She parallels this change in her own experience, as when she both celebrates and dreads the date on which her son was born and the attacks were carried out. She also contrasts our obsession with the stock market and our intention to "smell the flowers" (i.e., live each day to the fullest); she contraposes calling friends and hugging children with complaints about long lines at airports; and she sees an irony in the day—September 10—when, after a funeral and two near-death experiences among loved ones, she promises her daughter that they will "never have another day as bad as this one." This duality of feeling forms the substance of the essay.

15. Students may point to Quindlen's comment that although the crack in the bowl is scarcely visible, "I always know it's there." Her point is that the tragedy of 9–11 may fade from memory, as the line of the crack fades from view after gluing, but in our hearts the event never goes away. As she says elsewhere in the essay, we may fill our days with normal, mundane jobs like walking the dog, and this may soften the edge of our grief; but the "cracked" nature of the post-9–11 world can never be completely restored to wholeness. We remain "people of two minds," engaged in the mundane but not totally oblivious of the monstrous. The bowl, the day, the nation itself has been permanently "broken in two." So the answer she gives the questioner is, properly, not simply "yes" but "yes. And no."

"For the Love of Books" by Rita Dove
"Mother Tongue" by Amy Tan

Vocabulary Warm-up Exercises, p. 201

A. 1. aspirations

2. expressive

3. vivid

4. enticed
5. aspect
6. tolerate
7. contemplating
8. regrettable

B. Sample Answers

1. The <u>daunting</u> homework assignment promised to be extremely difficult.
2. His <u>passionate</u> performance showed that he truly understood the character.
3. Because I was <u>keenly</u> aware of my surroundings, I knew exactly where I was.
4. The audience was so <u>enthralled</u> that many sat on the edge of their seats.
5. The scientist was unhappy that others were <u>disproving</u> his main theory.
6. Her well-groomed hair looked as <u>impeccable</u> as her crisp new suit.
7. The alley was <u>forbiddingly</u> dark, so we walked a different way.
8. The reflection was <u>dazzlingly</u> bright, so we put on our sunglasses.

Reading Warm-up A, p. 202

Sample Answers

1. <u>goal</u>; *Aspirations* are things you hope will happen, *plans* are the specific steps towards making them happen.
2. (attracted); The opposite of *enticed* is *repelled*.
3. <u>feature</u>; Another synonym for *aspect* is *part*.
4. <u>brought the story to life</u>; (voice)
5. (vibrant); An antonym for *vivid* might be *dull*.
6. (accepted); Many people cannot *tolerate* cold temperatures.
7. <u>thinking about</u>; *Contemplating* means considering something or mulling it over.
8. <u>unfortunate</u>; A phrase with the same meaning as *regrettable* might be *a pity*.

Reading Warm-up B, p. 203

Sample Answers

1. (discouraging); A task that might be *daunting* would be to learn to program a computer.
2. (intense); A word that means the opposite of *keenly* is *uninterestedly*.
3. <u>flawless</u>; Someone's handwriting might be *impeccable*.
4. (discourages); The stack of dirty dishes was *forbiddingly* high.
5. <u>love and enthusiasm</u>; A phrase that means the opposite of *passionate* is *uncaring*.
6. <u>the statement that the language is too hard to learn</u>; *Disproving* means showing that something is not true or correct.

7. (fascination); I have often been *enthralled* by a good movie.
8. <u>brilliant</u>; A huge crystal chandelier could be *dazzlingly* beautiful.

Literary Analysis: Reflective Essay, p. 204

Sample Responses

1. She describes having to make corn tortillas although she does not know how. This makes her recall having to write a critical essay for her MFA.
2. These experiences made her feel anxious, trapped "like the woman in the fairy tale who was locked in a room and ordered to spin straw into gold."
3. These stories reveal that Cisneros is strong-willed, has confidence in herself, and has learned to trust her intuition and ability.
4. Dove realized that writers are real people, not just names on title pages or dust jackets.
5. Her reading tastes reveal that she values literature in its many forms.
6. They reveal that Dove was a shy and introverted child who found comfort in books and valued them for the boundless possibilities they represented.
7. The answers to math questions were precise and objective, whereas the answers to the English questions seemed to be a matter of opinion and personal experience.
8. In her adolescence, Tan was embarrassed by her mother's imperfect English; as an adult, she saw it as a part of her mother's unique way of expressing her thoughts and feelings.

Reading Strategy: Outlining, p. 205

Sample Responses

"For the Love of Books"

Main Idea: "I have always been passionate about books." Supporting Details: "warm heft in may hand"; "the warm spot caused by their intimate weight in my lap"; "I loved the crisp whisper of a page turning, the musky odor of old paper"; "leather bindings sent me into an ecstasy."

"Mother Tongue"

Main Idea: People in the United States who do not speak perfect standard English are treated with less dignity than those with a better command of English.

Supporting Details: Tan's mother has trouble getting desired results from her stockbroker; her mother is dismissed rudely by the hospital workers who have lost the film of her CAT scan.

Grammar and Style: Parallel Structure, p. 206

Sample Responses

A. "For the Love of Books": "My idea of a bargain was to <u>go</u> to the public library, <u>wander</u> along the bookshelves, and <u>emerge</u> with a chin-high stack of books. . . ."; ". . . she asked my parents instead, signed me and a classmate out of school one day, and took us to meet a writer."

"Mother Tongue": "That was the language that helped shape the way I saw things, expressed things, made sense of the world"; ". . . people in department stores, at banks, and at restaurants did not take her seriously, did not give her good service. . . ."

B. 1. Tan's mother is shown getting rebuffed and enduring rude behavior.

2. The writer hopes to achieve a sense of truth and to reach a receptive audience.

3. Amy Tan is recognized for seeing a world in which various cultures are of equal value and for astutely portraying of family relationships.

Vocabulary Builder, p. 207

A. 1. inscribe: to write in or on an object

2. manuscript: a document written by hand

B. 1. B; 2. A; 3. D; 4. C; 5. C;

Enrichment: Career As a Professional Writer, p. 209

Suggested Responses

1. Students might find fields such as nonfiction writing for special-interest magazines appealing because they enjoy writing and reading about particular topics.

2. Students might be most surprised to find out about technical writing because it differs greatly from fiction writing.

3. Making a living as a novelist or a poet might be difficult because of the time and creative effort involved in creating the work and because there is little guarantee that the work will be published.

Open-Book Test, p. 210

Short Answer

1. Students might include some or all of the following: the heft of a book in her hand: warm spot cause by their weight in her lap; crisp sound of turning pages; odor of old and new pages; leather bindings.

Difficulty: *Easy* **Objective:** *Reading*

2. In this passage Dove reveals her power of imagination, because the mere sight of a book could inspire her to imagine the many pleasures and insights it might contain.

Difficulty: *Easy* **Objective:** *Literary Analysis*

3. Dove was surprised by both the *Treasury of Best Loved Poems* and *by The Complete Works of William Shakespeare*; the former surprised her because of the many delights of feeling and language it gave her; the latter surprised her because it was not as difficult a— and much more interesting than— she expected it to be.

Difficulty: *Challenging* **Objective:** *Interpretation*

4. She identified with the boy because she, like him, was shy and isolated from the outer world but had a rich inner emotional and imaginative life that was not evident to most people.

Difficulty: *Challenging* **Objective:** *Literary Analysis*

5. Dove realized that writers are "real people"—not just distant, famous names on a book—and that it would therefore be possible to consider a career as a writer.

Difficulty: *Easy* **Objective:** *Interpretation*

6. Tan felt that standardized questions such as analogies focus only on the logical relationships of words, whereas she was more attuned to the expressive qualities of words. She felt that she approached language with imagination rather than with logic, so these logic-based questions were often difficult for her.

Difficulty: *Average* **Objective:** *Interpretation*

7. As a child and adolescent, Tan shared the perception of the outside world that her mother's "fractured" English was a sign that she was intellectually limited; as an adult, she came to realize that her mother's English was simply her distinctive way of expressing herself and did not reflect at all on her intelligence.

Difficulty: *Average* **Objective:** *Literary Analysis*

8. Students might include these examples: her mother has trouble getting desired results from her stockbroker; her mother is dismissed rudely by the hospital workers who have lost the film of her CAT scan.

Difficulty: *Easy* **Objective:** *Reading*

9. Students' answers might include the following: "The intersection of memory upon imagination"—standard English—literary analysis; "Not waste money that way"—nonstandard, informal English—everyday conversation; "Why he don't send me check, already two weeks late"—nonstandard English—conversation; "Yes, I'm getting rather concerned. You had agreed to send the check two weeks ago, but it hasn't arrived"— standard English—business conversation.

Difficulty: *Average* **Objective:** *Interpretation*

10. No, you would not expect it to be an easy test, because *daunting* means "dismaying, intimidating."

Difficulty: *Average* **Objective:** *Vocabulary*

Essay

11. Students should clearly identify which essay spoke most directly to them. They should cite details from the essay and from their own experiences with language and/or books to support their answers.

Difficulty: *Easy* **Objective:** *Essay*

12. Students should note that Dove focuses on the many ways in which books and writers sparked her own love of books and writing and how her encounters with ideas and a real-life writer gave her the confidence she needed to believe that she could really become a writer.

Students should note that Tan's essay focuses on the various kinds of English she absorbed growing up—the standard English of school and American society and the "broken," creative version of English used by her immigrant mother. Students might note that from reflecting on her mother's trials in trying to communicate in nonstandard English, she gained insight into the expressive and creative possibilities of language.

Difficulty: *Average*   **Objective:** *Essay*

13. Some students might suggest that Dove gained the more important insights because her experiences with books and with meeting a real-life poet clearly steered her in the direction of becoming a writer and poet herself. Others might argue that Tan's insights into the various kinds of English produced the more important lessons because she learned from her mother's "broken" English about her mother's intelligence and about the creative possibilities of language. As a result, she became both a more compassionate person and a better writer.

Difficulty: *Challenging*   **Objective:** *Essay*

14. Students might argue that the influences recounted in Dove's essay are not uniquely American but are more universal—a young person in any culture might be inspired to become a writer by a love of books and reading. They might argue that Tan's experience is more typically American: as the daughter of a Chinese immigrant, she was exposed to ways of speaking and thinking that were different from those of the mainstream American culture and that therefore forced her to think more creatively and compassionately about the differences in people and language.

Difficulty: *Average*   **Objective:** *Essay*

Oral Response

15. Oral responses should be clear, well organized, and well supported by appropriate examples from the selections.

Difficulty: *Average*   **Objective:** *Oral Response*

Selection Test A, p. 213

Critical Reading

1. ANS: C	DIF: Easy	OBJ: Comprehension
2. ANS: B	DIF: Easy	OBJ: Comprehension
3. ANS: D	DIF: Easy	OBJ: Interpretation
4. ANS: B	DIF: Easy	OBJ: Literary Analysis
5. ANS: C	DIF: Easy	OBJ: Comprehension
6. ANS: C	DIF: Easy	OBJ: Reading Strategy
7. ANS: C	DIF: Easy	OBJ: Interpretation
8. ANS: A	DIF: Easy	OBJ: Literary Analysis

9. ANS: D	DIF: Easy	OBJ: Literary Analysis
10. ANS: B	DIF: Easy	OBJ: Interpretation
11. ANS: D	DIF: Easy	OBJ: Comprehension
12. ANS: A	DIF: Easy	OBJ: Interpretation
13. ANS: B	DIF: Easy	OBJ: Reading Strategy
14. ANS: C	DIF: Easy	OBJ: Reading Strategy

Vocabulary and Grammar

15. ANS: A	DIF: Easy	OBJ: Vocabulary
16. ANS: B	DIF: Easy	OBJ: Grammar

Essay

17. Students might write about events that helped them realize that they had a special talent, such as winning an art contest or being asked to help organize a community project. Other examples might include realizing that one is a role model to a younger brother or sister, finding the profession one wants to pursue after school, or reading an article that inspires one to take on a new challenge.

Difficulty: *Easy*

Objective: *Essay*

18. Students might argue that the influences Dove mentions are not uniquely American. They could happen in any culture. A young person anywhere in the world might be inspired to become a writer by a love of books and reading. Students might argue that Tan's experience is more American. As the daughter of a Chinese immigrant, she was exposed to ways of speaking and thinking that were different from those of most Americans. That forced her to think more creatively about people's differences.

Difficulty: *Easy*

Objective: *Essay*

Selection Test B, p. 216

Critical Reading

1. ANS: B	DIF: Easy	OBJ: Comprehension
2. ANS: A	DIF: Challenging	OBJ: Literary Analysis
3. ANS: C	DIF: Challenging	OBJ: Interpretation
4. ANS: A	DIF: Average	OBJ: Interpretation
5. ANS: D	DIF: Challenging	OBJ: Literary Analysis
6. ANS: A	DIF: Average	OBJ: Reading Strategy
7. ANS: B	DIF: Easy	OBJ: Interpretation
8. ANS: A	DIF: Average	OBJ: Comprehension
9. ANS: D	DIF: Average	OBJ: Interpretation

10. ANS: D	DIF: Average	OBJ: Interpretation
11. ANS: C	DIF: Average	OBJ: Literary Analysis
12. ANS: C	DIF: Average	OBJ: Comprehension
13. ANS: D	DIF: Average	OBJ: Reading Strategy
14. ANS: A	DIF: Average	OBJ: Reading Strategy
15. ANS: B	DIF: Average	OBJ: Literary Analysis

Vocabulary and Grammar

16. ANS: A	DIF: Challenging	OBJ: Vocabulary
17. ANS: B	DIF: Average	OBJ: Vocabulary
18. ANS: D	DIF: Average	OBJ: Grammar

Essay

19. Students might point out that Dove, in the course of her essay, moves from the question, "What made you want to be a writer?" to the realization that it wasn't just books but an deep need for self-expression that sparked her love of books and writing.
   Difficulty: *Average*
   Objective: *Essay*

20. Students should use reasonable evidence to support their opinions. For example, students might believe that Tan reveals more about herself because she explores the influence of her mother's language on her writing quite deeply. She explains how she uses different Englishes for different audiences. She also discusses how her mother's language almost limited her possibilities in life. She explores her own attitudes and emotions regarding her mother's English as well as how other Asian Americans might react to similar language barriers in their lives. Tan demonstrates personal strengths that have defined her personality and helped her meet the challenges of her career as a writer.
   Difficulty: *Average*
   Objective: *Essay*

21. Students in agreement might cite Tan's interpretations of analogy questions, which were heavily influenced by her mother's use of English, and Dove's family's solarium library, which her family kept well-stocked with books and encouraged her to read. Those in disagreement might point to Dove's consuming interest in reading, which seems largely uninfluenced by her family, and Tan's ability to speak "different Englishes," which demonstrates her deliberate separation from her family's way of speaking English in order to succeed as a writer of American literature.
   Difficulty: *Challenging*
   Objective: *Essay*

22. Students might argue that the influences recounted in Dove's essay are not uniquely American but are more universal—a young person in any culture might be inspired to become a writer by a love of books and reading. They might argue that Tan's experience is more typically American: as the daughter of a Chinese immigrant, she was exposed to ways of speaking and thinking that were different from those of the mainstream American culture and that therefore forced her to think more creatively and compassionately about the difrerences in people and language.
   Difficulty: *Average*
   Objective: *Essay*

from "The Woman Warrior" by Maxine Hong Kingston and **from** "The Names" by N. Scott Momaday

Vocabulary Warm-up Exercises, p. 220

A.
1. divert
2. hovered
3. pastoral
4. exhilaration
5. outset
6. fleeting
7. accessible
8. principal

B. Sample Answers
1. The lovely setting <u>lured</u> us to have our picnic there.
2. Maggie's <u>cowardice</u> caused her to run in the face of danger.
3. The dancer in the bear suit was <u>lumbering</u> loudly across the stage.
4. Production at the <u>inefficient</u> factory decreased sharply.
5. The horse <u>shied</u> at the sound of a car backfiring.
6. The long, thin athlete could best be described as <u>rangy</u>.
7. When his watch fell to the bottom of the <u>ravine</u>, Will knew he'd never see it again.
8. During his <u>heyday</u>, the actor became extremely famous.

Reading Warm-up A, p. 221

Sample Answers
1. (redirected); <u>the direction of their lives</u>
2. <u>floating dream</u>; The neighbors *hovered* around, waiting for news.
3. (green fields); A word that means the opposite of *pastoral* is *urban*.
4. (open); An antonym for *accessible* is *closed*.
5. (joyful); Winning an election might give a feeling of *exhilaration*.
6. *Beginning* could substitute for *outset*; (initial) or (new)
7. <u>passing as soon as reality set in</u>; A synonym for *fleeting* is *brief*.
8. <u>biggest</u>; A *principal* cause of accidents is fatigue.

Reading Warm-up B, p. 222

Sample Answers

1. <u>brief period</u>, <u>stars</u>; In her *heyday*, Greta Garbo's picture was pinned up on many walls.

2. (long, thin); *Short and fat* means the opposite of *rangy*.

3. <u>drawn by</u>; People may also have been *lured* to dude ranches by fresh air and scenery.

4. (clumping); <u>moving with speed and grace</u>

5. <u>smoothly operating</u>; Because of *inefficient* methods, the bills did not get paid on time.

6. (strength and courage); The size and power of the horses made them face their *cowardice*.

7. <u>startled</u>, <u>thrown from the horse's back</u>; The horses might have *shied* in reaction to a loud noise or a snake.

8. <u>cliff, deep</u>; At the bottom of the *ravine* flowed a raging river.

Literary Analysis: Memoirs, p. 223

Sample Responses

1. The narrative point of view is the first person. This point of view is typical of most memoirs because the author is usually talking about incidents that he or she has directly experienced.

2. Students' responses might include some of the following: Event: receiving a horse as a gift from his parents; Significance: riding the horse allows him to see the world from a different, more independent perspective. Experience: Taking a long journey on his horse; Significance: Seeing new sights and meeting new people spurs his emotional and intellectual growth ("My mind soared"). Experience: Training his horse to race; Significance: It teaches him the value of discipline, teamwork, and working toward a goal.

3. The piece focuses on Brave Orchid's personal impressions. Students might note that passage in which Brave Orchid describes the habits of her American children or the passage in which she describes the young soldiers.

4. *The Woman Warrior* is different from other memoirs in that it is written in the third person and it is based on Kingston's mother and the "talk stories" Kingston heard as a child.

Reading Strategy: Relate to Your Own Experiences, p. 224

Sample Responses

1. The woman warrior in the title refers to one of the writer's ancestors in China—a brave heroine of one of her mother's "talk stories." The title might also refer to every Chinese and Chinese American woman in the book, including Brave Orchid, Moon Orchid, and their daughters.

2. Ellis Island is in the harbor off New York City. Brave Orchid and her husband went to Ellis Island when they first immigrated to the United States.

3. China was war-torn, and she wanted to join her husband in New York.

4. Students might mention any of a number of minor superstitions they have or have observed in others: counting, not walking under ladders, sitting in a certain chair while rooting for the home team, and so on.

5. Students might mention parents' disapproval of things like fast food, certain kinds of music, hair and clothing styles, and so on.

6. Students should describe any prolonged or anxious experience waiting for someone, whether in a public or private environment.

Vocabulary Builder, p. 225

A. 1. audiovisual
2. audiology
3. audience
4. audible

B. 1. D; 2. C; 3. A; 4. B; 5. C

Grammar and Style: Punctuating a Quotation Within a Quotation, p. 226

Sample Answers

1. The first, complex, sentence gives Kingston plenty of room in which to set the overall scene. The second, simple, sentence conveys the most important information with the added punch of brevity.

2. The first, compound, sentence allows Kingston to pose the various alternatives. The second, complex, sentence allows her to express Brave Orchid's anxious feelings about her son.

3. The first, complex, sentence allows Momaday to set the scene of the riding adventure. The shorter simple sentence that follows literally picks up the pace, as the content of the sentence indicates.

Enrichment: Memoir Writing, p. 228

Suggested Responses

1. Students should write the events of their story or make a detailed outline on the lines provided. Remind them that writing out the story first will set it firmly in their minds.

2. Students might point out the details of interesting characters, events, or settings. Remind them that the more interesting the details are, the more interesting the piece will be for readers.

3. Students should know that a traditional memoir is like an autobiography. It is usually a first-person narrative that recalls a significant event.

4. Students should describe the details in the piece that will be most interesting to their readers. They should describe what they need to emphasize in order to make their piece interesting.

Open-Book Test, p. 229

Short Answer

1. Brave Orchid applies the name "ghosts" to the caucasians of the United States because their

complexions seem so pale compared to those of Chinese people.

Difficulty: *Easy*   **Objective:** *Interpretation*

2. The excerpt from *The Woman Warrior* is written in the third person point of view. Kingston probably made this choice in order to allow her more creative freedom in portraying her mother's inner thoughts and feelings— it feels more like she is directly conveying her mother's experiences rather than her own.

Difficulty: *Average*   **Objective:** *Literary Analysis*

3. Students might mention some of the following: arriving in an overseas country for the first time; having parents who grew up in another country and who have never adjusted to American customs and values; waiting a long time at an airport for someone whose plane has been delayed; being reunited with a relative that you have not seen for many years.

Difficulty: *Average*   **Objective:** *Reading*

4. Students' diagrams should indicate that Brave Orchid keeps many of her Chinese customs, disapproves of many of her children's American ways, worries a lot, is superstitious, does not always believe what people tell her (for example, about where her son is stationed in the military), has a strong personality, and cares a great deal about her family.

Difficulty: *Average*   **Objective:** *Interpretation*

5. Students might note two of the following: the excerpt from *The Woman Warrior* differs from many traditional memoirs because it is written in the third person rather than in the first person, it focuses on the thoughts and feelings of someone other than the writer, it uses a great deal of specific dialogue, and overall has the feel of a short story rather than a personal memory.

Difficulty: *Average*   **Objective:** *Interpretation*

6. The significance of the opening section is that it connects Momaday to this horse-loving aspect of the Kiowas in a personal way.

Difficulty: *Average*   **Objective:** *Literary Analysis*

7. Students might suggest that having his own horse makes the young Momaday feel more independent, more like a man, so riding the horse colors his view of the world emotionally—it makes the world seem full of the possibilities of manhood.

Difficulty: *Challenging*   **Objective:** *Interpretation*

8. Readers who have been close to a companion animal or who have felt a sense of growing independence might identify more closely with Momaday's memoir.

Difficulty: *Easy*   **Objective:** *Reading*

9. Students might suggest that this section of the memoir shows that Momaday learned how to set his mind on a goal and achieve it through discipline and hard work. They might also note that the experience contributes to his emotional maturity by increasing his capacity to understand and work with an animal to achieve a common goal.

Difficulty: *Challenging*   **Objective:** *Literary Analysis*

10. No, you would not be listening closely, because *oblivious* means "lacking all awareness."

Difficulty: *Average*   **Objective:** *Vocabulary*

Essay

11. Students should clearly choose one well-defined episode from either selection, and then tell about an experience of their own that echoes that episode. Students should explain the connection between the episode in the memoir and their own experience—through similarity of circumstances, lesson learned about life, and so on.

Difficulty: *Easy*   **Objective:** *Essay*

12. Some students might prefer the more conventional first-person approach of *The Names* because it might seem more credible to them for an author to have detailed access to his own thoughts and feelings. Others might prefer the third-person focus on another person used in *The Woman Warrior* because it obliges the author to expand her perceptions to how other people close to her experienced an episode of life that she also lived through. Students should support their opinions with relevant quotations and examples from the selections.

Difficulty: *Average*   **Objective:** *Essay*

13. Students might suggest that Momaday's attitude toward his cultural heritage is mostly appreciative; he emphasizes the way in which his culture prizes horses in general—and his relationship with his horse in particular—broadened his horizons and spurred him toward a greater sense of independence and confidence and a deeper understanding of the world around him. Students might note that Kingston's portrayal of her heritage—largely in the person of her mother, Brave Orchid—is more mixed. Brave Orchid is superstitious (believing she can affect the flight of a plane with her will), suspicious (doubting her family's accounts of her son's whereabouts), and perhaps narrow-minded—she seems to find all things American distasteful: the food, the television, the conveniences that she thinks have spoiled her children. On the other hand, students might note the other side of the coin of Brave Orchid's old-fashioned ways: devotion to family, a firm sense of enduring values, great personal strength, and a bold sense of independence.

Difficulty: *Challenging*   **Objective:** *Essay*

14. Students should note that the places of The Names shape Momaday's outlook in a powerful fashion—being in close touch with nature and horses gives him a sense of spirituality and connection with the world around him. His sense of "coming of age"—of gaining a sense of independence—is connected with his training of and empathy with his horse and the new places and people he discovers riding the horse. For Kingston, San Francisco provided the opportunity for her to observe how a new place can sharpen a sense of conflict between cultures and generations—her mother, Brave Orchid, is uncomfortable in so many ways with the modern attitudes and conveniences of American culture, and she clings to many of her traditional

Chinese ways. Observing these conflicts surely sharpened Kingston's sensitivity to the way's in which place can shape people's attitudes toward life and other people.

Difficulty: *Average*   **Objective:** *Essay*

Oral Response

15. Oral responses should be clear, well organized, and well supported by appropriate examples from the selection.
    Difficulty: *Average*   **Objective:** *Oral Response*

Selection Test A, p. 232

Critical Reading

1. ANS: C	DIF: Easy	OBJ: Comprehension
2. ANS: D	DIF: Easy	OBJ: Literary Analysis
3. ANS: B	DIF: Easy	OBJ: Comprehension
4. ANS: D	DIF: Easy	OBJ: Interpretation
5. ANS: A	DIF: Easy	OBJ: Literary Analysis
6. ANS: D	DIF: Easy	OBJ: Literary Analysis
7. ANS: C	DIF: Easy	OBJ: Reading Strategy
8. ANS: A	DIF: Easy	OBJ: Comprehension
9. ANS: D	DIF: Easy	OBJ: Reading Strategy
10. ANS: A	DIF: Easy	OBJ: Interpretation
11. ANS: B	DIF: Easy	OBJ: Comprehension
12. ANS: C	DIF: Easy	OBJ: Reading Strategy
13. ANS: B	DIF: Easy	OBJ: Interpretation
14. ANS: C	DIF: Easy	OBJ: Literary Analysis
15. ANS: B	DIF: Easy	OBJ: Literary Analysis

Vocabulary and Grammar

16. ANS: A	DIF: Easy	OBJ: Vocabulary
17. ANS: C	DIF: Easy	OBJ: Vocabulary

Essay

18. Students should note that Brave Orchid remembers her sister Moon Orchid as Moon Orchid looked thirty years ago, when Brave Orchid left China. When Brave Orchid sees young Chinese women getting off the plane from China, she keeps thinking these women are her sixty-year-old sister. The narrator may be suggesting that our memories can fool us.
    Difficulty: *Easy*

    Objective: *Essay*

19. Students' essays should include a personal experience that relates in some way to Momaday's journey with Pecos. For example, a student might describe training a pet, learning to ride a horse, or working with animals in some way. Other examples might include going on a long trip, going camping for the first time by themselves, participating in races, and so on.
    Difficulty: *Easy*

    Objective: *Essay*

20. Studetns should note that the places of *The Names* deeply affect the way Momaday sees the world. He experiences being in close touch with nature and working with an animal. This gives him a sense of connection with the world around him. He gains a sense of independence during his journey. For Kingston, San Francisco gave her the chance to see how a new place can create a sense of conflict between cultures and generations. Her mother, Brave Orchid, is uncomfortable in so many ways with the modern attitudes and conveniences of American culture, and so she holds onto many of her traditional Chinese ways. Seeing these conflicts surely made Kingston realize how place can shape people's attitudes toward life and other people

Difficulty: *Average*

Objective: *Essay*

Selection Test B, p. 235

Critical Reading

1. ANS: A	DIF: Easy	OBJ: Literary Analysis
2. ANS: D	DIF: Average	OBJ: Interpretation
3. ANS: C	DIF: Easy	OBJ: Comprehension
4. ANS: B	DIF: Average	OBJ: Comprehension
5. ANS: B	DIF: Average	OBJ: Interpretation
6. ANS: B	DIF: Average	OBJ: Literary Analysis
7. ANS: C	DIF: Challenging	OBJ: Interpretation
8. ANS: C	DIF: Challenging	OBJ: Reading Strategy
9. ANS: B	DIF: Average	OBJ: Comprehension
10. ANS: D	DIF: Average	OBJ: Interpretation
11. ANS: A	DIF: Challenging	OBJ: Reading Strategy
12. ANS: A	DIF: Average	OBJ: Comprehension
13. ANS: B	DIF: Challenging	OBJ: Interpretation
14. ANS: D	DIF: Average	OBJ: Literary Analysis
15. ANS: A	DIF: Average	OBJ: Reading Strategy
16. ANS: D	DIF: Challenging	OBJ: Literary Analysis

Vocabulary

17. ANS: D	DIF: Average	OBJ: Vocabulary
18. ANS: D	DIF: Challenging	OBJ: Vocabulary

Essay

19. Students should say that this selection focuses on the feelings and impressions of Brave Orchid. Examples of her thoughts and impressions include her negative feelings toward the war in Vietnam; her belief that her children are restless, wasteful, disrespectful, and ashamed of her; and her feelings toward the immigration experience. From these impressions the reader learns about Brave Orchid's character—that she is conservative, put off by some parts of American culture, and afraid her children don't respect her values or their culture.

Difficulty: *Average*

Objective: *Essay*

20. Brave Orchid is a quiet woman who values the traditions of her culture. Her character is shaped by her Chinese ancestry and her immigrant experience. She is disapproving of many aspects of American culture, especially those aspects that have made her children difficult to understand. Brave Orchid's values are revealed by her thoughts on the Vietnam war; her determination to wait at the airport for as long as she does; her belief that she can keep her sister and her son safe by concentrating on them; and her disapproval of the fact that her children cannot sit still or save their money.

Difficulty: *Challenging*

Objective: *Essay*

21. Students should identify one of the experiences Momaday describes in the excerpt from The Names and relate it to an experience of their own. For example, a student might explain how training his dog to do tricks is similar in some ways to how Momaday learned to work closely with his horse to achieve a common purpose. Or a student might relate a story of the first time he or she went camping alone to how Momaday goes out on his own and learns to be independent. Still others might describe having to practice very hard to learn a difficult skill and explain how that is similar to Momaday showing determination to learn how to mount Pecos at a run.

Difficulty: *Average*

Objective: *Essay*

22. Students should note that the places of *The Names* shape Momaday's outlook in a powerful fashion—being in close touch with nature and horses gives him a sense of spirituality and connection with the world around him. His sense of "coming of age"—of gaining a sense of independence—is connected with his training of and empathy with his horse and the new places and peoples he discoveres riding the horse. For Kingston, San Francisco provided the opportunity for her to observe how a new place can sharpen a sense of conflict between cultures and generations—her mother, Brave Orchid, is uncomfortable in so many ways with the modern attitudes and conveniences of American culture, and she clings to many of her traditional Chinese ways. Observing these conflicts surely sharpened Kingston's sensitivity to the ways in which place can shape people's attitudes toward life and other people.

Difficulty: *Average*

Objective: *Essay*

Writing About Literature—Unit 6

Analyze Literary Trends: Integrating Grammar Skills, p. 238

Sample Revisions

1. In "Everyday Use," timid Maggie is nervous because her sister, Dee, is coming home. Although she envies Dee, she also believes that Dee is spoiled.

2. The girls' mother is physically strong, practical, and capable. Without a man to help her, she does everything that needs to be done on the farm.

3. Dee has always been smart and ambitious. Proud of her accomplishments, she tends to be contemptuous of the rural life she has left behind.

4. Dee is selfish. She thinks she should have the quilts because she appreciates their value, unlike her mother and sister, who put the quilts to everyday use.

Writing Workshop—Unit 6

Narration: Short Story: Integrating Grammar Skills, p. 240

A. Practice

a. A. I. "Unnnh," is what it sounds like. Like when you see the wriggling end of a snake just in front of your foot in the road. "Uhnnnh."

b. B. C

c. C. I. "Maggie can't appreciate these quilts!" she said. "She'd probably be backward enough to put them to everyday use."

B. Writing Application

"Why don't you take one or two of the others?" I asked. "These old things was just done my me and Big Dee."

"No," said Wangero. "I don't want those. They are stitched around the borders by machine."

"That'll make them last better," I said.

"That's not the point," said Wangero. "These are all pieces of dresses Grandma used to wear. She did all this stitching by hand. Imagine!" She held the quilts securely in her arms, stroking them.

Vocabulary Workshop 6, p. 241

A. Sample Answers

1. A *proliferation* of problems would worsen a situation.

2. A *didactic* poem is intended to educate.

3. *Corroboration* would help the witness.

4. *Indifferent* friends would ignore you.

B. Sample Answers

1. The hero returned to the *acclamation* of the crowd.

2. No one has been able to solve the mystery; it remains an *enigma*.

3. Our *itinerary* took us from Rome to Florence and then to Venice.

4. With such powerful athletes, they have a *potent* offense.

Spelling—Unit 6

Proofreading Practice, p. 240

1. fiction; 2. chorus; 3. glowing; 4. engrossing;
5. idealistic; 6. memories; 7. adolescence;
8. originality; 9. hysterically; 10. reflection;
11. unnamed; 12. rejection; 13. studies;
14. competing; 15. withdrawal; 16. expect;
17. disappearance; 18. politically; 19. committed;
20. unforgettable

Benchmark Test 12, p. 243

MULTIPLE CHOICE

1. ANS: D
2. ANS: D
3. ANS: B
4. ANS: A
5. ANS: B
6. ANS: C
7. ANS: C
8. ANS: D
9. ANS: C
10. ANS: A
11. ANS: C
12. ANS: C
13. ANS: C
14. ANS: A
15. ANS: C
16. ANS: A
17. ANS: B
18. ANS: B
19. ANS: D
20. ANS: A
21. ANS: C
22. ANS: B
23. ANS: A
24. ANS: C
25. ANS: D
26. ANS: D
27. ANS: A
28. ANS: D
29. ANS: A

ESSAY

30. Students' stories should describe the characters and settings and clearly establish the central conflict. The plot structure should include a series of incidents that build interest and tension, reach a high point in a climax, and end in resolution.

31. Students' essays should tell about a misunderstanding that occurred during their childhood. In the course of relating the events, they should extract some lesson or insight from that misunderstanding.

32. Students' essays should be instructive in tone. They should begin by designating the topic, explaining how it might be focused, and then developed through research questions. The essays should include help in finding online and print information sources.